My Life in Theory

My Life in Theory

Leo Rangell, M.D.

Edited by Fred Busch

A JAPA Book

OTHER

Other Press

New York

Copyright © 2004 American Psychoanalytic Association

Production Editor: Robert D. Hack

This book was set in 12 pt. Apollo by Alpha Graphics of Pittsfield, NH.

10 9 8 7 6 5 4 3 2 1

Library of Congress Cataloging-in-Publication Data

Rangell, Leo.
　My life in theory / by Leo Rangell.
　　p. cm.
　Includes bibliographical references and index.
　ISBN 1-59051-113-1 (hardcover : alk. paper)
　1. Rangell, Leo.　2. Psychoanalysts–United States–Biography.　I. Title
RC438.6.R357 A3 2003
150.19'5'092–dc22
　　　　　　　　　　　　　　　　　　　　　　　　　　　　2003022543

FOR ANITA, JUDY, SUSAN, RICHARD, AND PAUL

Contents

Toward a Unitary Psychoanalysis xi

Acknowledgments xv

1 Preview and Overview 1

2 The Early Course of Psychoanalytic Theory 15

  The Appeal of Theory 17
  At the Beginning 18
  Interpersonal Affective Tensions in the Early Soil 20
  Unity and Pluralism from the Beginning 25
  World War I: The Aggressive Drive 26
  Freud's Second Phase 27
  Post-Freud 28
  The Second Stage of Divisive Theories 29

3 The Methodology of Scientific Progression 35

  The Progression of Theory 37
  Ideation and Affects in Theory Formation 39
  The Expanding Field 40
  Four Flaws and Fallacies 45
  The Mainstream Is No Longer Main 50
  A Unified Theory, and Diversity in Unity 51

4 Personal Scientific Odyssey 55

  1940: The Field as I Began 57
  The Reporter-Narrator 59

Medical School   61
Neurology   63
To Psychiatry, and into the Field   66
   of Psychoanalysis
The Writing of Papers   68
Otto Fenichel   73
Genealogy   77

5 The First Half of the Second Half-Century: 81
   The 1940s to the 1960s

World War II   83
The Army Air Force, 1943–1946   84
A Prophetic Group Effect   87
After the War: Los Angeles, 1946   90
Ego Psychology   94
Psychosomatic Medicine and Medical   95
   Psychoanalysis
The Splits around 1950   99
The Fifties   105
A Reflection on the Sixties   111
The Presidencies   115
Stanford: The Think Tank   118

6 The 1960s Continue; Platform to the 1970s: 121
   The Stages of Decline of a Unified Theory

The Crest of the Wave and the Downward Turn   123
The Cracks Now Within   124
Los Angeles: The Sixties   126
Topeka   141
Prelude to Rome   144
Rome: Kohut, 1969   146
Anna Freud   155
Reflections on Theory from the Vienna Congress   175
The Spread and Radiation: Receptive Soil   185
My Parallel Work on the Evolving Mainstream: 187
   The Intrapsychic Process

7   The 1970s and 1980s: Divergences   191

   More of the Cumulative Theory; the Unconscious   193
     Decision-Making Function of the Ego; the
     Psychoanalytic Theory of Action
   The Compromise of Integrity   196
   Los Angeles from the Seventies   202
   A New Order: The American as Target   208
   My Contrasting Experiences in the American   212
   Multiple and Reciprocal Changes   215
   Toward Pluralism   216
   Lay Analysis   216
   Lawsuits   220
   Wallerstein   221
   Common Ground   223
   Chasing the Irrational   226
   How Many Theories?   227
   It Is What Each Theory Omits That Is the Problem   228
   The Positive Contributions of Many   229

8   The 1990s to 2000: Breaking the Bonds and Holding the Fort   233

   The Final Theoretical Path of the Century   235
   An Alternative to Alternative Theories   236
   Total Composite Psychoanalytic Theory   237
   Reason and "The Field" of Psychoanalysis: 238
     The Psychoanalysis of Public Opinion
   Changes in the Role of the Analyst: 242
     A Process Under Strain
   Knowledge and Authority   244
   Enactment   249
   Intersubjectivity   253
   The Altered Ground   256
   In the Meantime, Steady Advances   258
   My Outlooks: Some Social Extensions   259
     of Psychoanalytic Theory
   No New Paradigms   263
   Barcelona, 1997: Honorary President   265

9   The New Millennium   273

        January 1, 2000   275
        Comings Together: Modern Klein and   277
            Contemporary Freud
        Fusion and Secondary Revision: 279
            The Course of Schafer
        Unity with Disavowal: Fonagy   285
        Rapprochements: Continuing Conflicts   293
        Regrouping   302
        Loose Unity, the Latest Reversal,   304
            and Brenner's Change
        When the Dust Settles   309

Appendix I: Anita Rangell's "A Day with the Wolf Man"   315

Appendix II: Wolf Man's Letter (with translation)   325

References   329

Index   355

Toward a Unitary Psychoanalysis

This book is about the theory of psychoanalysis as I have studied it, practiced it, and participated in its development for more than half of the century of its existence. It is difficult to encompass a lifetime of engagement with such a complex phenomenon as psychoanalytic theory. The challenges intrinsic to that task are apparent in the succession of titles I considered during my work on this book. Ultimately the story that unfolded was a composite of all of them.

"A Unified Theory of Psychoanalysis." This refers to the fact that I espouse one unified theory of psychoanalysis, and that I differ in this from the pluralistic approach of many analysts today. I consider the current multiplicity of theories to be at the heart of the decline of psychoanalysis as an inspirational intellectual discipline, if not of its pragmatic and sociologic problems.

"Splits and Comings Together" came to mind as a subtitle while I was describing the experiences and travails of the psychoanalytic body during its long organizational life. Psychopathology can affect groups as well as individuals, and groups of psychoanalysts are not immune. The outcome of group psychopathology in our field has been recurrent splits—and related phenomena too, I would add now, having observed recently that the rapprochements and reunions now taking place may share the same determinants as the divisions that they purport to heal.

A major premise of this book is that there is a reciprocal relationship between two styles of theory progression: the scientific method, which Freud extended beyond the physical to the life of

xi

the mind, and the subjective and interpersonal factors that influence individuals and groups. In this history I will elaborate the workings of the subjective along with the objective because these are little acknowledged when the course of analytic theory is discussed. But I do not intend by that to diminish the role of the objective observer. The coexistence of these two styles, one objective and aiming at science, and the other subjective and fueled by affect, is an example of the general principle that a new discovery or thesis does not exclude or displace a valid older one. The violation of this principle incurs many difficulties.

"My Life in Theory." This has been the unswerving choice for title of all who read early versions of the manuscript. It highlights an important point. This is a record of the development of theory as I have felt it in my own life. I describe its progress and regress as I saw it, the ways that I feel I have influenced its course, and my experiences of the roles of others. In sixty years—more than half of the psychoanalytic century—of discussion and debate about theory, I have come to know firsthand almost all of the major contributors of this period. I have viewed their influences, positive and negative, with interest, and I want to report here what I have seen. In doing so, I must accept the inhibitions imposed by ethics and the law when it comes to recording the behavior of individuals. This is an unavoidable complication. The need for discretion exists in contrapuntal tension with the need for a real record of the interactions among the people who have shaped this significant intellectual discipline.

"Sixty Years as a Psychoanalyst." Some of my readers have emphasized this length of time, but not I. I would as soon forget it! The number, moreover, may mean nothing. When someone said to Freud that a dwarf sitting on the shoulders of a giant can see further than the giant, Freud replied, "Yes, unless he is blind." I once estimated that I have listened to some 175,000 hours of free associations. But if the tools of my listening are deficient or inaccurate, it might as well be zero.

"Ideas and People." This potential subtitle addresses the fact that people shape ideas; we are influential not only in enhancing ideas and their application, but also in diminishing their meaning and value. I mean to chronicle the ways that psychoanalytic groups, as assemblages of people, have worked sometimes to support, but also sometimes to inhibit, the optimum development of theory. My discussion of "people" includes the roles of individuals as I have observed them, directly during my own professional life and indirectly before that.

"The Decline, and a Path for the Return of, the Theory of Psychoanalysis" came to me toward the end. This is the primary message of this exposition—that *the* theory of psychoanalysis has been fragmented and is in a state of decline, and that revival requires reunification into one total composite theory, which I will discuss and describe. But this quite definitive sentence contained too much for a title; it did not capture my readers or induce them to go on. A more succinct phrase was desired by all.

"My Life in Theory," then, and for the subtitle its goal—a single theory. Should I call it a "unified" or a "unitary" theory? "Unified" seemed to imply that several complete theories exist that must be fused. "Unitary" seemed to fit better, as it did fifty and thirty-five years ago when I wrote of combining Freud's two partial theories of anxiety into one unitary one.

But I am speaking not only of theory, but of psychoanalysis in all its aspects. So, after a process of compromises and choices— the matter of choice is an underattended aspect of theory that I will discuss—the title of the book became *My Life in Theory: Toward a Unitary Psychoanalysis*.

This remained the title until almost the moment of closing. The practical publishing people then asked for a final change: eliminate the subtitle, in the service of streamlining and appeal. So be it. Whatever the book has to say can come under that, "My Life in Theory."

My wish is that this running account of my professional journey, including as it does all the thoughts and ongoing conflicts intrinsic to the subject, may conjure up in the reader's mind the interrelationships of the paths that have converged in the second half-century of our exciting and challenging field.

Acknowledgments

To think back about who nurtured and sustained an effort that has been nascent and diffused over a chunk of a century presents a challenge. This book has no sharp line or point of beginning, nor a place I can consider to be the end. I interacted with and was influenced by the social and professional contacts of a lifetime. I observed and participated with thousands, with every degree of closeness and distance, from intimate to afar, and in myriad ways. And over sixty years, the professional parade at every stage drew new people and lost old ones.

Behind them all were the personal nucleus. This book is about a large portion of "My Life." It is dedicated "To Anita, Judy, Susan, Richard, and Paul." Two of these are no longer with us. Richard passed away in 1977, at the age of 28, succumbing to an illness that had curtailed his life from age eleven. Anita left us in 1997, at age 81, from a process that took about three months, eroding quite rapidly a vibrant and sparkling person. My three surviving children, whose ages range from 50 to the sixties, are living effective and moral lives, including caring about their own children, my grand- and great-grandchildren. To them, too,—they are our future—I dedicate whatever good can come from this book.

This group, above all, brought me to this point. Any part of it that has been faulty or petty I brought with me. My wife Anita was like no other. A colleague recently referred to me flatteringly as "the North Star" of theory. In the turbulent waters of psycho-analysis of the past century, of which we were at the center during our whole married life, Anita was my unfaltering North Star. I could guide and right any move by seeing where she was. This is not an epitaph, of hers or mine. It is an observation.

In the active world around my home, I was influenced every day, every hour, every minute, by the lives of my patients, by endless interchanges with my colleagues and contemporaries, by scientific discussions on panels and meetings, on the platforms and with the audience, and by my lively coworkers in organizations, from the local to the national to the international levels. In the intervening personal times, every day, when I "came home from the office," my streams of thought were subject to comments and reflections by my close family surround, during all the years and phases of growth and development, against the backdrop of good times and troubled ones.

Small building blocks of this book had gradual developments. I know that the Simmel-Fenichel Lecture in Los Angeles in 1993 was a small stone in the structure of this book. The same was true of the Hartmann and the Freud Lectures of the New York Psychoanalytic, each adding its contents to the whole. Or of certain key papers on major subjects, such as anxiety, unconscious decision-making, or integrity.

As a more specific attribution, I wish to mention one person who came to me as a specialized and private editor, who came during the course of her work, to look into and smooth, if possible, the affective tone of the communication of these thoughts. Eve Golden, of Cambridge, Mass., herself a psychiatrist as well as editor, grew into the story, which she understood and absorbed. She labored with me for a few years, connected in microscopic detail to the unfolding events, while seeing and almost living the experience in a global sense. The book had been chosen to be the first in a new book series of *JAPA*, by its Editor-in-Chief, Arnold Richards and Book Editor, Fred Busch. But it was rough, and tough, and could feel harsh. It needed Eve. It is better now, while still saying what I believe. I am still responsible for every problem. But I am grateful to Eve for her skill, diligence, patience, and dedication.

For the rest, this book is dedicated to its readers. Toward the end of the book I speak of "the psychoanalysis of public opinion." This entity, as all other psychic outcomes, is multiply determined, ambivalent, and contains an internal tug-of-war, with pulls in opposite directions. This applies as well to the opinion of the analytic public, both inside and outside of analysis, toward psychoanalytic theory. This book aims to hone the special combination of the objective and subjective attitude that comprises the analytic approach, toward the end of establishing, defining, and maintaining the consistent growth of the theory of psychoanalysis.

I

PREVIEW AND OVERVIEW

In this book many streams of thought converge with the experiences of a professional life. The connecting thread binding them together is a direct observational history by a participant-observer of the second half of the psychoanalytic century. Since I have been at the vortex of the scientific and organizational issues throughout this period, this historical account is akin to an oral history. It is a chronicle of sixty years in psychoanalysis.

The apex of psychoanalysis is its theory. Every other aspect stems from the understanding that this provides, including the technical procedure that derives from it and the huge literature of applied analysis. Disagreements and debates about theory have been endemic to the social surround of our new science from the time Freud first began sharing and discussing his nascent views with his early collaborators, from Breuer and Fliess onward.

Now, at the end of its first century, psychoanalytic theory is in disarray. A person considering analysis is confronted by half a dozen alternative schools, frequently derisive of each other, and each laying claim to a superior or superordinate theory. Other disciplines outside of psychoanalysis offer competitive approaches. Public confidence in analysis is at a low ebb. In my view, it is today's widely held pluralism that has resulted in a fragmented and disorganized discipline; the acceptance of several or many concurrent psychoanalytic theories does not seem to me to have led to growth in the field. In contrast, I advocate one unified theory of psychoanalysis.

As psychoanalysis follows the path of an individual's development to understand that individual's life, the best way to comprehend the present state of psychoanalysis, and to assess its theoretical status, is to trace the developmental history of the field itself.

Freud started the mode for unification at the initial breakthrough of his discoveries. His earliest insights recognized the confluence of phenomena theretofore considered disparate. Symptoms, dreams, slips, jokes, character traits—all came from the same source. Freud's self-analysis led him to the same understructures he discovered in his patients. The "normal" also thus fused with the pathological. Unity was the theme.

Over the next forty years of his theoretical odyssey, Freud continued this process of integration. As new discoveries were made, the theory grew by accretion, refinement, and modification; there was no finiteness, either of observation or of explanatory additions. Yet all elements were synchronous and continued to be parts of a unified, cumulative whole. Expanding from the neuroses, Freud applied his theory to the total psychology of humankind.

After his initial discoveries, as his work continued Freud advanced the knowledge he had begun in a new context, that of the relationships that arose around his discoveries. With the formation of the earliest pioneer group, a new and major determinant of the course of theory was added to the observational techniques on which Freud had relied—this was the power of group relations. One of my reasons for writing this book is to document the influence of the interpersonal on the development of theory. Having entered the field in 1940, I can discuss its development from that time on from the point of view of a direct participant and a central one, as I served as president of the American Psychoanalytic Association (twice, five years apart) and of the International Psychoanalytic Association (for two successive terms). I write about this era of our history with poignant personal feelings.

I will describe the history and course of the theoretical splits that have brought us to the current day: the dissents of the pioneers who left Freud near the beginning; the views of Horney, Sullivan, and their cultural and interpersonal schools; the Alexandrian splits of the late 1940s; and the disagreements at the end of the 1960s that finally ended the cohesive unity of the Freudian orientation of American psychoanalysis.

I will point to three loci where divisive theoretical and interpersonal activities intertwined and then coalesced into new paths for developing alternatives. These places (and people) were the Topeka group that gathered around David Rapaport and began to split off around George Klein in the fifties and sixties; Los Angeles, where the British analysts entered in the late sixties; and Rome and Chicago, where Heinz Kohut respectively began and continued his own new theoretical direction.

The activity in Topeka introduced the possibility of two theories rather than one: that is, a clinical theory and a separate abstract theory. This was the first chip in the central trunk, and the first division of the existing main theory into two. In Los Angeles, for a variety of reasons with a large interpersonal component, a few individual analysts brought about an invasion of English analysts; this was the window through which international Kleinian theory entered American psychoanalysis. Beginning in Rome and culminating in Chicago, Heinz Kohut moved away from classical theory and into the new theoretical school of self psychology. Newly available data on the personal circumstances in which this development took place cast illumination on some hitherto unanswered questions.

The mushrooming movement toward theoretical pluralism received quasiofficial sanction in 1987 in Wallerstein's Presidential Address at the International Psychoanalytic Congress in Montreal, when Wallerstein posed the question "One Psychoanalysis or Many?" (1988) and supplied his answer: "Many." No one theory, Wallerstein felt, had the right by logic or performance to claim superordinacy over any other.

"Transference to theory" (Rangell 1982a), a mechanism that occurs regularly in psychoanalytic group life, plays a major background role in theoretical divisiveness. Positive and negative transferences to training analysts or institutes may be displaced by candidates—in fact by all members of the analytic family, young and old—to the theories that these mentors or institutions stand for. The entire span of affects from idealization to calumny may get involved, crisscrossing the analytic population, and resulting in cliques based on vertical and horizontal alliances.

Waelder (1967), in a sweeping survey of the history of civilization, stated that progress has victims as well as beneficiaries, and that progress is an alternation of excesses. In what can probably be considered the postmodern phase of development of psychoanalysis, the basic aims and method of its theory and practice have indeed been molded by degrees into meanings almost opposite to what they were. The original analytic attitude, carefully developed to be correct and unimpeachable—that is, as objective as possible given a human observer—in order to preserve the new discoveries against a torrent of resisting forces, did lead over time to a rigid stance that called forth justified criticism as analysis was assimilated and became more familiar and less needful of such protective measures. But the path of reform on this issue as on many others tended to eschew adjustment and turn instead to an opposite extreme, with a discarding of gains won in the past, and a depreciation of many of the original assumptions and goals of psychoanalysis.

The existence of a specific psychoanalytic body of knowledge, and the analytic authority that derived from this, have been questioned in favor of a more egalitarian relationship between the two participants in the analytic alliance, and an atmosphere of mutual negotiation of interpretation and understanding. Analytic inquiry into the repressed past, which seeks recovery of the psychic contents behind repression, has been downplayed in favor of the analysis of transference and a focus on the here-and-now. There has also been a rejection of the goal of reconstruction and the theory of the efficacy of recovered memories associated with it. Paradoxically, at the same time that transference was being elevated to its superordinate role, the neutral position of the analyst that makes exposure of the transference possible was being opposed and depreciated. This is an example of how a misuse may be pushed to an opposite excess instead of being corrected. Similarly, the recommendation of anonymity, which had also often been overdone to the point of caricature, instead of being more finely tuned was generally downplayed. Eventually even the assumption of a reasonable professional role yielded to recommendations for self-disclosures that at the height of their popularity made the two participants in the psychoanalytic exchange virtually interchangeable. I do not question the increasing definition of the affective role of the analyst, which permits greater depth of understanding. I do demur, however, at the replacement of accretion by substitution in the evolution of theory. Expansions may be added, but the indispensable cannot be dispensed with.

Relational theories often substitute objects for drives. In my view, however, no psychoanalysis, either in theory or practice, can do without both drives and objects. The roles of instinctual drives, for example in the gamut of sexual conflicts, are absent or obscure in most of the new theoretical systems. In a paradoxical recent development, many of the same analysts who discard drives, either because of cultural preference for object (that is, social) relations or because drives are too "biologically" oriented, evince great interest in the neurosciences; dismissal of the biological on one score is ironically matched by its embrace on another. Cerebral accompaniments of psychopathology are prematurely invoked to explain psychological phenomena at the same time that Freud's (1915) recognition, in his instinctual theory, of "the frontier between the mental and the somatic" is considered psychologically unacceptable. I find the logic rather dubious. Many modern and postmodern revisions seem to me in similar ways to be regressions rather than advances, to turn back the clock on some of the most valuable achievements of psychoanalysis.

It is not what each alternative theory contributes or emphasizes that makes for competitive systems, but what each omits. When substitution replaces accretion, one of the results is omission. The very first dissidents began establishing differences by leaving out essential elements that had been discovered early in the development of psychoanalysis. The major point of contention, and historically and recurrently a source of passion, is whether a theory without the Oedipus complex, or sexual drives, or defenses against these, is a theory of psychoanalysis. The early cluster of dissidents (Jung, Adler, etc.) and their successors (the relationists and self psychologists) have made significant contributions—the drive for mastery, the overriding importance of self cohesion, and so on—but they have made them at the expense of intrapsychic sexual or aggressive conflicts and the anxieties that result from them.

The final result of theories that omit (rather than accumulate) is the disintegration of psychoanalytic theory. Theory is deintegrated, rather than the reverse. Integration and the integrity contained in it—both in the sense of wholeness, and also in the moral sense of consistency, discipline, and principle—diminish. The observed data behind the original formulations are not contested, nor are they obliterated by argument; they are simply replaced by other formulations that ignore or obscure the observed reality of sexuality and aggression. Theory is gradually denuded of its underpinnings, resulting in fragmentation and a discontinuity in the theoretical history of psychoanalysis. Only a seamless attention to infancy, preoedipal, oedipal, and beyond, can rationally embrace the entire span of ontogenetic development. Focusing on infancy or the preoedipal alone is not enough.

In the ongoing debate over "one theory or many," I favor one "total composite psychoanalytic theory" (Rangell 1988, 1997a). This theory is unified and cumulative, and aims at completeness with parsimony. Such a unitary theory is not monolithic, as some fear. Built into it are many principles of multiplicity, leaving room within it for an infinite complexity and individuality.

My observations of psychoanalytic history will move between the local, the national, and the international spheres, outlining the scientific and human factors that intertwine at every point of progress and regress. Analysts today cannot know firsthand the subtleties of the interrelationships among the pioneers—between Freud and Ferenczi, say, or Freud and Jung, or between Ferenczi and Abraham, or Jones and the central Europeans. Yet these subtleties may have played major roles in theoretical and scientific developments. While historical documents and the vast published correspondences among many of these individuals have taught us much about their interpersonal constellations, this is not the same as direct observation. And when direct observation is impossible, as over a long span of years, individual witnesses may sometimes act as bridges between generations. The complex personal struggle between Melanie Klein and Anna Freud, the most divisive conceptual split in psychoanalysis, has benefited from such a personal description (King and Steiner 1991). I have tried to offer descriptions of such social and interactive factors as I have observed in my own experiences among the leading analysts of the second half of the century.

I will also discuss a few aspects of my own contributions that seem important to me, and that I feel demonstrate theory by accretion. One is the matter of unconscious agency and the role of the active unconscious ego: specifically the view of ego, not person, as agent. Another concerns the moral dimension of human conflict, and psychoanalysis as a moral discipline. Both of these subjects require that the analyst's concerns include individual responsibility, an area not well understood and sometimes even avoided in analysis.

History has taught us to expect pendular swings, and so it should not be surprising that after a long era of pluralism we are now seeing a distinct trend toward repair of the splits and dissensions of recent decades—a trend toward unification and the re-creation of theoretical harmony. As psychoanalysis enters the new millennium and its own second century, leaders of separatist factions are softening intransigent positions and expressing support for unity and the termination of divisiveness. Many analysts have openly reversed radical departures and moved back toward more central positions on enactment, self-disclosure, and the intrinsic asymmetry of the analytic pair.

Such moves toward rapprochement cannot but be welcome. But it seems a necessary caution to examine them with the same analytic eye we will turn on everything else in this study and investigation. Agreements do not always heal or bridge differences, nor do they automatically imply substantive synchrony. References to "common ground" are often quite loose as to what constitutes a common theory of understanding. Some psychoanalytic societies that split decades ago and have grown apart are seeking to merge once again—not because they have resolved their theoretical differences, but out of the economic and logistic pressures of the current climate. Primary process can operate as much in new comings together as it did in the original splits. Variations in theory, whatever they may be, may come about more for social reasons than for scientific or intellectual ones, and therefore they must be examined for their specific contents.

If psychoanalysis has had irregular swings, however, it has managed to keep to a steady path between them. Every analyst, entering the field at some certain point in his or her own life, forms alliances and convictions (the two are related), and emerges as a practicing clinician who uses a learned theoretical armamentarium as it has filtered through a personal characterological makeup. The bottom line, the base of observed data from which each analyst's theory continues to evolve, is, we hope, the stream of clinical experience that constitutes our daily life. This is an ideal. Our ongoing professional and social relations are formative as well, and contribute also to a resultant analytic identity.

In my sixty years of practice, I too have both changed every day and traveled a steady line. My own evolved identity and theory are the subject of this book. I conceive of this achieved identity not as "contemporary Freudian," as today's definition would have it, but as "developed Freudian." That is, my theory is not a blend of Freud with Klein, Fairbairn, Kohut, and Stolorow that reflects the omissions and attenuations that the latter have imposed on various parts of the theoretical whole. It is rather the system of theory that I consider to have accumulated over a century. This includes in one overall conceptual plan drives, objects, the self, the full developmental cycle of the individual, all functions and component psychic structures of the internal world that have been identified and found useful, the unifying interstices that bind these together, and the external environment in which the organism or person is nourished and sustained.

My clinical stance as a psychoanalytic therapist has also been cumulative, and it too derives from this total guiding orientation. I started out as a young analyst in the forties. My emphasis on the objective was in keeping with the general interest of new discipline at that time to protect itself from the pressures that beset it from all sides. But subjective factors were there too, and were always an integral part of "the analytic instrument" (the best definition at that time was Isakower's in 1938). That the patient's data and concerns each hour filtered through the analyst's unconscious, affects, and total history, and that all of these contributed to his or her formulations, was part of our understanding, and we were taught to facilitate those processes and use them.

I am a very different psychoanalyst today in my 80s than I was in my 40s. All aspects of psychoanalysis, its theory, its techniques, its areas of application, have developed and grown as the field has continually expanded. Theoretical additions explode continuously, and therapeutic modifications continue to be enthusiastically proposed and tried out. The theoretical "center" has developed, as well as the periphery. And the past half century in which all this has been happening is the one in which I was a developing analyst, always interested in, and ready to deal with, these changes and challenges. While I still enter each hour ready for and open to whatever the patient will bring to it, the analytic attitude includes empathy as well as objectivity. I always did more than listen, but I am freer now than I was in the past. I am more apt to move things along and get them going. If the patient finds it hard to start, I no longer consider it taboo to open the hour myself, though typically I still do it to get at what was holding the patient back. I am not averse to introducing something, although it will usually be related to the stream of talk going on. It might be from today's newspaper, or an outside event, and it might include my feelings about these. I am still not apt to introduce a new subject, or a momentary interest of my own. But I do let the patient see more about me. I may joke, volunteer a story, illustrate a point freely with anything that has relevance. I could say defensively that I always did this, but it is true that I do it more freely now, and I know that I have been too stiff at times in the past. When one of those inevitable major events occurs that affects an analyst over a long analysis, I am more inclined now to share it than to withhold it, or try only to get the patient to free associate about it. I have occasionally noted pieces of what can be called conversations. These moments do not impede the analysis; they can help it open up, reach new depths of protected affects, experiences, and fantasies. At 90, I am currently having one of the most analytic experiences of my life with a patient who comes twice a week, and sits up. Do I owe these changes to the relationists, to the push of intersubjectivity, to Owen Renik? I rather think not. But who knows? Maybe to some degree I do.

This book spans the period from 1940, when I entered the field, to the early years of the new millennium. The turn of the century saw the one hundredth year since the discovery of psychoanalysis and its adoption into the intellectual armamentarium of man. In three years, a century and a half will have passed since Freud's birth. The centennial of Anna Freud's birth passed over eight years ago, and Heinz Hartmann's hundredth birthday was celebrated about the same time. Other big-number anniversaries of individuals and of institutes have come due, and more will soon. Such milestones, along with the end of a century and the beginning of a millennium, call for a long-range assessment and perspective.

At the end of this "Century of Freud," the status of psychoanalysis is ambiguous, both within the family of science and in the surrounding intellectual world. Some medical, physical, and social scientists (psychoanalysts among them) consider psychoanalysis to be on the wane—of some intellectual value, perhaps, but impractical or irrelevant. Others, however, remain convinced of the validity and enduring quality of its central tenets, and that its clinical usefulness and vitality, and its broader intellectual applicability, assure it a secure and permanent place in the scientific understanding of man and his place in nature.

The unsettledness of the scientific status of the discipline stems in part from the same striking divisiveness, the warring over basic assumptions, that I have been describing within the field itself. While psychoanalysis has always manifested cycles of growth and decline, the three and a half decades since the mid-sixties have in my opinion seen a major, lasting, and qualitative change in the style of its development; this change has made for divergence and fragmentation.

This book describes my personal course through the tumultuous developments of the last half-century, and the theoretical positions I have come to hold as a result. Looking back I see some surprising outcomes. While I have held many central administrative positions in the field, I know that I am seen now as representative of a distinctly minority view. Most of the theoretical positions I believe in and the scientific credos I espouse, accepted by consensus at one time as "mainstream," are today quite universally referred to in unflattering terms. The thinking and observations I offer in this book are directed toward just such contradictions.

2
THE EARLY COURSE
OF PSYCHOANALYTIC THEORY

THE APPEAL OF THEORY

To many, among whom I include myself, the appeal of psychoanalysis has always been its theory. The most exciting aspect of the new science, the one that galvanized the intellectual world, was the understanding it promised of the human mind. Everything that followed stemmed from that. Therapy and prevention were part of the new field's potential, and so was its applicability to many other dimensions of human activity. But the search for knowledge, in and for itself, was always in the forefront of the psychoanalytic quest. In this case, the excitement was over knowledge of the locus of knowledge itself: the mind, as derived from the physical organ, the brain.

But not long after the theory of psychoanalysis made its entry onto the intellectual scene, theory found itself no longer automatically welcome, and its very existence a matter for debate. There was concern that in a treatment directed by theory, intellect would override emotions; this fear has led repeatedly to periods in which understanding is considered suspect, as is anything that smacks of intellectuality. As far back as 1915 Jung was seeking to "protect" spirituality from the intellect, and Ferenczi (1926) spoke for emotions over cognition. In mid-century, Fenichel (1941) devoted much of his classic monograph on technique to countering Theodor Reik's denigration of ideation and insight in defense of affect. Today the same issue appears in the agreement of many with Bion's

(1970) well-known recommendation that the analyst eschew memory and understanding. A potentially useful metaphor is embraced literally. The danger of intellectualization as a defense is used against the appreciation of, and need for, theory.

Similar misunderstandings contributed to the splits of the 1950s, in which neutrality was misunderstood as coldness. At an international congress in the 1970s, one Kleinian discussant told a Freudian, "You are carpenters; we are poets." In the 1990s, even the possibility that the analyst might possess special knowledge, and thus the "authority" to make an interpretation, came to be questioned and seriously opposed. One result of this position, when efforts at rationality fail and discouragement sets in, is the cynical conclusion—encountered more often than one would wish—that theory does not matter.

This perennial controversy, like many false or misleading dichotomies, demonstrates the exaggeration of a proper caution and restraint into a fallacious principle. Cognition and affect are both intrinsic to mental life and behavior, and indeed typically appear in them fused together. Both are proper objects of psychoanalytic study and both are addressed, although in different ways, by psychoanalytic methodology. Psychoanalytic theory directs itself to the understanding of thought, feeling, and action, not any one of the three alone. Psychoanalytic understanding, transmitted through its theory, aims to encompass and comprehend the total sequence: the ideational stimulus, the affective arousal, and the meaning of any ensuing behavior. Thinking without feeling, or feeling without thinking, arouses the analyst's interest and curiosity equally, and the analytic approach to these conditions itself consists of a unique combination of the cognitive and affective. Psychoanalytic theory, which contemplates the totality of human mental experience and behavior, cannot do without either.

AT THE BEGINNING

As I mentioned earlier, Freud's earliest insights involved the recognition that phenomena that had once appeared separate in fact arose from a common etiologic bed. That such disparate phenomena could all be traced back to a common source was as astonishing as it was novel. Each new insight, and the interest it evoked, stirred a new wave of disbelief and opposition. Freud's developing vision of integration also led to his enduring insight that obstacles to progress must be seen as data in themselves, and added to the integrated whole. It was his refusal to yield or bend to opposition, whether it came from without in the form of external criticism, or from within in the form of discouragement, that led him to the two pillars of the psychoanalytic method, resistance and transference. Anger toward the analyst—or love or submission, for that matter—did not cause Freud to turn back, as they had Breuer. They too were findings, and they led to further discoveries: displacement, reaction formation, and more.

These were the beginnings: the first plowings of the new field by the man who had discovered it. Freud's next tasks were two: to advance the knowledge he had acquired, and to steer his way through the complex relationships that necessarily and inevitably developed around his breakthrough. His experiences in those two contexts—as individual researcher and as group participant—were to have very different lines of development. Freud's relations and cooperative endeavors with his original early colleagues varied from positive ones with the likes of Abraham, Jones, and Ferenczi, and early with Rank, to the difficulties that ensued shortly thereafter with Jung, Adler, Stekel, and, before the end, with Ferenczi and Rank as well. These relationships were not much like the one with Dora or Anna O. or indirectly (since in this case he observed through a parent) with Little Hans. In the therapeutic dyad, relationships were defined, roles established; the observer, the first analyst, controlled the conditions under which he would observe. Analytic patients were required not to translate feelings into action. Peer groups, however, operate differently. There could be no such constraints in psychoanalytic groups, either the very first ones or any that followed.

It was not the positive contributions of his new colleagues that Freud felt the need to oppose, but what they left out of their ongoing formulations. This distinction, in my view, is one that bears watching as our history unfolds. At that time it was necessary that the specific new discoveries most prone to produce opposition and resistance (the Oedipus complex, childhood sexuality, repression, the unconscious, sexual conflicts, latent perversions in neuroses and the normal) be protected and preserved from those who would suppress them, whether they were objectors from within the new field, or outraged critics from without. This is no less true today.

In the first phase of theory building, from 1890 to 1920, Freud and his original close collaborators constructed a good part of the edifice of early psychoanalytic theory, which is summarized best in Chapter 7 of "The Interpretation of Dreams" (1900). Observed phenomena of dreams, clinical data from free associations of patients, and insights from Freud's self-analysis were all understood to be a single kind of data. The explanatory system—the theory— offered to address this accumulated data included at various times early instinct theory, the dynamic, genetic, topographic, and economic points of view, repression as a defense against instincts, the first theory of anxiety as a direct physiological transformation, and a problematic and abortive attempt to penetrate the interrelationship between the psychological and the somatic.

INTERPERSONAL AFFECTIVE TENSIONS IN THE EARLY SOIL

A veritable industry has grown up around the never-ending interest, both scientific and historiographic, in the interpersonal relationships and struggles of early psychoanalysis. Various chroniclers' visions of the young psychoanalytic community can be found in *The Secret Ring* (Grosskurth 1991), the minutes of the Vienna Psychoanalytic Society (Nunberg and Federn 1967), and in the published correspondences of Freud with Fliess (1887– 1902), Jung (McGuire 1974), Freud and Jones (1908–1939), Ferenczi (Brabant et al. 1993–1996), and Abraham (Abraham et al. 1965). Moods ran the gamut, and the bonds among the members of the small group were strong, but ambivalent and labile. Rank went from one of Freud's most trusted colleagues to one of the most rebellious and disappointing. Jung was of course the historic example of a bipolar relationship, since Freud accorded to him first his highest, and eventually his lowest, esteem. Wilhelm Reich's standing, too, swung from valued colleague to persona non grata, and the relationship with Adler also had a negative outcome. Freud's relations with Breuer, Fliess, and Stekel—and even with Jones, who later became his biographer—all displayed different degrees and kinds of ambivalence. All of these relationships affected and influenced evolving theories, and led to a variety of group splinterings. Rank and Jung espoused formulations that looked to earlier and more amorphous developmental determinants than Freud's Oedipus complex, while Ferenczi, and in a sense Adler, preferred concepts developmentally lateral or subsequent to the oedipal. The former were the forerunners of Klein and her focus on infancy and the preoedipal, and the latter of Alexander, Kohut, and later correctivists and interactionalists.

I relate this background because it is upon this interpersonal soil that I propose to construct a unitary theory of psychoanalysis. Is it possible, is it desirable, is it necessary, is it helpful, is it appropriate to aim at such a global and all-embracing conceptualization? I think that it is. From the very beginning of psychoanalysis there have been theoretical divisions that led to splits of various kinds; these did not begin with the modern splits of the 1950s. Today, when we are encountering serious, pervasive, and quasiofficial divisions and fragmentations, it seems advisable to examine the methodologies of these early competing theoreticians, as well as their explanatory efforts. If we look at the original divisive events as a baseline, perhaps we can discern some important tendencies: how the theoretical and the personal mingle in psychoanalytic theory; how far the earliest alternative theories followed the scientific method gradually built by Freud; and to what extent it was new methodologies that led to subsequent divergence.

Many of the theoretical problems that would prove perplexing in the future—and the complicating role of interpersonal factors—were already present then, either in nascent or developed form, at these earliest stages, although they could not yet be fully understood. The questions that vex us today were already starting to burst out. The universal interest and curiosity in this original group is in part motivated by interest in the scientific nature and origins of Freud's discoveries and formulations, but it seems too to indicate some recognition of the influence of the group process among the pioneers on the way psychoanalytic theory developed.

What was Freud's goal as he disseminated his findings and ideas to the colleagues he was eager to enlist? Did he want only agreement, or was he open to new ideas and developments? Opinions on this—often based on projected attitudes—vary; views of Freud range from selfless scientist to complete narcissist who would accept only a subservient following. Confronting these questions as they arose in the relatively simple stage of the early days might prepare the way for an understanding of the more complex manifestations of the same issues as the century advanced. But it is clear that from the beginning, both the main body of theory and the early competing systems developed out of a combination of factors that included attempts at scientific method admixed with affective pressures. The proportions were not always the same, but the two contributing paths were: the cognitive-rationalistic on one hand, and the affective-inspirational-identificatory on the other.

These paths did not always run in expected directions; political or social alliances did not necessarily delineate, for instance, who followed Freud and who dissented. Whatever conclusions followed from it, the ideational route led to conviction on the basis of clinical observation and self-introspection or analysis, and this became the basis of rational growth in the psychoanalytic field across theoretical lines. It can hardly be said, however, that all who were in agreement with Freud's evolving formulations came to this position from a mainly cognitive direction. The working opinions of some of Freud's followers at that early stage must have been at least in part a function of their attachment to a scientific trailblazer who was beginning to command wide attention. The same was true for the followers of other individualistic leaders in psychoanalysis, such as Adler and Jung early on, and Lacan, Klein, and Kohut later. (Six members walked out of the Vienna Psychoanalytic Society together with Adler at one time, and Freud wrote Jones [Freud and Jones 1908–1939] that he was happy to see them go.)

In the interest of the science of psychoanalysis, it is useful to look back past the personalities to the complex empirical issues involved. Did the early divergent theories derive from the same method and data as Freud's evolving theories? Or did they derive from another method, or from different data, from the start? To what extent did new alternative explanations follow the scientific method that Freud had gradually built up: a sequence of first collecting data, then subjecting the cumulative observations to the cognitive process of theory formation, and thus intellectually encompassing the data obtained? On what empirical commonalties can the different paths be compared? For instance, the competing explanatory systems of Adler, Jung, and Rank were never based on clinical reports comparable to the major case histories that Freud presented; there were no new presentations from their own practice and experience fortifying their deductions with equally compelling clinical data. The clinical substrates from which their alternative theories were deduced seem to have been the same as Freud's. Also in common, to the extent that such clinical data were forthcoming, they were all obtained by the same method of data collection that was current at that time, en route to the method of free association. Their claims to separateness, therefore, seem strained.

From common methods of observation and shared data, different early analysts extracted different messages and different explanations. Breuer walked away from the field, unable to contain the anxiety and conflict aroused by his countertransference to the transference, neither of which had yet been recognized conceptually. Jung turned to the spiritual and cosmic for explanation of the observed data, rather than to internal biopsychological forces. Ferenczi, at first very much in tune with Freud and his method of attempted objectivity, saw fit early to make exceptions to this stance that increased steadily in number and scope toward a more active analytic role. This variance led him (perhaps the first psychoanalyst to do so) to alter significantly the method of data collection by supplying gratification, offering reassurance, and intervening to the point of having adrenaline handy to treat the various crises he felt he could expect his patients to experience.

One conclusion emerges: agreement about how to expand the developing theoretical edifice was not easily achieved. In addition to variations in individual judgment and creativity, there were elements of interpersonal friction and attraction that did not lend themselves readily to rational processes of comparison and critique. And the force that leading figures exerted upon friendly colleagues and followers acted to further these individual differences. The result was divisions, separations, and splits that started early and would become endemic and institutionalized, waxing and waning as groups formed and reformed, over the next century—a century at the end of which we still have achieved no consensus or resolution.

It is also worth noting that time has cast doubt on the veracity (or if not that, the relevance) of Freud's early clinical experiences. As psychoanalysis expanded its study from the symptoms of a narrow group of analyzable patients to the characterologic makeup of the general population, theorists of applied psychoanalysis widened their scope too, setting their sights on the study and explanation (analysis) of biography, history, art, literature, aesthetics, philosophy, sociology, politics, civilization. The clinical case, while maintained as a base by many, was overshadowed further and further, and recently has come to be considered secondary as a source of analytic data. In its most revisionist form, this trend touches upon an undercurrent of suspicion about the validity of Freud's original case histories, to a point where some institutes now minimize or even eliminate these in their curricula. Michels (2000) has demonstrated the complexities intrinsic over time to the use of case histories as data, and the need to consider the intentions and scientific aims of the authors in relation to the clinical material and experiences they elect to describe.

UNITY AND PLURALISM FROM THE BEGINNING

Soon after his initial discovery, therefore, and at the beginning of his development of a unified theory, Freud was surrounded by theoretical pluralism. This was not yet eclecticism: that is, there was as yet no argument that the various theories were equivalent. However strongly the early dissenters pressed their claims of validity, none of their theories were sufficiently strong or developed to claim equivalence, let alone dominance, with confidence. None of the leaders were themselves prepared, nor were their groups advanced or coherent enough, to make ambitious and exclusionary claims. Convictions were not yet strongly developed. And democracy was not yet a superordinate force, pressing to make all theories equal.

While the role of the observer and his influence upon the observed have since that time been lifted into prominent view, the influence of the group surround on the affective attitudes of scientists has been less examined. Certainly biographical interest in the psychoanalytic pioneers and later analysts, and in their friendship groups, has not been lacking, but the writings on these people as individuals and on their group allegiances have generally not considered the influence of relationships on theoretical and scientific development. The interest in the relationships among the early analysts has been an inquisitive one, and it represents a different (nontheoretical) field of historical interest and inquiry—curiosity about the private lives, flaws, and intrigues of heroic figures. These had theoretical import as well, as the two streams affecting scientific progression, rational creativity and interpersonal influences, are never completely independent. In psychoanalytic history, at least, they have always blended and influenced each other, and together have been responsible for theory's irregular course. But an (appropriate) wariness of ad hominem commentary has left us with a gap in our understanding of the role of persons and groups in the history of psychoanalytic theory.

This division between the rational and affective modes that affect theory development does not overlap with divisions that can be drawn between normal and abnormal or even between realistic and unrealistic, at least when psychoanalysis is the subject. Psychoanalysis discovered and introduced a second reality, a *normal* irrational reality, with its own radiating span of effects. The influence from within of primary process thinking has caused many vicissitudes in the development of the psychoanalytic theory of the mind—turns, arrests, and reversals as tortuous as the most serpentine paths of human "progress" in any of our other intellectual endeavors.

The course of psychoanalytic theory has been defined by both of these channels of methodology and motivation—the ideational and the affective, the rational and the irrational, the discoveries and reflections of individuals formulated autonomously and the opinions fashioned by group adhesions and identifications. Contributions of both types were added both before his death and afterward to the structure Freud had built, and to the contributions of his colleagues and successors, who expanded the scope of psychoanalysis into every field of human effort.

WORLD WAR I: THE AGGRESSIVE DRIVE

World War I interrupted the flow of psychoanalytic theory as it was developing among this first group of interconnected colleagues. Communication among the early analysts was disrupted while their nations fought to destroy each other; it was not by happenstance that Freud added the aggressive drive to his instinct theory during those years. In spite of many objections to Freud's formulations of the instincts, and in spite of the many proffered alternative views of the basic nature of humans, I offer the opinion that the concept of instinctual drives in psychoanalytic theory has not been significantly improved since then, either by retraction of one or the other drive in the now dual-instinct theory, or by the serious addition of any further instinctual drives alongside the sexual and aggressive ones.

Freud's double description of Thanatos (on the one hand as contrasted with Eros, on the other as a death instinct, rendered operative by the turning of the aggressive instinct against the self) has always been a theoretical, empirical, and philosophical puzzle. Fenichel (1945) was one of the significant adherents of this concept, which has been downplayed by most other theorists. And the exigencies of history brought a further poignant and successful early application of psychoanalytic understanding out of this period of world conflagration. Psychoanalytic principles were applied to the "war neuroses," which made their first appearance in the context of a degree of analytic comprehension. In 1918, Ernst Simmel (1944), a young psychiatrist in the German army, described the dynamic role of castration anxiety in what had until that time been thought of as "shell shock," brought about by petechial hemorrhages in the brain from artillery blasts in combat. Focusing on "a microscopic picture of the war ego," Simmel quotes Freud: "One can dare say that in war neuroses, what is feared is an inner enemy. In this way war neuroses differ from traumatic neuroses, but are similar to transference neuroses" (p. 248). (This paper had a personal meaning for me, not only because I used it in future writings, but because twenty years later Simmel joined Fenichel in seeding psychoanalysis in Los Angeles, where I was able to benefit from the inspiring thinking of these two important pioneers.)

FREUD'S SECOND PHASE

Freud's second phase of theory building, from 1920 on, converged upon psychic phenomena from multiple directions, rounding out but not completing his metapsychology. In "Beyond the Pleasure Principle" (1920) and "The Ego and the Id" (1923), he added to his metapsychology the structural point of view, and laid it down for future generations of psychoanalysts to clarify and integrate. This was his most ambitious, complex, and controversial concept, and the one most in need of elaboration and clarification. The beginning of this second phase was when Freud first described the ego in depth; after these papers its role in psychic life would be studied and taken into account as a psychic system in ongoing interaction with the id. With the delineation of the superego as a separate system from the ego, along with the very important central shift from the first to the second theory of anxiety, Freud came to his tripartite division of the psychic apparatus, the formulation from which all future modifications would take off, and against which all revisions would be measured and compared.

The theory of anxiety, one of the central insights of Freud's psychoanalytic theory of motivation and behavior, was amended in his (1926) second theory to a view of anxiety as a signal of danger. Freud did not, however, either withdraw his first theory of anxiety—the direct transformation of repressed libidinal impulses—or successfully integrate the two theories; rather he put the first theory aside. Of the now two theories, Freud wrote, *"non liquet"*—it does not flow—that is, the two do not flow together. This unsettled status of a centrally important concept would eventually be elaborated by a number of later authors, including myself.

POST-FREUD

That is where Freud left it in 1939, the beginning of the post-Freud era. Two major monographs, almost coinciding with his death, fixed the place of the ego in the theoretical firmament. These two brief but signal contributions were Anna Freud's *The Ego and the Mechanisms of Defense* (1936), published a few years before her father's death, and Heinz Hartmann's *The Ego and the Problem of Adaptation* (1939). The first looked inward, to defense; the second outward, to autonomy. Together these two works announced and set the tone for the new central subject upon which advances in psychoanalytic theory would focus for decades to follow. When I entered the field a year after the publication of Hartmann's book, at the fifty-year mark of the psychoanalytic century, ego psychology had been widely embraced as the successor to the phase of the id in psychoanalytic thinking.

THE SECOND STAGE OF DIVISIVE THEORIES

The early colleagues who had veered away from Freud were only the first in a series of disagreements and divisions. Dissident movements based on differences over theory or technique followed one upon another. Before Freud's death, even before his own theory had reached its final stage (the structural theory), another divergent movement began to escalate in the United States, overlapping with previous separatist movements. The theories of Sullivan (1953), Horney (1937), and Fromm (1941) had their roots in the 1920s, and matured in the 1930s and 1940s into the interpersonal school of Harry Stack Sullivan, and the William Alanson White and Karen Horney institutes. I might call this phase of coalescing groups the second stage of competing theories. All of these second-stage theories stressed the external environment, the interpersonal and the cultural, over what they felt to be the innate, biological base of Freudian psychoanalysis, and they emphasized the pressures of the outer world rather than of the instinctual drives. Sexuality was downplayed as a source of conflict. Aggression was not considered a drive, but a result of frustration.

Despite its divisiveness, this was actually an active and fertile period for theory. There was no organizational unity and there was little sense of theoretical integration, yet a good deal was laid down that would return repeatedly in different forms in future developments. While many new claimants concentrated on distinguishing variant theories from each other, some voices did note the points in common among current theories and previous ones. Clara Thompson (1950) attempted to do so in a lecture series at the Washington School of Psychiatry and the White Institute in New York. In my opinion, however, she did not pinpoint the crux of the difficulty that was making for the dissension: namely, that it was not what each theory *added*, but what each *left out* that made for controversy and isolation. The interpersonal is of course important, but is not also the intrapsychic? Culture certainly plays a part, but why not also the drives? Environmental factors are inescapable, but they do not obviate an innate base. More specifically, the Oedipus complex, which is determined biologically, developmentally, and experientially, found little place in any of the new systems. Every element of the new theories, every aspect of cultural input, is included in the Freudian system, but the reverse was not true; that is, crucial Freudian components are excluded in many of the new theories.

This second wave, the group of alternative interpersonal theories, can be seen as a transitional group, linked to alternative theories that had preceded them, and pointing to related alternative theories still to come. There were overlaps as well as differences among the new views themselves, and between them and the developing central theory. Clara Thompson pointed out that Horney's views on cultural conflict merged into Adler's on power and mastery, and linked the writings of Rank and Fromm with Jung's. Sullivan's interpersonal school presaged future object relations theory, while his description of a self system was a prelude to self psychology, however strongly Kohut would later disavow any connection with him or with Alexander. Rank (1947) introduced the concept of "will," but in a context different from the total psychoanalytic theory of intrapsychic dynamics, and not integrated with it; although the thinking is quite different, there is a generic relationship with my own (Rangell 1969a,b, 1971a, 1986) later descriptions (within the structural theory) of the place of unconscious ego will in intrapsychic thinking and processes.

The setting up of straw men that become the center of needless arguments flourished from era to era. One example is the notion that an analyst does not admit mistakes. (It may be that there once was such a belief in the *technical* need for such a stance in some early practice, and that this became incorporated into a fantasy of the omniscience of the analyst.) Ferenczi and Rank felt it necessary to write in 1923 that analysts do need to admit their mistakes. This carried forward, so that many current theorists (viz., Gill 1994) continue even now to emphasize the need for caution, stressing that an analyst should admit mistakes and be on an equal basis with the patient. I do not believe that Freudians consider themselves immune from the expectation that they be human and fair. In my opinion, analysts then and now take on the responsibility of being considerate and decent, yet aim for the analytic attitude as well. The two are not incompatible, and both are intrinsic to the analytic process.

Many of the concepts and issues that confront us today came up early and recurred later in modified forms. Fromm spoke of the "true self," a link to the "false self" described later by Winnicott (1965). Horney considered values and the role of idealized objects, which would be stressed by Kohut (1971, 1977). Many of these early emphases were preludes to the later here-and-now and social constructivist theories, with their stress on empathy, intersubjectivity, and energized transference–countertransference interactions. Consistent with the hypertrophy of some elements and atrophy of others that is common to every phase of theory modification, both of those periods, the early one that emphasized the interpersonal and the modern one that emphasizes intersubjectivity, downplay the intrapsychic and the roles of reconstruction and insight, nuclear centers of the psychoanalytic method and understanding.

These interpersonal groups gained enough momentum, and eventually felt themselves sufficiently different, to separate themselves from the main theoretical stream. In their strength and cohesion, the dissident movements of these decades resembled those of the early years, except that the earlier movements had not been sufficiently cohered or differentiated to split off into officially separate groups. Where once had been Jung, Adler, Rank, and Ferenczi were now Sullivan, Horney, Adolph Meyer, William Alanson White, Erich Fromm, Frieda Fromm-Reichmann,

Edith Weigert, Clara Thompson, and Abraham Kardiner. I remember some of my early teachers returning to the New York Institute after a year or two with the Horney group. Some returned for theoretical reasons, such as Sydney Tarachow, who became an admired teacher and productive psychoanalyst of the central tradition, and an important formulator (1963) of psychoanalytic psychotherapy. Others seemed to return for the prestige of the New York Institute and the contacts it offered for their professional futures.

For despite the splits, the American Psychoanalytic Association maintained its dominance, and continued to be the administrative structure under which the still-developing "Freudian" theory was preserved. This was still a total theory in the post-war period and into the thirties. It centered neither on id (that is, drives) nor ego alone, although this was sometimes misunderstood and misrepresented; it encompassed all central discoveries to that date. It stressed the psychic interior as the specific and unique area of psychoanalysis, while including—it did not overlook— the interaction and reciprocity of this internal core with external experiential factors. Within this intrapsychic center, however, the minute understanding of unconscious conflict was being increasingly studied and continuously expanded.

Yet during this same time, the American was solidifying an administrative position that would have a long-range divisive effect on the growing profession. While on the one hand representing, preserving, and guarding the Freudian theoretical orientation, the American was moving toward a medicalization of psychoanalysis that countered Freud's strong espousal of lay analysis. Following a policy of exclusion that had begun with A. A. Brill decades earlier, as described in Richards (1999), the American in 1938 voted to limit training to physicians.

This was an official policy that would strain the affective mood and internal harmony of the body of practicing psychoanalysts until it was finally reversed half a century later, and it meant that during a period of rapid growth, an anomalous state held sway in most of the important training centers in the country. At the same time that many of the world's leading analysts were flocking under conditions of calamitous duress to American shores, the official administration of American psychoanalysis was sowing seeds of conflict and disharmony. Even as rescue operations took place, bringing endangered analysts from Europe and providing a new home for the expanding but displaced new profession, psychoanalysis in this country was claimed for medicine, to the exclusion of all the other social sciences whose members practiced freely as lay analysts in the International Psychoanalytic Association.

So an anomalous ecology arose in almost every American city with a psychoanalytic culture. Each major institute established a central nucleus of European emigrés as its leading thinkers and teachers. Some of these were medically trained and some were not, but they were often the intellectual and inspirational models of their psychoanalytic communities. Among them, to name a sample across the country, were Sachs, the Bibrings, and the Deutsches in Boston; Hartmann, Kris, Loewenstein, and Nunberg in New York; Waelder in Philadelphia; the Katans in Cleveland; the Sterbas in Detroit; Alexander in Chicago and Los Angeles; the Eisslers in Chicago and New York; Spitz in New York and Denver; Buxbaum and Schmidl in Seattle; Bernfeld, Berliner, and Windholz in San Francisco; and Simmel and Fenichel in Los Angeles. The medical-only admissions policy was thus not only inconsistent but also highly ironic, and it took its toll on several generations of aspiring analysts.

People, events, relationships, social groupings and stratifications, rivalries, common enemies, frustrated ambitions, regroupings: all of these have been as determining and influential in directing the course of psychoanalytic thinking and theory as has the scientific method of observation—data collection, examination of results, and proposals of explanation. Social and organizational experiences have been crucial to the development of psychoanalytic science, and demand their share of any historical study and reflection. I have described this type of labyrinthine dynamic background and its effect on psychoanalytic theory in "Transference to Theory" (1982a). Displacements from attachments and relationships to institute figures, and transferences to the theories they represent, are a ubiquitous and underarticulated influence on theory. A related mechanism was pointed out by Reider (1953) about transferences to institutions. As all transferences are derivative of attitudes toward earlier formative objects, such displacements are what analytic theories are often made of, as much as of the clinical experiences and consensual validation to be hoped for in their origins. While clinical investigations and experimental and research approaches—all scientific methods—have been used commendably by various workers in the field, these too are often overshadowed by transference alliances and identifications in the hustle of psychoanalytic practice and organizational life.

3
THE METHODOLOGY
OF SCIENTIFIC PROGRESSION

THE PROGRESSION OF THEORY

When I say that the course of psychoanalytic theory has been driven by an amalgamation of the scientific method with interpersonal and political influences, I mean "politically" not pejoratively, but in reference to the art of living in a group, being civil, a civilian, a citizen. While theories—most pointedly theories in the social sciences—are generally a fusion of these two processes in various ratios at different times, it is important to establish a line of demarcation between them. This is a broad band rather than an absolute one, but a "good-enough" separation between the two poles can nonetheless be made. (This stricture applies also to the oft-repeated observation that measurement is always subjective, influenced as it is by man, the measurer.) In my view, the failure to separate adequately the scientific and sociopolitical has led to theoretical ambiguity and affective divisiveness. While the subjective is intrinsic to the study and understanding of human affairs, it need not preclude the objective, nor should it be allowed to block or obscure the scientific method of observation, data collection, and theory formation. Science can be used to understand the political, but group processes do not always further the understanding or progress of science.

My experience has led me to believe that the political in our field has encroached upon the scientific to the detriment of our discipline; the unfortunate effects are apparent especially in a new

public skepticism about its validity and its unique place alongside other scientific acquisitions of mankind. Psychoanalytic
theory stands upon an observational base, both clinical and from
life, that serves as the understructure from which its data are
derived. In this subjective and humanistic science, however, personal and interpersonal input are not always easily distinguished
from theoretical formulations arrived at objectively. While both
streams make contributions that need to be acknowledged and
accounted for, their influences need to be kept apart insofar as
possible so that proper judgment and validation may proceed. As
countertransference shapes and complicates the productions of an
analytic hour, so do the affects and motivations of theoreticians—
and their relations to their social surrounds—color the opinions
and theories they offer. The goal of psychoanalytic science, in
common with other humanistic sciences, is to draw as direct a line
as possible between data and explanation, even when the data,
as in this case, include the observer. The analyst is part of the
observations to be explained, but (ideally) he does not distort the
explanations to suit his needs. On the contrary, to the extent that
the observer affects the data, which to a variable degree is routinely the case, this influence and its effects must be included in
the explanatory theory. The theory should explain objectively the
subjective data observed—in the patient, in the clinical observer,
and within the working pair.

Fashions and fads and political correctness, familiar in other
forms of group life, are a commonplace in psychoanalysis as well.
Both progress and lags have been brought about by interpersonal
affects and effects. This was seen early in the personal relationships
between Freud and Fliess, Breuer, Jung, and others. It appeared in
a more distant way between Freud and Charcot, and then among
the early pioneers themselves. As relationships grew more numerous and more complex, rivalries and hostilities arose among the
first cadre of supporters: between Ferenzci and Jones, Abraham
and Jung, Abraham and Rank, and, after a close friendship and
collaboration, between Rank and Ferenczi. A number of the early
analysts turned so decisively with Freud against Rank after he

published *The Trauma of Birth* (1952) that Rank, encountering Ferenczi in New York City's Pennsylvania Station on one of his frequent visits to the United States, felt that Ferenczi pretended not to see him (Eisenstein, in Alexander et al. 1966). Competition and hostile rivalry also arose between psychoanalytic cities—between Budapest and Berlin, for instance, and Zurich and Vienna, foreshadowing the London/Vienna rivalry of later psychoanalytic history.

IDEATION AND AFFECTS IN THEORY FORMATION

Ideation and affects, thinking and feeling, hold equal status as objects of study by any theoretical system that would understand and encompass human behavior; however, this is less true of the roles of ideation and affects in the *formation* of theory. There is no automatic and equal fusion of the two in creativity, in discovery, or in scientific breakthroughs. The scientific method is built upon observation, which is followed by conceptualization and then by theory formation. Freud made observations, in practice and in life, and proceeded from hunches about them to the explanatory theories that he eventually offered. These theories led to further observations, which led in turn to expansions and modifications of the theories. Individual analysts repeat this progression, which can be regarded as the scientific method as it applies to psychoanalysis. Both observations and explanations are continually subject to consensual validation and testing. This sequence does not preclude a role for affect, conscious and unconscious, and for unconscious processes in general, which are indeed central and ever-present elements in the creative process. But affect as an object of study is not equivalent to, or interchangeable with, affect within the explanatory tool.

Nevertheless, the development of psychoanalytic theory, as observation itself, is subject to two simultaneous streams of influence: one ideational, which enlists the "rational," and the other affective, which opens the door to the "irrational." This is not to downplay the role of affect in the creative process or in the living of a life. But affective reactions should not be permitted to replace ideation in scientific progress. The value of theoretical insights, even the most abstract, achieved by a synchrony of affect and cognition, needs to be asserted against the tendency to denigrate their intellectual nature. Affect separated from or dominating cognition blunts, distorts, and impedes the rational. In the unique case of psychoanalysis, this is the very realm at which the light of the new understanding is directed. But these forces, and the resulting compromises and distortions, are the objects, not the means, of psychoanalytic study and progress.

THE EXPANDING FIELD

Development of the psychoanalytic discipline, both its theory and its practice, has always proceeded irregularly—at times in linear fashion, at other times in tortuous turns. The number and kind of psychoanalytic practitioners have changed: they are no longer exclusively physicians but representatives of the entire spectrum of psychologically expressive disciplines. The body of theory that comprises psychoanalytic understanding, which had begun to divide almost at once, has continued to do so, blossoming into a multiple array of alternative theories. Patients are no longer chosen from the narrow group of the early days, but from a much wider one. Applied psychoanalysis has similarly broadened its scope, following Freud himself in his wide search for cultural data to which to apply his new discoveries: Leonardo, Moses, group psychology, the discontents of civilization all came under his scrutiny. However, Freud's own researches never strayed for long from the clinical method, where the direct observation of data, cognitive and affective, provided with the aid of the psychoanalytic process the most authentic and reliable method for extension of the theoretical tree. The clinical process was also the most closely and reliably monitored source for validation of the results and claims of the derived therapeutic procedure.

Can a theory of psychoanalysis keep up with this endlessly proliferating, almost limitless agenda? Can psychoanalytic theory continue to encompass the increasingly broad phenomena that it scrutinizes? Is the theory of psychoanalysis a general theory of man, as Hartmann (1939) declared at the time of Freud's death? And crucially and most pragmatically, did psychoanalytic theory remain one theory, or did it in order to fill an expanding field split of necessity into more than one—several at the very beginning, then one major one for some time, then a division into two, then more, then many, and finally into an indeterminate "eclectic" group of alternative, interchangeable theories, to be chosen for the varying phenomenology they selectively attempt to understand and explain? The same questions apply to psychoanalytic technique. Did there develop one healing profession of psychoanalysis, or many separate fields of practice related to the multiplicity of theories (or even unrelated to these)? Is there one discrete, unitary, specific entity called psychoanalysis, or is there a theoretical league of nations, made up of a potpourri of disciplines related to each other, but each a different and separate whole?

It is difficult to assess the present status of psychoanalysis; contradictory trends can be both seen and felt. On the one hand, there is widespread derogation, even reviling, of the claims and aims of psychoanalysis—a feeling that it has failed in its promise, been a false idol, even a hoax. At the same time, large numbers of young people, looking to make their own places in society, are strongly drawn to the science and profession that more than any other aims to understand and treat human mental problems in depth.

This ambivalence about the field, in my opinion, stems in essence from widespread uncertainty as to the validity of its theoretical core. There is no doubt that the center of psychoanalysis, its explanatory theory, is not today at its peak. We are dealing not only with hostile appraisals from outside, but also with a crisis of spirit and morale within the profession itself. There was a time when a psychoanalytic referral was a fairly predictable process. Analysts shared a common theory from which a common treatment could be confidently expected. There were individual variations among analysts, of course, but "psychoanalysis" meant a view and a means common enough to all of its practitioners that it defined a profession: analyst and patient would look inward, hoping to expose and resolve unconscious conflicts.

As psychoanalysis rounds the turn of its first century, the practice of analysts is less homogeneous, and the theory is less coherent. Patients are neither as confident nor as plentiful as they were, and the prognosis for psychoanalysis is considered by many guarded. One obvious factor is the economic, political, and social milieu. But the issue is overdetermined; the *science* of psychoanalysis is not as secure in its moorings as we would wish, or as it once was. This background condition of scientific uncertainty is in my opinion a major source of instability within the discipline. It is not hard to believe that a public that sees psychoanalysts themselves sharing a theoretical base and consensus would feel more confident than one that witnesses the theoretical disharmony of the field. One major determinant of the plight of analysis resides not in our external surround but within our own field, and this is the one that we can influence.

This opinion is not shared by all. Many, probably most, analysts feel otherwise. They point to a rich diversity in our theory and science, and see this as creative advance. Psychoanalysis, in this presently dominant view, has broken away from restricting bounds, and is becoming more realistic and more useful. There are multiple theories, alternative explanations, many understandings. The current theoretical ambience, which holds this condition to be healthy, views these multiple points of view as equal, interchangeable, and a matter of preference or choice, based on experience, taste, or scientific conviction. A referring source, whether doctor, friend, advisor, or another psychoanalyst, needs to decide not only on analysis as opposed to the many competing treatments (both psychological and somatic-pharmacological), but also on what school or theory of psychoanalysis, and only then on which analyst. Despite everything written about "common ground," patients sent for a treatment to classical analysts, self psychologists, Kleinians, Lacanians, and Jungians will receive different treatments.

While those who defend diversity may say at this juncture that our definition of common ground allows a free intermingling of patients with anyone called a psychoanalyst today, and that this attitude of latitude and tolerance is operationally in effect across the field, empirically this is not the case. A self psychologist refers to others in that school; the same goes for classical, Kleinian, and object relations practitioners. Schools stay together; this has been so in Great Britain for decades, and is currently the case in this country and abroad. Even "contemporary Freudians" and "modern Kleinians" have failed to establish an operative and workable fusion of identities and clinical practice. Within the societies or institutes labeled "eclectic," each student (and later each analyst) comes with, or soon acquires, a more or less specific analytic identity. Indeed, it would be more to the credit of the science of psychoanalysis if theory and practice *did* coincide. When divergent theories do not result in qualitatively different treatments, that is, when there is little or no relationship between what one thinks and what one does, there is reason to wonder why.

It is also not the case, as some claim, that patients are distributed according to diagnosis: that is, that the neurotic go to the classical, "oedipal" analysts, the narcissistic to the self psychologists, the borderline to the Kernbergians, the deeply disturbed to the Kleinians, or the socially problematic to the object-relations theorists. In practice, patients go most often to an analyst of the school of the referring analyst. Nor are different patients of the same analyst treated with different theories according to their individual psychopathology, as some analysts theorize. Every patient with a particular analyst is looked at through the lens of that analyst's theory.

Clinical practice and debates over theory run different courses. What is "done" in actuality needs to find its way into the refinements of the theories that purportedly guide therapeutic procedures. Theorists often start out developing new theories for limited situations, then extend their conclusions more widely, and finally come to apply their thinking to all patients. This new thinking eventually extends, as Freud's theories did, to all people, and comes to comprise a new general psychology as well as a new clinical one. Self psychology, object relations theory, Kleinian concepts, like classical theory, have come to apply their thinking not to specific and limited clinical phenomena but to all development, normal as well as pathological. This developmental line is characteristic not only of entire theoretical systems, but of part-theories as well: that is, of specific concepts, for example projective identification. Starting out as limited mechanisms, or theoretical expositions of specific states or syndromes, they ultimately become global explanations of diverse behavior.

Another ironic set of conditions adds to the inconsistency and confusion; this has to do with the demographics of psychoanalysis today. Most institutes now call themselves eclectic, partly out of conviction, and partly in self-defense. There is currently a paucity of patients, an overabundance of psychoanalysts, and in some cases a dearth of candidates. The "core" institutes, those that have adhered most closely to "Freudian" concepts, suffer more than the others from too few applicants, and many cannot muster enough for a first-year class. Some of the most actively "eclectic" institutes, however, have waiting lists, and are turning people away. Even the American Psychoanalytic Association, reflecting this trend, has changed its scientific focus drastically in an eclectic and multitheoretical direction. This wider theoretical view is the postmodern, liberal position favored by most analysts today. However, to a minority (within which I include myself), it appears to be a trend toward scientific laxity. I suggest that there is a relationship between the resistance within the field to Freudian classical psychoanalysis, the fact that few seek training in the Freudian schools, the fact that large numbers respond to the offers and publicity of the new schools, and the confusions and divisions within psychoanalytic theory. And without ignoring the competitive pressure of faster treatments by medication or other means, all of these, in my view, are related to the simultaneous drop-off of the number of patients who desire analytic treatment, which had been strong and positive for many years.

At the same time, I wish to point out—and it is an important distinction to maintain—that the current pluralistic ambience is *un*related to the fact that a large number of new nonmedical analysts came into the fold of American psychoanalysis in one movement as a result of the legal and administrative changes of recent years. This influx, based on the successful resolution of an inequity that altered the face of American psychoanalysis, is not to be confused with, or ascribed to, the theoretical conflicts with which in some circles it is mistakenly conflated. From my direct experience, I can attest that the same theoretical issues and divisive conditions, in similar proportions, exist within the new groups of nonmedical analysts as in the older groups of American medical analysts, and for the same complex reasons.

FOUR FLAWS AND FALLACIES

As background for the exposition of what I consider to be the negative aspects of theoretical multiplicity, I wish to take note of several modes of thinking that I view as relentlessly active in psychoanalytic group thought and affect. These have bedeviled the course of our theoretical history and, almost from the beginning, have made for the infiltration into our theory of a mixture of reason and unreason and flawed group logic. These modes of thinking can be characterized as two fallacies and two flaws of logic, and they run through the history of our theory building, diverting it repeatedly in less than rational directions.

The first of these, a basic and common fallacy yet also a major modus operandi in psychoanalytic theorizing, is the replacement of a preexisting set of observations or piece of explanatory theory by another *when both the old and the new apply.* A more rational accumulative method of theory growth—the retention of findings and theories that are still applicable as new or more advanced ones are discovered—would lead to a more comprehensive and less incomplete or internally conflicted theoretical system. Such an approach does not reject new ideas or formulations, but it does discourage untoward deletions while encouraging the accretion of new, needed, and valid components.

This type of fallacious thinking took hold early in the evolution of Freud's thinking during the history-making Freud/Fliess (1887–1902) correspondence, when Freud (1897) "changed" from the seduction theory to his recognition of the role of unconscious fantasy in the etiology of the neuroses he was treating and studying at the time. I use quotes because it is neither clear nor in fact vital whether Freud, at the very beginning of his new insight, *replaced* the role of seduction, or *added* the role of fantasy to it. It is my opinion from all that followed that, after a brief vacillation, Freud settled into the belief that both applied. He himself stated later (1917) that it did not matter. Nevertheless, crucial for the future group development of the field, the internal–external dichotomy, precursor of the nature–nurture controversy, was born, and has never ceased to arouse passionate debate. A variety of reasons are offered and conclusions reached to explain Freud's change in, or addition to, theory. The factual history is ambiguous in itself, and this has led at times to a questioning of Freud's motives. Some believe that Freud invented fantasies, or even projected his own on to his patients (and the world), and Masson (1984) suggests that Freud covered up his seduction findings to cater to the medical establishment. The insistence on either/or with regard to this subject has not only kept it cloudy but has enabled it to confuse all of the other polarities and dichotomies that exist in the wider mental landscape.

This faulty style of reasoning can be applied to a wide range of phenomena, where it tends to encourage new findings at the expense of older ones. In a recent article (Harris 1998), much attention was paid to the rather arresting assertion that it is not parents who have the major effect on children's behavior, along with their genes, but the children's friends and peers. It happens that friend and peer relationships are a particular interest of mine, and I wrote one of the rare papers (1963a) in our literature on that most important object-relationship called *friendship*. But this example shows how replacement rather than addition can lead to distortion instead of cumulative insight. Both parents and peers play contributory roles; neither should be overlooked.

This leads me to the second pathogenic fallacy, which has also produced division and discord as long as psychoanalysis has existed. This is the mechanism of *pars pro toto*, the selection of a part and its substitution for the whole. One partial explanation (or several) is taken to be an entire explanatory system. A correlate of this faulty concept is the discarding of elements previously discovered to be necessary to the whole, as encapsulated in the common metaphor of throwing the baby out with the bathwater. The importance of the first years of life hypertrophies, and the oedipal period atrophies. Self-disorders take center stage, and intrapsychic conflicts are overshadowed, or gone. This fallacy is easily seen to be related to the preceding one. In the Freud example above, fantasy became the only explanation, while seduction, previously identified as operative in some cases, was eliminated as a possibility.

Freud himself, comparing Klein's work to Jung's in 1927, wrote to Jones, "All our apostates always grasped part of the truth and wanted to declare it as the whole truth" (Freud and Jones, 1908–1939, p. 635). Earlier he had commented, "In scientific matters people are very fond of selecting one portion of the truth, putting it in the place of the whole and then disputing the rest, which is no less true, in favour of this one portion. In just this way a number of schools of opinion have already split off from the psychoanalytic movement, some of which recognize the egoistic instincts while disavowing the sexual ones, and others attribute importance to the influence of the real tasks of life while overlooking the individual's past" (Freud 1917, p. 346). He said the same about Adler: "There must, of course, be *something* correct in this theory of 'individual psychologists'; a small particle is taken for the whole" (Freud 1933, p. 142). "It is an almost human characteristic of these 'secessionist movements' that each of them takes hold of one fragment out of the wealth of themes in psychoanalysis and makes itself independent on the basis of this seizure—selecting the instinct for mastery, for instance, or ethical conflict, or the [importance of the] mother, or genitality, and so on" (Freud 1917, pp. 143–144). This kind of fallacious thinking has been pointed out by many authors since then.

The importance of the oedipal stage was not invalidated as the importance of the preoedipal phase became better recognized and acknowledged; a second etiological focus was added. Ego psychology does not obviate the study of the id, nor object relations the psychology of drives. The increased role that Freud attributed to the ego added to his original formulation a new knowledge and appreciation of how ego and id interrelated. Acknowledgment of such additions leads to a different theoretical culture than do clusters of competing theories, in which alternative systems of explanation continuously vie with each other. In the latter case, each new system replaces and discards, leaving itself devoid of specific elements necessary for a comprehensive theory.

A third logical deficiency obtains when knowledge and insight gained in one sphere are not applied—or at least not applied without significant delay—to related relevant situations. Freud's insight of the complementary series, for example, which he applied to the dichotomy of genetic vs. experiential in producing sexual deviations, can fruitfully be applied to many other dualities. "I propose . . . that we should name a series of this kind 'a complemental series,' and I forewarn you that we shall have occasion to construct others of the same kind" (Freud 1917, p. 347). Elsewhere he said (with regard to the relative influences of the sexual drives and life experiences) that "the diminishing intensity of one factor is balanced by the increasing intensity of the other" (1905a, p. 240). Covering all the possibilities, he continues: "There is, however, no reason to deny the existence of extreme cases at the two ends of the series." Much is lost and overlooked in theory development when this insightful formulation is not applied to other conflicting or dichotomous pairs. Would this thinking, for example, not go a long way toward bringing clarity to the ongoing and charged disagreements about the roles of historical and narrative truth, or the duality of "objective" and "subjective"? In such dichotomies both poles must coexist, and any specific manifestation usually represents a combination of both.

The fourth logical flaw and obstacle to advance is the failure to follow up one's thought or actions with the consequences that could be expected from new discoveries or insights. For example, Waelder pointed out the fact that every theory is a combination of clinical and abstract, experience-near and experience-distant. This observation should do away with the separation of theories into clinical and abstract, yet it mostly fails to do so. Such failure to acknowledge the consequences of insight is a routine condition in every individual analysis, which is why attention must be paid to the phases that follow the acquisition of insight; I have addressed this in a previous study (Rangell 1981b) on the phase between insight and change in clinical life. In group life, however, questions of consequentiality remain more elusive; a group can dismiss a challenge more easily than an individual can. While there may be much verbal exchange in the extended psychoanalytic family, for example, it is less likely that reparative changes will follow debates and discussions.

Ernest Jones (1920), in an editorial in the first issue of the new *International Journal of Psycho-Analysis*, wrote that there were two forms of opposition to psychoanalysis. The first, direct opposition that denies the new truths as false, is the less dangerous. The second form, the "more formidable" one, is "to acquiesce in the new ideas on condition that their value is discounted, the logical consequences not drawn from them, and their meaning diluted" (p. 4). In the present context such opposition may be seen as an institutional denial mechanism, which by weight of numbers is stronger than an individual resistance. This attitude, I submit, is endemic today; but not, as Jones had it, in response to the *new* and disturbing. In the current ambience it is the persistence of the *old* and disturbing ideas that is apparently acknowledged but operationally denied. It is more difficult to address and influence group pathology than the individual pathologies that are the subject of an individual analysis.

THE MAINSTREAM IS NO LONGER MAIN

Current wisdom has it that we live in a period of theoretical pluralism. In truth, group movements, organized around alternative theories often based on the above fallacies, coalesced into a steady stream of change and innovation in the last two or three decades of this century, bringing about a major alteration in the look, theory, and practice of psychoanalysis. In his official opening of the 1995 International Psychoanalytic Congress in San Francisco, the chairman said explicitly that "the main theme of this Congress was chosen to encourage pluralism as well as to stimulate the development of new ideas compared with the more classic ones" (Grinberg 1995).

This situation is widely accepted in the present psychoanalytic culture. Indeed, the celebratory mood that accompanied this announcement was such that it has led to the impression that the approbation is unanimous. This is not, however, the case, and I will try to make clear why I for one do not share it. Due to a reversal in recent years of what is considered "politically correct" in psychoanalysis, my contrasting view will hardly induce a mood of ready acceptance in most of my readers. Still, I believe that this is the direction our profession will take into its future. My own effort in psychoanalytic theory throughout my sixty years in the field has been to tease out and advance the progression of the unitary theory begun by Freud, retaining what has proven to be enduring (not necessarily ideal or complete) and accruing to this developing whole whatever new discoveries also prove valid and enduring. My goal has always been, and it is in this book, to present a view of a unitary psychoanalytic theory as this has cumulatively grown and progressed over the century. I want also to delineate the impediments to cumulative growth imposed by conflicting methodologies and group phenomena. During the first half of my professional life, this orientation had much company, and was in fact the "correct" view among the most influential analysts of the time. This was not because it contained and continued Freud's evolving theories, but because it was considered the theory that best fit the psychoanalytic method of empirical observation, leading to the most satisfying and useful explanations of the data obtained.

Yet even in its heyday the psychoanalytic "mainstream" never earned its position by numbers or popularity. Existing within a hostile surround, its adherents had to comfort themselves with an affinity based on commonality of thought. After a golden period of centrality, a peculiar turn of history has made this traditional, cumulative view a minority interest once more, this time within psychoanalysis—a minority that at times seems to be dwindling down toward zero. The mainstream, although it is still called that, is no longer main. However well attended our psychoanalytic congresses may continue to be, psychoanalysts are still a small group, an island in the larger ocean of psychiatry, social work, and psychology. But unlike before, our core beliefs now are fragmented and shattered. In that fact, in my opinion, lies the most important of our problems, not in the sociology or the external political turbulence usually held to blame. We are still isolated, but can no longer warm ourselves with closeness within our own field. How this has come to pass has not been generally or sufficiently the focus of investigation.

A UNIFIED THEORY, AND DIVERSITY IN UNITY

My life experiences as a psychoanalyst in continuous clinical practice and searching always for unity in diversity have converged into a personal scientific credo. I call this overall point of view a "total composite psychoanalytic theory" (Rangell 1988, 1997a, 1998)—"total" because it contains all nonexpendable elements, "composite" because it is a blend of all valid discoveries, old and new, and "psychoanalytic" because it fulfills the criteria of psychoanalysis. While intellectual progress often appears irregular and uneven to outside observation, and while this is true in the special case of psychoanalytic theory as well, this total theory, which continues to develop alongside of the alternative partial ones, is I believe a parallel and more desirable development of the psychoanalytic science than the current resort to theoretical pluralism.

The term *unitary* today seems to many to be tainted with autocracy and authoritarianism. There is a similar bias against "classical," which denotes enduring value and permanent appeal, but implies to some a crumbling ruin—this is ironic, as analysts, along with archeologists, seek and see value in the buried old. The unitary and the classical are now explicitly called reactionary, and pluralism is considered liberal. Politics mixes with science, deflecting theoretical discussion in untoward and confused directions. The idea of a unified theoretical formulation not only fails to evoke in others the quiet satisfaction of the (at least potentially efficient) comprehensiveness of the past, but in fact produces a distinct aversion and arouses an oppositional affective response.

Yet a unitary theory need not eschew complexity, in psychoanalysis any more than in any other science. A unified psychoanalytic understanding may include an array of internal forces, structures, and processes sufficient to encompass the immense complexity of its subject, human psychology. There must be room in this unitary theory for all the diversity of human nature and all its infinite complexity. The claim of a common practice based upon diverse understandings, however, as the concept of the "common ground" underlying multiple theories suggests, leads in quite other directions. These are opposite formulations: one view asserts that clinical behaviors may differ, but that one understanding applies to them all; the other that the clinical technique is the same in all cases, whatever the understanding that informs it. The former, which coincides with my view, is congruent with Fenichel's (1945) dictum, "There are many ways to treat neuroses but there is only one way to understand them" (p. 554). That way is the psychoanalytic way; the central quest of the psychoanalyst is to make the fullest possible determination of what that way is. Such a unified view is never complete, but it strives for completeness, with as much economy as possible.

A historian can focus an investigation in two ways: with microscopic views of a limited area, or with more global overviews of a larger one. I feel that in psychoanalysis we have seen ample and copious studies of circumscribed theories, minutely dissected and accompanied usually by intense debates about their contents. We have also seen plenty of microscopic dissection of abstract general theories of understanding and therapy. One such fine differentiation, commonly stressed when I was a candidate, comes to mind as an example—the differences between introjection, incorporation, and identification. We felt so knowledgeable and victorious in being able to separate these closely contiguous entities one from the other! There has been less study and less assessment, however, from the macroscopic end—the overview from a more distant vantage point, comparable to an aerial view of a geographic or military area, in which certain trends and large installations can be discerned that are not visible (or recognizable) on the ground. Individual trees and species have been closely studied in the landscape of psychoanalysis and have come to be well known, while entire forests, the relationships among them, and the interconnecting paths and bridges, have been missed.

I feel that we must examine our general "field" with the same care, purpose, and methods that one turns on specific subjects or on the contributions of individual analysts; such efforts direct our attention to the base of the psychoanalytic population pyramid that gives group opinion its strength and importance. In applying analytic study to sociopolitical life, I (2003) have come to feel that the psychology of public opinion must be much more broadly emphasized than it has been. Too often only the prominent and most visible are looked to for their roles in the unfolding and consequences of events; not enough attention is paid to the actions of everyone else, the people who absorb and react to ideas or quietly formulate their own, normal or pathological, and who are mainly responsible for group attitudes and conditions, and for subsequent outcomes.

Like the multiple metapsychologic points of view that converge upon a single psychic element, I will approach the state of theory itself by following a number of converging paths; these come together in my view of a unitary theory. These multiple points of view and vectors of experience are interactive and re- ciprocal, and they converge around particular theoretical and historical foci. In a 1993 lecture in Los Angeles, I described the psychoanalytic journey as a composite of several paths: (1) Freud's discovery of psychoanalysis; (2) the history and vicissitudes of psychoanalytic thought from Freud to the present, its expansions and development, progressions and regressions; (3) integrated with these, actually the raison d'être behind all of them, the jour- ney of a patient through psychoanalysis; and (4) the role of the present generation of psychoanalysts in carrying the future of psychoanalysis forward into the next century.

Each of these paths proceeds, in its own characteristic way, from uncertainty to knowledge, through anxiety (which both obstructs the journey and guides it) to integrity. This can, most importantly, be said to be the path of a patient in analysis. It also happens to highlight two of my own key theoretical concepts, the theory of anxiety (Rangell 1955b, 1968b) and the syndrome of the compromise of integrity (Rangell 1974a). I believe that the irregu- lar, inconstant, erratic external course of psychoanalytic history, which has affected both our theory and our derivative practice, contains within it a steady, developing, evolving theme that once was, *and still remains*, its central trunk. It is this "enduring arma- ture" (Rangell 1983) of psychoanalytic theory that I aim to out- line and delineate. And it is this defining central structure that will continue into the future.

4

PERSONAL SCIENTIFIC ODYSSEY

1940: THE FIELD AS I BEGAN

As I was entering the field in the early 1940s, Karen Horney had just seceded from the New York Institute, and a number of young analysts and students had gone with her. Horney represented analytic interest in the importance of cultural input to the conflicts of the individual. It was a moment of potential apocalypse; Hitler had invaded Czechoslovakia and Poland, and the tendency to see cultural, rather than individual, input as the etiologic center of the mental disorders reflected, as many felt it, the sociopolitical pressures and conflicts of that historic time.

Those of us contemplating training in psychoanalysis faced several dilemmas. We had to reconcile our sense of duty with the wish to use this crucial time for personal professional advance. But behind this, a more abstract question confronted us: was it external pressures or intrapsychic dynamics that caused the symptoms we would see in our practices treating the "nervous and mental diseases"? The ominous rise of fascism and the social ferment that it engendered competed during these charged and anxious times with scientific interests in the minds of my generation of future psychoanalysts, just as social consciousness and antifascism influenced the thinking of the socially oriented psychoanalytic theorists of that period, focusing them upon environmental contributions to mental life. This was the context in which the cultural and interpersonal schools arose and engaged the minds of adherents who felt that the answers to these existential questions lay in that direction. In these schools, the dominant role of culture was emphasized, and the intrapsychic model correspondingly underplayed. In a more specific sense, to many in my generation of young, eastern, liberal-to-left mental health trainees, the conflict was whether Freud or Marx would be the intellectual beacon that could lead us toward a rational world.

I myself was of a mind to combine the two: to focus on internal mental conflicts and their resolution, but to make myself available to fulfill my social responsibilities as well. As for the conflict over theory, at that time I felt (rather than knew) that psychoanalysis, in its theory of understanding, could embrace the totality of life, and would explain, and influence, the social as well as the individual behavior of its subjects. This belief did not preclude, but rather facilitated, my stance toward the impending call for military duty.

The same ideological struggle and intellectual dilemma, but in a different form, confronted older analysts as well, inside the cauldron of central Europe. Closer than we to the scene of the impending apocalypse, a leftist group of leading European classical analysts were also caught in an agonizing conflict between scientific and political beliefs. In their case, however, the conflict seemed to exist not *within* psychoanalysis, but between it and political action. Humanism was felt to be securely established within psychoanalysis; it was a matter of how psychoanalysis and psychoanalysts were to survive and endure. Otto Fenichel, as one of that group, held a central goal: to protect scientific psychoanalysis and its role in cultural criticism (Reichmayr and Muhlleitner 1998, CL 7/1). In his travels ahead of the advancing Nazis, he struggled over whether to support or oppose the continued existence of the International Psychoanalytic Association, on the basis of its conservative stance in the face of actions of "Aryan" members of the DPG in Germany. Only after considerable debate with others and within himself did Fenichel decide to make common cause with the political left, but to maintain solidarity with other analysts in professional matters. Wilhelm Reich, who experienced a more extreme conflict between psychoanalysis and political action, had already given up analysis, and started on the road to the individual compromise formations that eventuated finally in his psychotic symptoms.

THE REPORTER-NARRATOR

Just as it is helpful to be aware of the personality of the analyst-presenter when assessing a clinical report, I think it will be helpful to the reader many times over the course of this narrative to have some knowledge of the psychological instrument through which the facts and opinions in it are filtered.

Since I aim to demonstrate how my experiences as a developing analyst dovetail with the development of my theoretical convictions, this account is the experiential memoir not primarily of a private life, but of a public scientific one. I offer it not as an indulgence in autobiography, but to supplement the record of my theoretical path that I have left in the literature with the personal experiences that illuminated that journey. While the element of personal history that I am introducing is not usually included in a scientific exposition, I feel that it belongs here, and furthermore that a history of the particularly human science of psychoanalysis is incomplete without it.

I offer my own story also because the ranks are thinning of those who participated in this era first-hand, or who can reach back to direct contact with the generation that preceded us. But only through such reaching back is continuity extended to the founders and pioneers. Newcomers to the field can benefit from a knowledge of what preceded them. Comparable interpersonal issues of psychoanalysis in Great Britain have finally been exposed and studied, first by King and Steiner (1991), and then by Baudry (1994) and Reed and Baudry (1997). Reed and Baudry (1997, p. 488) have said that "The record of controversies in psychoanalysis, more often than not, reveals the conflicts of human beings in action, not of analysts in good-enough neutrality." But it took fifty years for that truth to be recognized and studied in England after the controversies there. It is now three or four decades since the American version of similar problems began and burgeoned. It is not too soon to begin to reflect on them. A new generation in psychoanalysis arrived on the scene as the actions of the previous one were eventuating in splits. In the city where I live and work, a "lost generation" of analysts was caught in a storm of conflict during their training years in the sixties and seventies. While the effects were not uniform, and some retained individual creativity, many others were demoralized and succumbed to an apathetic future.

As I have said, I entered the field in 1940. My path then—at mid-century, in this country, in urban New York where I grew up—was, as for many of us, a recapitulation of the serendipitous yet crucial one followed by Freud. In the late thirties and early forties, the course was typically from medicine, to neurology, through psychiatry, to psychoanalysis. We became interested in behavior initially through a fascination with the nervous system and the amorphous line between the brain and the mind. We had a subliminal (if not overt) conviction that there was a long way to go before that line could be crossed or understood, that the intellectual ground was murky, and that a world of clarification was needed. But there was no dearth of applicants ready to embark upon this study at that phase in the history of our science. The field was compelling, mysterious, and infinitely desirable. Its prestige at the time was such that the best and the brightest were seduced by its challenge and its potential. I have learned since then that these attributes were not without another element. I know that for me at least there was a sense that this new field offered a window onto unnamed questions with which we all live—mysterious questions that have in common the unease and anxiety they evoke—and that in it might lie at least some of the answers. There was lively dissemination of this intriguing new system of understanding and therapy, and its affective and intellectual impact were increasingly evident, but since acceptance by the public had not yet hit its stride and so there was no deep pool of patients, the prospect of a thriving practice was not yet a motivating temptation.

MEDICAL SCHOOL

My medical education began in 1933 at the University of Chicago. It did not directly point me toward psychoanalysis, but it did evoke an interest in the central nervous system and its extensions, the spinal cord and peripheral nerves. This interest turned out to be a first step in that direction. I was interested almost at once in the embryology, and then in the anatomy and neurophysiology, of the brain. This was the most special, the most fascinating, the most compelling organ. It was the core and somatic center from which so many things—behavior; life almost—radiated. (I note with interest as I use the word "core" here, that this word has been an important organizing theme for me, recurring in my writings over almost a lifetime. A collection of my papers in 1990 was titled *The Human Core*.)

This cumulating interest in the brain coalesced out of a series of studies presented from the first year by, as I remember, George Bartelmez, professor of anatomy, who taught us embryology, histology, and neurology. (I looked his name up; with the wide interest of everyone today, myself included, in checking himself for Alzheimer's, I was relieved that this memory of seventy years ago was accurate.) I remember being impressed at the very start by the role of the brain stem in maintaining life; this may be one of my first thoughts about a "core." William Bloom (of the text by Maximow and Bloom) taught histology, and the dramatic A. J. (Ajax) Carlson and Arno Luckhardt physiology. A crucial and inspirational figure later, but also a cold and intimidating one, was Percival Bailey, professor of neurosurgery. He was known to have come directly from Harvard's Harvey Cushing, the father of neurosurgery, who had created the first classification of brain tumors, and through them of brain functioning.

I remember thinking, first vaguely but soon in a more formed way, that I would like to head toward brain surgery (no pun intended). The brain seemed to control it all. It made and directed the human being. The most special specialty was neurology, I thought, and above this, looming as the ultimate, was neurosurgery, in which one can act and do as well as think. That seemed to me an epitome, an infinite mystery and challenge, the power to affect things at the source. By working on pathology here, one could set things straight, and turn what had gone wrong back to normal. (I wonder as I write this where this high aim came from, since, although my parents were hard-working, loving, and supportive, my origins were humble and without intellectual stimulation. My parents were both immigrants—my father from Russia, my mother from Poland. They met at around the age of twenty on the teeming Jewish east side of New York. I am the oldest of four.)

Bailey, scientist that he was, years later came also to be known for his vituperative criticism of the Freudian opus, which he considered a fraudulent pretender to the status of a science. I remember Bailey's lively second in command, Paul Bucy, as a kinder and more accessible person, if less inspirational, and more of a communicator. Neurology, more passive than neurosurgery but more scholarly, was represented by Roy Grinker, who was Chief of Neurology and Psychiatry (which were fused into one department) and whose textbook we used. Grinker, I heard vaguely, had recently returned from a psychoanalysis with Sigmund Freud in Vienna. No more than that was communicated explicitly, but some negative sense came through about this experience. Grinker was an authoritative neurologist. His textbook was one of two that we knew about, the other being Israel Wechsler's of New York. These two authors were contemporaries, and both Jewish. Neurology seemed to be a scholarly, Jewish, talmudic specialty—the most intricate crossword-puzzle type of specialty, the most challenging intellectual pursuit. The main specialists practicing in that field were known to be Jewish; along with Wechsler and his colleagues in New York, and Grinker, I knew of George Hassin, also in Chicago, and Eugene Ziskind in Los Angeles. This was emphatically not so, however, among the leading surgeons and internists, or in most of the other specialties. Even less was it true for neurosurgery, which was known to be the most inaccessible field of any to Jews, or indeed to anyone without connections.

Psychiatry was not a great presence in medical school during that period. I had a clinical course in psychiatry from Jules Masserman, to whom I presented a case of schizophrenia that he praised, but I did not yet see the connection of psychiatry to the rest of life. In contrast with the negative feelings we absorbed about Grinker's psychoanalysis, an experience with some positively tinged emotional connection came in a course by child psychiatrist Douglas Buchanan. He was a dry Scotsman who did not look the part, but his class is the only one in which I recall any reference to feelings. I remember him speaking in one lecture of difficulties experienced by children in relation to love, and I have a memory of feeling an embarrassed silence in the room. Or perhaps it was entirely my own embarrassment. But I do not remember any discussion or question or follow-up. The lone reference to psychoanalysis that came up during those years was the name of Franz Alexander who, as I learned later, was the active leader at the Chicago Psychoanalytic Institute further north in the Loop. But he played no part at the university or in the medical school.

NEUROLOGY

After my graduation in 1937, I returned to my home city for an internship at Brooklyn Jewish Hospital, to be followed by continued training in my chosen specialty. Leo Davidoff was the much-respected head of neurosurgery there—an island of Jewishness in a gentile field. A residency with him was shaping up as my goal. The first step on this path was to be neurology, about which I already felt positive and motivated. One of my fellow interns was Victor Rosen, who was also planning for neurology, though in his case with the goal of neuropsychiatry. We both applied and were accepted for the highly praised Montefiore Hospital neurological residencies, and began there on January 1, 1939.

At Montefiore, we meshed with a sparkling group of residents, interns, and young staff members. Importantly for this saga (and, I soon learned, typical of this forward-looking and avant-garde group), many of them were very interested in psychoanalysis. Particularly close to me and to Rosen—we became something of a triumvirate—was Jacob Arlow, who had already had a psychiatric residency at the U.S. Public Health Service on Ellis Island. Jack had been deeply inspired by psychoanalysis, and intended to apply for psychoanalytic training after psychiatry and neurology. He would "analyze" the dreams of anyone who volunteered them! Among the young staff members and teachers of the residents were Samuel Atkin, Sydney Tarachow, and the hospital's neuropathologist, Charles Davison, all of whom, while they were trained neurologists, were also either graduates of, or candidates at, the New York Psychoanalytic Institute. It did not take much to lure any of them, during their teaching of clinical neurology, into psychoanalytic side-meanings. And the brilliant Nathan Savitsky had just as much to do with influencing us toward analysis, albeit in a negative way, by his compelling and entertaining antipsychoanalytic stories. One day in the residents' cloakroom he regaled an enthralled audience with the story of how George Gershwin had died of a brain tumor after being told by his analyst that his headaches were neurotic. I did not know then, but was not surprised to learn from the principals themselves after I had settled on the West Coast, that Gershwin's analyst in Los Angeles, Ernst Simmel, had kept sending Gershwin back to his neurologist, who kept returning him to the analyst as neurologically negative, and insisting that the headaches were psychogenic. Gershwin was finally operated upon by Howard Nafziger in San Francisco, who found the malignant brain tumor from which Gershwin died.

My preconscious plan, not fully articulated at the time, was to apply after neurology to work with John Fulton at Yale in neurophysiology, and then go on to neurosurgery. I had already had several preliminary interviews toward neurosurgery residencies, but a number of factors led me to a shift in direction. One was my being Jewish. This had been an issue in my applications to medical school, and it was clearly a greater one at many sought-after residencies. I felt it most overtly in my interviews for a neurosurgery residency at the Neurological Institute at Columbia and at the University of Pennsylvania. Another personal factor that played a definitive role at this crucial juncture was that I had just married, a month after starting my neurological residency at Montefiore. I felt a new sense of urgency, and the neurosurgery path now seemed the longest and most arduous one of all.

The resultant of these forces was the decision to join my close colleagues and switch to psychiatry, from which I would move on to psychoanalysis. Without much *sturm und drang*, I had made a crucial choice—away from a life work, as I looked at it then, that aimed at pinpoint localization, complete reversal of pathology, and instant gratification by a definitive cure, to one at the opposite pole of indistinctness, ambiguity, multiple causation, and interminability. I did not know this at the time, nor did I appreciate the enormity of the change, but my new course in life was established. I had thought that neurosurgery would require too many years of study and training; ironically, what I entered instead was a field that would call for study for the rest of my life. From the point of view of intellectual scope, what I gained was limitless. But my wife and I played the "what if" game for fun and speculation more than once, especially during discouraging scientific-political times, which were not infrequent during our long shared career. What if I had made the alternative decision? Every time we played our mental game, the outcome was different.

Although I made this decision unexpectedly, it was actually not as completely sudden as this narrative may suggest. A seed of interest in psychoanalysis had been planted during my college days at Columbia, although it did not germinate until ten years later. I have a small but definite memory of an intense brief exposure to Freud, which, while only a glancing occasion, left its mark. I remember absorbing, from a quick scanning of parts of a book—

it might have been "The Interpretation of Dreams" or A. A. Brill's *The Basic Writings of Sigmund Freud*—certain striking references to sex and dreams. I knew that the text was right, and that it was speaking to me. But there was no conscious thought to move in that direction at that time.

TO PSYCHIATRY, AND INTO THE FIELD OF PSYCHOANALYSIS

From the neurological residency that turned out to be my entry into the field of neuropsychiatry, I proceeded to a pair of psychiatric residencies. The first one was broadly oriented, providing brief exposure to many patients, and the opportunity to learn diagnosis and acute treatment across the diagnostic spectrum. I followed this with a second residency that concentrated on long-term psychotherapy, and the treatment of fewer patients in depth over the entire year. Such complementary training experiences were the mode at that time. The acute-turnover residency was in 1940 at Grasslands Hospital in Valhalla, New York, a Westchester county hospital with a busy urban service facility. The second one was in 1941 at the New York State Psychiatric Institute of Columbia University, a teaching hospital with a program of intense individual psychotherapy; it also, however, included insulin shock and other somatic modalities. Electric shock therapy was introduced into the therapeutic armamentarium during that year, and the Psychiatric Institute took a lead part. After a brief separation while I was at Grasslands, Jack Arlow and I came together again at the Psychiatric Institute, while Victor Rosen, who at that time was thinking more about academic psychiatry than psychoanalysis, went ahead from Montefiore with his plan to train with Adolph Meyer at the Phipps Clinic in Baltimore.

At Columbia, I found myself again with an ambitious and eager group of young neuroscientists-in-training, with ultimate aims toward psychoanalysis. Jack Arlow was there, and some former classmates from medical school whom I had not seen since then, such as the brilliant, energetic, and inquiring Louis Linn. We all settled into the intense treatment of our small complements of patients, feeling more or less unrestrained about time, as there were few external constraints to determine the length of therapy except the length of the residency itself. The atmosphere was inquisitive, congenial, fairly free, encouraging of scholarship. Analytic thinking was dominant, and it permeated and influenced the intellectual atmosphere.

Looking back, I can see that I started the practice of psychoanalytic therapy in stages, even before I was completely clear as to exactly what that was. First there were the therapies conducted in the two psychiatric residencies. At Grasslands treatments were relatively acute and brief, with occasional sharing of the hour's material (I would not call it supervision, or even consultation) with the resident a year ahead of me. That happened to be Samuel Futterman, who had already started analytic training in New York; I met him again later in Los Angeles, where we lived near each other. Strange as they were for me then, I think those initial sessions did qualify as analytic-type treatments, starting several patients on the road to self-inspection and insight.

In these early experiences, I already thought in terms of "the hour." "The material"—that is, what the patient spontaneously said, while I listened and (by my stance and attitude) encouraged—was "data." The rest was up to me; it was for me to "understand" what the patient was saying, at a different level and in a different frame and context than he or she could. I learned a great deal about the main outlines of what my patients and I were trying to do. Our roles quite easily became defined, as did some big concepts about what I was hearing. Today I understand with greater subtlety how we, those first patients and I, were intertwined. I remember an hysterical young woman with a shy smile, perhaps my first "analytic" patient. I was a young male doctor, and her therapist. We were connected—by a bond that it would take me many years to learn to dissect into its complex components. I was very motivated toward a therapeutic goal, as much in these early days as ever afterward. It was only later that I began to understand the dangers, or at least the analytic undesirability, of what Freud (1900) called "therapeutic zeal." But I still believe, now as I did then, that therapeutic intent is no bad thing.

Formal analytic training began for many of us during our residencies; we wasted no time to get going into the "real" thing. Soon after beginning my second residency at Columbia, I applied to the New York Psychoanalytic Institute (there never seemed any doubt among this group as to which institute to join; the New York Psychoanalytic was automatically the place), and I began my analysis and formal analytic matriculation a month after that residency began. Arlow and I entered the New York Psychoanalytic Institute together. We started our analyses on the same day, February 1, 1941. We took the subway together to Columbus Circle, went our separate ways from the subway station, and met again after our analytic hours for the train ride back to the hospital. Traveling together on the subway to and from our respective hours every day for a year, we were the first psychoanalytic study group I knew of.

THE WRITING OF PAPERS

The writing of papers began early for me compared to most, and soon became a steady interest. Although this desire to write arose partly in response to outside stimulation, I know that the process came mostly from motivations within myself. An impulse to communicate, share, and discuss accompanied my interest in scientific and theoretical learning as I progressed along my chosen path through medicine and psychiatry. It had its start perhaps when I was an intern in medicine, continued during my residencies in neurology and psychiatry, was in evidence as well during military service, and blossomed as I became a student of psychoanalysis and human behavior. The desire to write was for me such a continuous one—almost the central professional activity of my life, I would say, and the one that brought me to the attention of my peers and colleagues in the scientific and organizational structures in psychoanalysis—that I am curious about its origins. Psychoanalysts have always had a zeal to hear and discuss papers, and they argue. Their main quest is to understand, and their goal is to solve riddles. Was it not this same curiosity that led Freud to the riddle of the sphinx, and directly to Oedipus?

The wish to organize and transmit my own thoughts on a subject of general interest came to me early; the first time in my professional life that I can recall was during my general rotating internship after medical school. Sulfadiazine had just been introduced, and there were excited discussions about the new "antibiotics," and the claims made on their behalf. I was asked—perhaps I volunteered—to present a case on rounds in which this new treatment was being tried, and I remember thinking that I could just as well describe and organize *all* the cases I then had, which were several, and try to evaluate and discuss the subject. I remember, how accurately I cannot say, some fleeting (I would now say preconscious) twinges of anxiety and self-doubt about the *chutzpah* of this thought. But I also remember suddenly asking myself why I thought anyone else would know more about this treatment, which had just been introduced, than the interns on the ward who were closest to the patients. While we interns listened with awe when staff members pronounced "facts," in this case all of us were seeing the method and its results for the first time. What would make the doctors on the outside better authorities on the new subject than the interns, who were on the front lines with the sick patients? I remember reporting on several patients and giving a "paper" on the subject at rounds; it was a satisfying success.

I believe I was coming personally to the scientific method, the method of making clinical observations of one's own and drawing conclusions based upon them—that is, the acquisition of direct data and then the interpretation of them. A cognitive need to organize and make coherent, and an affective wish for feedback and confirmation (and no doubt personal notice), converged in a method and a course of action, with accompanying gratifying results. Whatever the exhibitionistic instinctual drive component, mastery was enhanced and object relations enormously stimulated.

Today in my ongoing deep curiosity about inner workings, I can see in retrospect a motivation to observe, to learn from seeing, and to organize my findings and thoughts—and along with this a drive for action, expression, and external communication.

This mode continued and developed during my residencies, applied each time to new subjects of study. At Montefiore, I was probably the least resistant of the house staff to presenting interesting and talked-about cases. I remember presenting at grand rounds to Moses Keschner, the toughest of our teachers, whom everyone loved and feared. One presentation involved a young female patient who had been admitted to the neurological service as a case of Sydenham's or possibly early Huntington's chorea, with a rather acute onset of involuntary tic-like movements of the neck and throat muscles, but whom I came to diagnose as a case of globus hystericus. I took a careful history, influenced by both of my guiding disciplines (psychiatry and neurology), and elicited an acute conflict about fellatio in her immediate premorbid life. The interchange between Keschner, me, and the audience is remembered to this day by some of the participants, as the whimsical Keschner, who was no doubt aware of his students' latent interests, noticed the suppressed giggles and said, "OK, Rangell, give me the *schmutz*." We had fun. And with our spreading psychological interests, we probably twisted the findings and data occasionally to fit our involved and inquiring young minds. I don't think that the motivation of *anyone*, individual or group, is ever *purely* scientific!

To present, to compare cases and stimulate discussions, became a way of life. We were all learning in these provocative exercises and exchanges about human behavior, as well as about the brain. We were an enthusiastic and close group, and no one voluntarily missed the conferences, seminars, and discussions that were our fare. I loved them, and I came also to love to do them. My wife reminded me more than once that I postponed our honeymoon to give a talk to a journal club at Montefiore. (That one I don't remember!)

Presentation soon became publication. I started to publish at Montefiore as a coauthor with the ebullient Savitsky. We produced several papers (Savitsky and Rangell 1950a,b) on ocular findings, including homonymous hemianopsia, in multiple sclerosis, a subject he knew well and allowed me to help him write up and publish. I continued writing during the residency at Grasslands, where I wrote my first paper (1942) on my own. This further whetted my appetite to formulate, write, and publish observations or ideas that I felt might be new and of interest. This case at Grasslands combined neurology and psychiatry. A woman had been admitted after midnight as an acute schizophrenic: disoriented, seemingly hallucinating, and rather wild. From a careful interview conducted on admission in the middle of the night (we had a schedule of alternating night duty), I made a diagnosis of cerebral air embolism: air, I thought, had been sucked into engorged pelvic veins while the patient, who was postpartum, was exercising in the knee-chest position to improve her pelvic muscle tone. I concluded that she had a toxic organic syndrome rather than a psychogenic thought disorder. Savitsky's tutelage kept me ever alert not to miss a neurologic episode and so besmirch the name of psychiatry (or psychoanalysis). The patient recovered quickly, and I was—briefly—a hero.

Once I had started writing, both the motivation and the process intensified. The next year at the Psychiatric Institute, I met as a new staff member a recent émigré from Germany—the young Margaret Mahler, with whom I was to have a meaningful and lifelong relationship. Mahler was in private psychoanalytic practice, and had sent to our hospital a 7-year-old boy with the multiple tics and coprolalia of Gilles de la Tourette's disease. The patient was assigned to me for long-term therapy, which Mahler supervised. The combination of her analytic insights into "motoric" symptoms (as she called them) and my still-fresh neurologic interests led the two of us to coauthor a paper (Mahler and Rangell 1943) on the "*Maladie des Tics*," discussing both its psychosomatic (neurologic) and psychoanalytic aspects. This was the first psychoanalytic paper on the subject, and it remained the only one for many years. (Only decades later did great interest in that syndrome appear, when pharmacological treatment with haloperidol came into prominent use and stimulated psychotherapeutic interest again along with it.) My interest in child neurology, first tapped in medical school, began to overlap with a new (and permanent) interest in child analysis. It was this link and its aftermath that prompted Heiman Van Dam (1988) to call me many years later "a crypto child analyst." Mahler went on to a major interest in tics. For me, however, the war intervened, and to my regret, I could not accept her invitation to pursue this subject in further depth.

I allow myself this digression about writing and communication because it has a twofold relevance—a scientific one and a pragmatic one. The capacity to communicate ideas, important in the private work of analysis for its own sake, is also important for analysts who aspire to higher positions in the public arenas of psychoanalysis, be they scientific, teaching, or administrative. In the quest for recognition and appointment, the most common bottleneck among analysts is caused by anxiety about presenting clinical work or scientific papers to evaluators. Various institutes and associations today, in an effort to deal with this problem, hold courses and symposia at such august venues as the congresses of the American and the International. Writing also relates to one of the negative aspects of group process that I am describing and dealing with in this book—the way political adherents at times cluster around writers and their writings, resulting in the group influences that supersede the scientific method in determining the professional course of a psychoanalyst navigating through the historical periods of developing psychoanalytic theories. The actions of writing, formulating, making original observations, and drawing one's own conclusions serve as a counterweight to the tendency to go along with the conclusions and formulations of others. I do not mean that one may not accept, or be guided by, the theoretical work of others. But one's own discoveries and the application of one's own scientific method is the best antidote against over-suggestibility. In this area—that is, in the acquisition by individual analysts of autonomy and independence in consolidating their own experiences as well as in assessing the plethora of theoretical writings that surround them—in my opinion lies the future of the scientific life of psychoanalysis.

I am moved to reflect that the motivation and growing habit to write, speak, and publish that I have annotated here went along with, and probably itself stimulated in me, an increasing confidence in observing, formulating, and offering results to be tested by the opinions of peers—a combination of attitudes and activities that were helpful both in increasing my confidence in my professional activities, and in moving me into prominent positions. These attitudes stemmed, I think, from an active rather than a passive nature, and a tendency to initiate and choose, rather than to accept and concur. I see these as a fortunate set of directions, results perhaps in part of having been the first-born, having had a father I had neither to fear nor imitate, and having being allowed and encouraged, but not forced, to pursue education, every stage of which was remarked by my parents with quiet praise and satisfaction. I am grateful, and aware that not everyone is so fortunately situated.

OTTO FENICHEL

During my residency at the Psychiatric Institute in 1941, I encountered for the first time the name of Otto Fenichel. Psychoanalytic books were becoming available in the turbulence of Europe as analysts, including Freud, were being hurriedly displaced, and the Institute was developing an important Freud library in New York under the watchful eye of librarian Jacob Shatzky. There I came across Otto Fenichel's future classic *The Psychoanalytic Theory of Neurosis* (1945), which he had published in preliminary form in the *Psychoanalytic Quarterly* as "An Outline of Clinical Psychoanalysis" (1933). This series of chapters was for me an avidly read source. The case nuggets Fenichel presented, and the direct and succinct conclusions he reached, were to me entirely convincing. They seemed to be direct and logical cause and effect. They made the irrational rational. They made sense, however uncommon this new sense might be. I did not know then that this treatise would develop into the most admired psycho-analytic summary presentation of my life—almost a scientific credo. I also learned at that time—I am not sure at what level of consciousness this stayed with me—that Fenichel lived in Los Angeles.

I did not know then the role that Otto Fenichel would play in my professional identity, how much he would come to represent the spine of my guiding theoretical system, the distillate in the modern world of what Freud had laid down during the previous half-century. Another aspect of Fenichel's leadership has emerged more recently (Jacoby 1986, Harris and Brock 1992), related to the challenges and moral conflicts of the Hitler years. As the Nazi storm began to build, Fenichel and Wilhelm Reich found them-selves locked in a titanic struggle over the Marx vs. Freud dilemma I mentioned above. An émigré, moving ahead of the storm from Berlin first to Oslo and then to Prague before coming to Los An-geles, Fenichel first took the position that the Marxist group of psychoanalysts should leave the I.P.A. in opposition to politically (as opposed to analytically) conservative forces within that orga-nization. Considered by some as autocratic, but more prescient in the face of the events of the times than Freud seems to have been, in the end Fenichel used his power to hold the I.P.A. together against the divisiveness that grew with the developments in Ger-many, choosing to unite divergent factions rather than to disrupt the entire analytic movement. Fenichel's adherence to psychoana-lytic thinking remained steadfast and survived the pressures and agony of the times. Detailed accounts of the conflicts and activi-ties of an influential group of Freudian-Marxist analysts, includ-ing among others Fenichel, Wilhelm and Annie Reich, and Edith Jacobson, have been documented in a recent study by Reichmayr and Muhlleitner (1998) of a *Rundbriefe* of letters circulated by Fenichel to this small scattered group during the late thirties.

Fenichel had an encyclopedic mind and superb talents for organizing and interpreting clinical data. His classic textbook, *The Psychoanalytic Theory of Neurosis*, summarized what was known of psychoanalysis up to that time. In the forties, at the halfway mark of the psychoanalytic century, the field and its literature were still encompassable by one individual. I think that Fenichel also saw the future. Many of the principles and problems to come were presaged in his two classic volumes on theory and technique. I have mentioned the perennial affect-ideation controversy, for example. Fenichel (1941) debated this subject vigorously in his monograph on technique, arguing persuasively against the views of Theodor Reik, who felt that theory, ideation, and intellectuality stood in opposition to the affective life in psychoanalysis and worked to stultify and invalidate emotional experiences. Fenichel knew that both were indispensable. Fenichel also foresaw the coming overemphasis on transference, comparing it to the prevalent early misunderstanding that psychoanalysis was only about sex. The lifting of any one element out of the whole at the expense of other necessary ones was recognized and opposed by Fenichel as it had been by Freud. Fenichel spotted the intrusion of the irrational into the theory of psychoanalysis, and warned against it, foreshadowing many of the divisions to come. "The subject-matter, not the method of psychoanalysis, is irrational," Fenichel (1945, p. 4) wrote. This has been a beacon to me through the years since.

I had the good fortune to meet Otto Fenichel not long afterward in an unexpected way. The war in Europe broke out during my first (neurological) residency, and America entered it during my third, when I was at Columbia. I left New York for the Army a year after I finished my residencies, on New Year's Day, 1943. In 1945, I met Fenichel at an Air Force base in Colorado and spent a few days with him there. He was visiting as a civilian to observe our treatment of airmen with war neuroses— a treatment based on psychoanalytic principles, of course. We interviewed returnees from combat and hospitals abroad who had undergone traumatic experiences in air warfare under sodium pentothal to release repressed memories, much as Freud had used hypnosis in his early cases. The film *Home of the Brave* was based on this work.

I had never subscribed to the widely held myth that all classical analysts are closed and rigid. But if I had, my experience with Fenichel during those days, as brief as they were, would have dispelled it. To me, even before we met, Fenichel *was* psychoanalysis. And now here was Fenichel himself, an open, amiable, somewhat raucous man, eager, enthusiastic, with a quick, ready laugh and open to any good use or practical expansion of psychoanalysis that could be made.

I felt honored to be able to arrange on the spot to continue with him the training analysis I had begun at the New York Institute before entering military service. (I had already planned to move to Los Angeles after the war for other reasons; the image and now the person of Otto Fenichel were the icing on the cake.) Forty years later (Rangell 1986a), I wrote that a life history is shaped by psychic determinism, ego will, and chance events. All three of these played their parts for me in this determining life move. My intended move to Los Angeles was confirmed and solidified in my meeting with Fenichel. Tragically, however, he died suddenly of a ruptured cerebral aneurysm at the age of 48. This was in January 1946, five months before I arrived in Los Angeles. Chance played its hand twice, first in the brief presence and then in the absence of Fenichel.

Fenichel has remained for me an inspirational model; not the man, whom I met but cannot say I knew, but his psychoanalytic way of thinking. By serendipity, the text that had come to mean so much to me was published that very year I met Fenichel and planned to begin work with him. Fenichel, and this book which was his zenith, have served me, in a way, as a model for this book. He looked back from 1940, and so will I—but I can look forward from that year too—not only toward all that preceded his epic summation, but also toward the developments that followed it. In this wide historical view, I do not aim to be inclusive, or to be substantive and thorough about specific theories. Instead I will examine the course of the scientific method and its vicissitudes, its use and misuse in the formation of alternative and competing theories, and the obstacles that must be overcome if we are to achieve an operative unity at the present time. I will try to use this viewpoint not so much to detail each theoretical system, but to trace the evolution of psychoanalytic theory in a global and macroscopic way. In particular I want to explore the implications of one question: Is theory best advanced by retaining durable past elements as knowledge advances, or by discarding prior discoveries? To this end, I will summarize the first half of this history from afar as background, and then describe the developments of the second half from the position of a participant-observer. I will also venture to opine upon the future—psychoanalysis in the next century. The developmental history provides a platform for allowable predictions, and for my own preferred formulation for the psychoanalysis to come.

GENEALOGY

As I prepare to establish my view of this analytic half-century, looking from 1940 both backward and forward to what lay ahead, I have already enunciated the main defining name for me of Fenichel. I think that naming the authors who have influenced me the most (after Freud) may be the best way to conjure up for my analytic readers the essential nature of my theoretical leanings and the general spirit of my scientific stance. My evolving view of a central developing trunk of theory, with multiple radiating derivatives encompassing all observable phenomena, progresses, in part, from Freud, through Hartmann, Anna Freud, Rapaport, and Fenichel; it bridges through more recent colleagues Waelder, Greenacre, Jacobson, Lewin, Edward and Grete Bibring, Spitz, Zetzel, and Mahler; in the next generational group, more or less my own, it connects to Stone, Arlow, Brenner, Gray, and, with certain qualifications as to timing, to Gill, Wallerstein, and Sandler; and then finally it attaches to the work of younger colleagues who link this thinking to the future: Blum, Boesky, Richards, Shengold, Busch. With all of these authors, while I may differ on certain points, there is (or in a few cases has been) major agreement and overlap with their general orientation and philosophy of theory.

Several of the distinguished contributors on this list have made significant changes in their theoretical centers over the course of this last half-century. Three of them have traversed wide swings in their long and productive writing careers—Wallerstein and Sandler followed biphasic courses, and Gill passed through multiple phases. I was in quite complete harmony with the early views of all three of these. Gill was the most eloquent supporter and interpreter of Rapaport in his earliest stage, during which time I felt us to be in complete unison. I disagree with several subsequent developments in his thinking, upon which I will elaborate later. Both Sandler and Wallerstein were leading representatives of the views of Anna Freud in symposia at Hampstead and elsewhere; at that time the three of us were in theoretical harmony. Sandler was probably the most authoritative and articulate spokesman for the Freudian position, other than Anna Freud herself, during the British controversies that spanned the middle decades of this period. However, Wallerstein later espoused the equality or equivalence of an array of abstract theories, and Sandler became a powerful object-relations theoretician—both of these developments occurring during the shifting alliances after Anna Freud's death—and my views and theirs diverged. During the long gestation of this book, one of the most consistent proponents of the classical view, Charles Brenner (1994), came first to offer, and then to embrace, the opinion that the structural model of the three psychic systems of id, ego, and superego be dispensed with. After reviewing Brenner's reasoning and the extensive discussion his recent papers received, I find his new advocacy neither necessary nor useful for reasons I will make clear in Chapter 9. Our divergence may have been foreshadowed many years earlier, in Arlow and Brenner's 1964 formulation, which coincided with Gill's (1963) view on this same subject—all three favored replacement of the topographic view by the structural. In agreement with Anna Freud, I have always been of the opinion that the original five, which became six, metapsychological points of view *all* exist simultaneously, each offering an avenue of understanding that converges with the others in the explanation of any specific psychological datum. In that overview, the structural point of view continues to furnish an important segment of total understanding.

If I were to choose which of my colleagues in modern times I consider the closest to myself in the content, internal consistency, and total esprit of their psychoanalytic thought, it would perhaps be: in the generation just before me, Leo Stone; in my own generation, Jack Arlow; in the generation just after, Harold Blum.

5

THE FIRST HALF OF
THE SECOND HALF-CENTURY:
THE 1940s TO THE 1960s

WORLD WAR II

Less than a month before I finished my residency at the New York Psychiatric Institute, Pearl Harbor exploded and the United States entered World War II. One year later, having just dipped into private practice and begun to get the feel of it—enough to experience an exultation about the limitless world of professional work and intellectual interest ahead—I joined the United States Army Air Force, and was off to the Service.

I left New York with my wife and less-than-two-year-old daughter on New Year's Day 1943, on an airplane, in a snowstorm. I had orders to proceed to an Air Force station in Miami Beach, Florida. The first time in a plane, the first time to Florida, I was off on a great adventure. The plane made many stops; at every landing, the people on the ground wore less and less clothing, as we headed toward the warm climes. As I left New York, I already had a feeling I might not come back there to live, a preconscious (as I have gotten to know my preconscious!) plan to resettle in Los Angeles. I had an uncle there who had become for me a pleasure-ego ideal. He visited New York from California periodically, and always left a beckoning Southern California impression on my siblings and me.

But I did feel that I had made a permanent imprint for myself in New York that was by this time professional in addition to personal. The group of friends who trained together would remain closely knit into the future. Victor Rosen and I went off to the war in the early forties, I from my analytic training and a beginning private practice in New York, and he from his residency at the Phipps Clinic in Baltimore. Jack Arlow stayed, continuing his analytic training at the New York Psychoanalytic Institute. Charles Brenner came from Boston to New York during the war years, at which time the association between himself and Arlow began to develop. In fact I did not return to New York after the war, but relocated in Los Angeles as one of a large wave of Easterners. But a strong link between the two coasts had already been established among our small group, out of our common starting soil and our original roots in psychoanalytic thinking.

THE ARMY AIR FORCE, 1943–1946

Three and a half years in the Army did not impede my professional life; they enhanced it, challenging and furthering my intellectual development. Psychoanalysis had struck a chord in the military, and the dynamic psychiatry intrinsic to it was much on the minds of certain important policy-making individuals. This fortuitous circumstance did not mean that there was no ignorance or resistance among the uninformed, whether lay, medical, or military. But in a remarkable development for the small field of psychoanalysis at the time, William Menninger was Chief of Psychiatry in the Surgeon-General's office, and the dynamic John (Jock) Murray of the Boston Psychoanalytic was his counterpart in the Air Surgeon's office. Both were eager to make as much use as they could of psychiatrists with any smattering of psychoanalytic training.

I had started toward becoming an analyst at exactly the right time. I learned later that my brief exposure to analysis at the New York Psychoanalytic—I left for the Army after just less than two years as a candidate there—had been enough to label me a "key man." That seemingly tiny appellation was a very advantageous one: it meant that I, and the others in that category, could be assigned to posts only by the department heads in Washington; we were immune from the haphazard distributions of assignments in this country and abroad. Analytic thinking was deemed relevant, and an important desideratum. The uncovering of repressed conflicts was valued in the service of the war effort. I had various assignments, all at centers that knew, and made use of, a dynamic psychiatric approach. From Wichita Falls, Texas, a very lively and heterogeneous airfield base with a dynamic psychiatry department watched over personally by Jock Murray, I proceeded to Fort Logan, outside of Denver. This was a major assignment, where I was sent as one of four analytically oriented teachers for the School of Aviation Psychiatry, and where I eventually met Fenichel. At both of these Air Force posts, the intention was to expose and treat the unconscious conflicts of soldiers insofar as these impeded the goal of the time—to pursue and win the war.

I spent a meaningful and intense year in Denver, teaching young military doctors a dynamic psychiatry based on psychoanalytic theory and thinking. We tried to demonstrate, in a simple and innovative way appropriate to the goal-oriented demands of the work, how motivations and conflicts and obstacles can come from the unconscious. The cause was exciting, the intellectual challenge strong, and the people involved were all enthusiastic and receptive in the extreme. The four colleagues on the faculty quickly became close: Ralph Greenson, from Los Angeles where he had already been in psychoanalytic practice; Lewis Robbins, staff member at Menninger's and analytic candidate, whom I had known at medical school in Chicago ten years before; Sydney Berman, an analytic candidate in training in Washington to become a child analyst; and myself, a candidate in the New York Psychoanalytic Institute. The four of us gave a structured and formal course of training to medical officers enrolled in the School of Aviation Psychiatry. This was a lively introduction to psychoanalytic thinking, and it was eagerly received by an audience consisting not only of doctors in every field and specialty, but also of the administrative military "brass" and enlisted personnel from various interpersonal and public relations departments on the base.

But another intellectual group activity, running parallel to our main educational function, also was gaining momentum. This took an intense and biphasic course, and offered an interesting preview into the future. Alongside the formal teaching, Greenson, whom we called Romi, began to give spontaneous seminars, initiating informal lectures, and holding evening discussions, usually in his home. These extra get-togethers were both instructive and entertaining. Conducted with his lively wit, they attracted a wide and eager audience, and rapidly acquired a "not-to-be-missed" status. Not the least of the mélange Greenson offered was a dash of Hollywood: tidbits about the personalities, characters, and problems of celebrities here and there (one never knew exactly the source of this stream of information, or the relationships involved). But there was plenty of excitement and stimulation in these voluntary group activities, which spread out from our unit to the post in general. The film *Captain Newman, M.D.* was inspired by the narcosynthesis treatments of returnee airmen at Fort Logan that I described in the last chapter, and was made in the film capital from a script by Greenson's friend Leo Rosten. Captain Newman, played by Gregory Peck, was of course Romi.

Many of those who took our course went on to become analysts, going first into psychiatry and then into analytic training. Quite a few later went through Menninger's in Topeka. We all had a fond and personal feeling for that institution in the middle of the country (I had considered a residency there before choosing Columbia) and the unique unifying influence it seemed to exude, fusing analytic and American thought not only in psychiatry but culturally as well. It was said (Seeley 1967) that Karl Menninger "Americanized the unconscious." This statement later took on an ambivalent tone, in subtle identification with Freud's (1930) negative attitude toward America, but at this time the atmosphere was all in its favor. Topeka, in the heartland, was supporting analysis, not diluting it.

A PROPHETIC GROUP EFFECT

All of these accomplishments and pleasures, however, turned out to be transitory, and they were followed by a less joyous phase of group experience. As Romi's assumed leadership of the group turned into dominance, what came to pass was a gradually changing group atmosphere that in retrospect can be seen as an interesting social experiment. Following a period of excitement and exhilaration, the collective affective atmosphere and mood gradually changed—first to a generalized restlessness and irritability, and ultimately to aggression, rebellion, and increasing rumbles of discontent. Smaller groups and clusters formed, based mainly on their perceived or felt relationship to the leader but with ambivalent affective streams toward each other as well. These effects were irregular, inconstant, and often camouflaged, but they led to either internal moods or external acting-out, directed horizontally and vertically within the group.

The lightning rod was of course the inspirational and seductive Romi, whose love and acceptance became the currency for self-esteem and perceived standing in our intellectual and affective society. Greenson was one of a pair of twins named Romeo and Juliet, and he lived out his role in his exciting psychoanalytic life. Everyone, myself included, was attracted to him, and we all quickly came to need his approval. My wife warned me to take it easy—he had been flattering and teasing to her while I was away from the post on a trip; that was his general way, and she felt the pull of his spell as well. But as he came to perceive me as a potential rival in the capacity to attract notice, his pull to attach me as an adherent grew particularly strong. This was quite successful for a time, and was aided by a reciprocal push from me, as I was an eager participant in these stimulating, unexpected activities. I was very excited by all of this new professional experience, and considered myself fortunate to have left New York. The Army had so far not been something to be suffered, but a source of enjoyment and benefit. As I had already made plans to move to Los Angeles for reasons having to do with the lure of the West

Coast, the convergence of these professional circumstances was an unexpected bonus.

But the group effects of a charismatic leader began to stand out in increasingly bold relief in this intense and artificial group. It seems to me now in my long look back that the experience was an adumbration of phenomena that would later prove deeply meaningful in the further development of psychoanalytic history. In a natural unplanned experiment, intense psychoanalytic input was introduced to a receptive and intelligent audience. The group members were away from home and their normal environments, and exposed to a forceful and stimulating leader. Dynamically it seems to me—a group interpretation, as it were—that the repressed conflicts, sexual and aggressive, that were the subject of our ongoing discussions were received in a personal way by the members of the group, bypassing each individual's defenses. What gradually evolved, subtly and covertly at first but more openly over time, was a palpable group anxiety, and frustration, disillusionment, and splintering among the membership. People turned against each other according to shifting vertical and lateral alliances, defined by variable degrees of standing with the leader and derivatively with each other. The results foreshadow in an almost signal way the etiology of larger psychoanalytic splits. In this more limited case it did cause divisions within the group, shedding some light in retrospect on larger, more official splits to come.

As these discontents emerged into the open, the group esprit soured, and some friendships were painfully broken. I can speak of this last outcome with unhappy familiarity. As Greenson saw what was happening, he turned against me with wrath and criticized me for not having told him what was happening. As his "special friend," he said, I should have warned him. I myself had had all I could do to contain my own disturbed and mixed feelings, having inwardly been both appreciative and critical of his role in fostering this group psychodynamic education. The result was a considerable strain in our personal relationship, and by the time post personnel were being reassigned and dispersed, we were on very uneasy terms. My decision to move west was darkened by this episode, and it suffered another blow shortly afterward. Otto Fenichel, whom I had met during this sojourn in Denver and with whom I was looking forward to continuing my training, died suddenly in Los Angeles in January 1946. I was to be discharged from the Army shortly, however, and I decided that I would carry out my plan to move to Los Angeles.

Despite the dramatic goings-on, I never lost my interest in observation and communication. I wrote a few papers while in the Army, mainly on neurology (the new psychoanalytic orientation was still fused with my old neurologic one). One paper (Rangell 1945) discussed the case of a soldier with weakness in both lower extremities, who had been regarded as a hysteric. I diagnosed an epidural abscess following a spinal tap, and the soldier recovered after proper surgical treatment. Another article (1947) considered a small series of cases of peroneal palsy in tall airmen. These men had to sit in a cramped position in the narrow cockpits of combat planes with their legs tightly crossed. The resulting symptom of foot-drop was traced to a crushing of the peroneal nerve between two opposite knee bones that occurred in people with a certain type of lanky anatomy.

These kinds of cases were not my bread-and-butter anymore; such neurological consultations came my way only occasionally now. Steadier and more important to me was my growing exposure to the ubiquity of psychic conflict, and the need to keep the psychoanalytic eye focused on its unconscious base. In this unusual setting I came to appreciate the unconscious roles behind the rampant anxieties and surface decompensations, and the separation and castration understructures fueling them, in those returned from combat missions—and those expecting to be sent on them. In this I joined my later colleague Ernst Simmel, who in World War I had delineated the castration anxiety that underlay the war neuroses. During this intense period of clinical exposure, almost four years, my conviction of the role of the unconscious deepened and widened in scope, as insights derived from it could be applied externally in daily work. A bonus of this exposure was the relationships I made with colleagues across the nation, which were personally invigorating at the time and later facilitated my involvement with national and international psychoanalysis.

AFTER THE WAR: LOS ANGELES, 1946

In 1946, Los Angeles was *the place*. Southern California was the paradise that people came west to be part of. I arrived in June 1946. It was all optimism. The atmosphere, the climate, the profession, the colleagues, the warm southern California sun—they all spelled "go." The daily commute from my first house in Santa Monica to my first office in Beverly Hills passed through a fairytale lane. We were on the crest of a wave.

Psychoanalysts of all ages and degrees of training were leaving the Army and migrating west from New York, Philadelphia, Chicago, and Topeka to find the sun. Swelling the small ranks already here, they formed the nucleus of what would become one of the most populous psychoanalytic foci in the country, and, more importantly, one of the most publicized. Being in analysis in Los Angeles was not to be hidden; people wore it like a badge, and many were people one reads about. During the years to come they would not shy away from capitalizing on their analyses as they did their movies and plays. They gave psychoanalysis a positive press, and *Lady in the Dark*, for instance, became a major hit on Broadway. There were connections to psychoanalysis everywhere.

The years after our relocation were rewarding in every sense. There was practice: ever increasing, always interesting and challenging. There was continuous writing and speaking, there were willing and receptive colleagues, and there was a prescribed course toward becoming a certified psychoanalyst. I started at the Los Angeles Psychoanalytic Institute after the war in 1946, resuming what I had started at the New York Psychoanalytic, and moved smoothly along this path. By 1950 I was ready to present a graduation thesis.

The graduation paper was at that time a requirement, and preparing it was a compelling professional activity to me. It made for an optimum pulse of learning, to continue to combine my clinical work with efforts to encompass in writing what I was seeing and experiencing. Early in this period after the war, after a few years of clinical psychoanalytic work and still fresh from psychiatry and neurology, I wrote a paper called "The Psychiatric Aspects of Pain" (1953), which was a fusion of my civilian and military experiences. Another paper published during this period was on the psychosomatics of cardiovascular disease (1951); this reflected my continuing openness to medical problems and my having been drawn to the psychosomatic area previously by Flanders Dunbar at Columbia, who was a pioneer in that field. This brief period, however, was a transition, a bridge to a more psychoanalytic center. In all my subsequent writings, it was the unconscious that took precedence.

The class of candidates that I joined in 1946 immediately became close friends. The young Los Angeles institute was cohesive and united, and so was our group. In light of its future history, however, the membership of that society/institute looks interesting, and I can say in retrospect that lines of differences—almost of separation—were in evidence very early. I bring this out because I believe that the composition and structure of individual societies have much to do with their subsequent histories. Twenty-five years later, when I was president of the International, I got to know the members of the newly approved Venezuelan Society; speaking at their initial meeting as a newly accepted Society, I told them only half in jest that I could already see the lines of their future split.

In our Los Angeles Society in the mid-forties, the most respected nucleus was the Freudian core composed of a number of European émigrés and a few Americans: Ernst Simmel, Ernst Lewy, Frances Deri, Hanna Fenichel, Margaret Munk, David Brunswick, Charles Tidd, Carel Van der Heide, and Ralph Greenson. Otto Fenichel was the departed spirit. Simmel, who was always mentioned in the same breath as Fenichel but who was modest and less visible, had been sent to Los Angeles by Freud from the Schloss Tegel Sanatorium that Simmel had founded in Berlin in 1927 to seed the nascent

L.A. group. Freud himself, warmly appreciative of Simmel, had stayed at Schloss Tegel several times when he visited his dental surgeon in Berlin. There was plenty of activity and enthusiasm during my early years in Los Angeles, but the members of this group, who were the leaders in things educational, were, with one exception, conspicuously inarticulate in open scientific discussion. This inhibited many of the younger people who wished to speak; and for those few who dared, it made for problems of anxiety and guilt. Greenson was the voice of the older group; he was almost the only one who spoke at Society meetings. On more than one occasion I ventured to bring up the issue of the older analysts' reticence and what it brought about, as these people had quickly become close friends to me and my wife Anita. But Deri or Hanna Fenichel would explain, "He [Romi] speaks for us." I do not think that language was the issue or the inhibitor; Siegfried Bernfeld of San Francisco and David Rapaport of Topeka were close friends of this émigré group and were frequent visitors to Los Angeles. Both had distinctive European accents, and both were brilliant and inspiring speakers and formulators. Both became distant models for me.

There was a group in Chicago, close to and aligned with Franz Alexander, that was not yet openly opposed to our Freudian nucleus, but that was becoming so. Martin Grotjahn and Norman Levy were prominent members of this group, which was supplemented in thought and spirit by May Romm from the Columbia Institute in New York, and Judd Marmor, a former Horneyite from New York who had rejoined the New York Psychoanalytic Society before migrating west. He had not, like Tarachow, changed his views, but had made this administrative change for other reasons. Marmor was a brilliant and ready speaker, and by nature and conviction was already an obvious leader of the "neo-Freudian" segment. These analysts were a free-speaking, conventionally friendly group, not particularly hierarchic, and they did not take well to the more authoritarian European contingent in Los Angeles. Their spiritual kinship with Franz Alexander led them to bristle against "rigidity," which is what they felt a theoretical goal of neutrality or objectivity implied. I should point out that there were European analysts in both groups, and that not everyone from Chicago supported Alexander. Carel Van der Heide, from that city and institute, who had come to Chicago from Holland, was very much with the Freudians. There was overlap in the lower echelons as well. Candidates generally (but not always) sided with their analysts, and their friendships spanned the dividing lines.

After my move to the West Coast, I came to New York often to see my parents, friends, and family, whom I had not left without guilt and backward looks. I visited my New York colleagues too at those times, and expanded these relationships as I began in the early fifties to participate in the American Psychoanalytic Association and attend its meetings. My links to New York felicitously furthered both my personal and professional interests, and, as a bonus and a secondary gain, kept solid my connection with colleagues and teachers there and my identification with the likes of Jacobson, Greenacre, Mahler, Spitz, Hartmann, Kris, and Loewenstein, the formidable group who cohered at the New York Psychoanalytic after the war. Leo Stone was there too, in a class by himself and rapidly becoming the analysts' analyst, and so of course was the next generation of theoretical leaders, by whom I mean Arlow, Brenner, and soon Victor Rosen again, who after a few years' detour into Adolph Meyer's psychobiology had come back to New York after the war and followed his friends into psychoanalysis at the New York Institute. The three of us, Arlow, Rosen, and I, became presidents of the American Psychoanalytic Association in close succession in the early and mid sixties, and so did Brenner, whose elegant summaries of the central tenets of psychoanalytic theory, written in these early years from his teaching lecture notes, became definitive statements of Freudian thought, noted for their clarity and felicitous style.

This relatively small but increasingly well-known nucleus of analytic thinkers in New York to whom I felt close seemed to be a group intellectually united, although not necessarily all close to each other personally. Rooted in the scientific method, they represented an analytic attitude that became a model around the country. Somehow they call to my mind the New York school of abstract expressionists, also a regional, closely knit group, who were looked upon by the rest of the country in the thirties and forties with the same type of respect. My own experience with the analytic group taught me that these individuals carried a humanistic outlook so deeply fused within them that there was no need to question it or make anything special of it. However, even the increasing attention that their combined writings commanded did not keep them from becoming stereotyped as symbols of authoritarianism and rigidity. This drew reactive opposition and then even calumny, which I knew to be unjustified. I became linked with them for better or for worse as their man in the west, a characterization of which I was, and remain, proud. To my mind, they have worn well in analytic history. My identification with this group, fused with the identification I was forging with Fenichel and Simmel, and through them with Freud, went a long way toward fashioning my analytic identity.

EGO PSYCHOLOGY

Theoretical progression and extension of the body of Freudian thought took off again as the dust settled after the war, first into relief and then into a boom. The ego, which Anna Freud and Heinz Hartmann had lifted to a vigorous start, was off on a fast and exuberant trajectory. Recognition of the centrality of the ego, as it directed and regulated the activities of the id and superego while adapting to stimuli from the external world, solidified over the next two decades. The psychic model fashioned and defined as Freud's last major contribution before his death in 1939 was examined, dissected, and expanded into many of its potential ramifications (but not all—that task is still unfinished). The role of the ego as the executive (my word [Rangell 1986]) hub of the psychic structures was integrated into theory; it also came to be seen as the central agent of the psychoanalytic method—as indeed it was, consonant with Fenichel's (1945) terse and undisputed observation that psychoanalytic treatment occurs through the rational ego: "In a direct sense the analyst works *exclusively* upon the *ego*" (p. 54); or, ". . . all analysis is really ego analysis" (p. 56). This was the general belief at the time, both theoretically and operationally—at least in American psychoanalysis. Freud's theory, which with the addition of the structural theory had been brought to a tentatively rounded-out form by the time of his death, had by now been reacted to, absorbed, and accepted, and was the fulcrum of mainstream psychoanalytic thought. The system ego, which would be singled out for both elaboration and opposition from many angles in the years to come, was during this period accepted and used; in the light of what was to follow, this success was perhaps an ominous portent.

One post-war phenomenon, a sequel to the usefulness of analytic thinking in the emergency and topical war neuroses, was a greater acceptance of the relevance of psychoanalysis in civilian life. One manifestation of this spread was the increasing appearance of psychoanalysis in major medical schools, where analysts were beginning to come to prominence as heads of departments of psychiatry. From Columbia and Cornell in New York, to the University of Colorado in the Rockies, to U.C.L.A. and the University of California at San Francisco, psychiatry departments joined Karl Menninger, who had brought psychoanalytic thinking to the heartland, in bringing the idea of the unconscious to the intellectual fore at the more traditional levels of American science. Fears that had concerned Freud from the beginning were placed on hold as America, partly under the influence of the émigré analysts, became after the war the stronghold for the preservation and advance of Freudian analysis.

PSYCHOSOMATIC MEDICINE AND MEDICAL PSYCHOANALYSIS

Psychosomatic medicine was one derivative of the new fusion of analysis and medicine that emerged as a prominent new field of interest and inquiry. Arising from sturdy roots dating back to the 1930s, this new specialty was spearheaded by Franz Alexander (1950) in Chicago and Flanders Dunbar (1954) in New York. I had first heard of Alexander when I was a medical student. A clear, forceful teacher and an inspirational leader, whose influence in university circles extended well beyond medicine for twenty-five years, he built a spirited and enthusiastic psychoanalytic institute in Chicago, close to medicine but independent of academic ties. I encountered Flanders Dunbar a few years later when I was a resident in psychiatry at Columbia; she was introducing psychosomatic medicine and psychodynamic research into medical conditions, at New York Presbyterian Hospital there, next door to the Psychiatric Institute.

Alexander had spent several summers in Southern California, and in the late fifties he migrated to Los Angeles. He started and headed a strong department of psychiatry at the new Cedars-Sinai Hospital, where his active psychoanalytic research program set a new tone. His presence was a stimulus for psychoanalytic research, in medical circles as well as among psychoanalysts, and a focus for debate within the energetic young psychoanalytic milieu that had begun to develop in the city. Alexander's psychoanalytic credo brought Ferenczi's active psychoanalysis into modern times, years after the original closeness between Freud and Ferenczi had dissolved and their differences been sharply acknowledged. That being so, his views and those of his disciples quickly and naturally came into direct opposition to those of the group around Fenichel, Simmel, and the other analysts who had been sent to Los Angeles by Freud.

Alexander was born in Budapest but he had trained in Berlin, and his scientific point of view followed and advanced the theories and orientation of his countryman Sándor Ferenczi. Continuing where Ferenczi left off, Alexander opposed the Freudian position (of objectivity and the supplying of insights toward the resolution of inner conflicts) in favor of a more active and directive approach. In his view, treatment would compensate for the patient's pathogenic history. The analyst would provide corrective emotional experiences to counteract the particular deprivations or traumata suffered by the patient during the childhood years. This "therapeutic" aim, which was in keeping with "medical" goals but which had been considered by Freud to be secondary and so left to come automatically, was for Alexander the preeminent one, and it dictated his therapeutic approach. The unconscious conflicts and fixation points in development that led to psychopathology were sought for in analysis, and reparative attitudes and roles against them were deliberately assumed by the therapy-minded psychoanalyst.

These two simultaneous developments—the establishment of an analytic psychosomatic medicine and the ascendancy in psychoanalysis of ego psychology—were championed by medical and lay analysts alike. The problem of lay analysis was always in the air, but had not yet been confronted. Lay analysts were leaders and models in local societies and institutes, but remained for the most part outside the American Psychoanalytic Association. Yet it was during this same period that the American, still embracing its medical identification but largely spurred by the teachings and contributions of the displaced medical and lay analytic population, was growing to be the central locus of Freudian psychoanalysis. It was within the *American* Psychoanalytic Association that "ego psychology" was finding its home, not the *International* association, which the refugee analysts had left behind. There is no more ironic symbol of this brewing split than the fact that the émigré Otto Fenichel, a physician, took an internship in Los Angeles so that he could acquire a license to practice medicine here, and so give legitimacy in this country to the psychoanalytic leadership of the analytic émigrés, many of them lay. It was during the course of this internship that Fenichel died in 1946.

These two issues—opposition to nonmedical psychoanalysis, and advocacy of (Freudian) ego psychology—arose in juxtaposition. Although they are commonly misconstrued as one, they are separate, and we need to keep them clearly so in order to follow the courses of these contiguous issues and the developments to come. The theoretical spirit of the American leadership during those years was predominantly Freudian; the anti-lay bias that had preceded those years persisted in spite of that leadership, not because of it. Preeminent lay analysts from Kris to Waelder to Anna Freud were allied with the American on the basis of its guiding theory, in spite of its still-present iniquitous stance toward nonmedical analysts. Because the American was self-serving and wrong on the medical issue does not discredit its efforts to preserve the central psychoanalytic theory. In the mid-fifties, in fact, it was the *non*-Freudian segments in the American that split off into the Academy, which remains medical to the present day! In any case, to Freudian theorists of that day, medical or not, the American was home.

American psychoanalysis at this period addressed without conflict both the soma and the ego. To attend actively to the body did not deny the role, or the separate intricacies, of the mind. The course of theory did not seem to be affected either by geography, as Freud had feared—Freud is reputed to have said to Jung as they first entered New York harbor, "Don't they know we're bringing them the plague?"—or by issues of turf. The psychoanalytic idea was being widely seeded.

At the same time as the administration of the American was rejecting the training of lay analysts, ego psychology in psychoanalytic theory was taking root in that institution, where it was introduced and elaborated largely by European theorists, many of whom were nonmedical analysts. Kris, Waelder, Erikson, Rapaport, and Anna Freud, none of them physicians, were icons of analytic theory as revered within the mainstream of American ego psychology as any medical leaders, American or European. While the views and influence of A. A. Brill and the Flexner report on American medicine effectively hindered American acceptance of lay analysis, this did not in any direct way determine the course of psychoanalytic *theory* in this country. The struggle between Freudian trends and divergent ones, both the original divisions and those brewing in the present, was a parallel struggle, and it developed independent of geography or professional degrees.

Freud had both medical and nonmedical adherents, and of the proponents of the opposing theoretical systems, some were one and some were the other. That is still true. Similarly, there are both European and American "Freudian" analysts, and European and American dissenters. Jung and Adler, both physicians, opposed Freud. For every Waelder (a physicist and a nonmedical analyst who knew and defended Freud as much as any), there was also a Rank (an artist, nonmedical, who troubled Freud and eventually left him). The traditional Freudian view was advocated and protected in the United States in the postwar era as it was not in Europe. But in every major city in the United States, it was a European individual or couple who maintained and led this Freudian view. Some of them were medical and some were lay. There were child analysts among them, with their own variety of theoretical orientations. All refugees from Hitler, from many disciplines, the European analysts brought to this country the central body of the evolving psychoanalytic theory, as well as the seeds of the alternative directions in which some of them would later proceed. Yet it was the energetic theoretical leadership of this inchoate group of displaced analysts, in combination with the receptivity of their new home to the still-inspirational body of central psychoanalytic thought, that was to establish the main trunk of American psychoanalysis in the middle of this eventful century.

THE SPLITS AROUND 1950

Only a few years after the war ended and the wave of new settlers had established itself on the west coast, already seeds of dissension, both personal and theoretical, were beginning to divide this expanded and strengthened analytic center. I believe that this was the case everywhere, although the trend manifested itself differently in different places. In Southern California, there was another stream, increasingly dark and ominous, running alongside the sunny one of advance and consolidation. The informal groupings that I outlined above within the Los Angeles Psychoanalytic were taking more definite form, and real divisions began to grow between them. With the deaths of Fenichel in 1946 and Ernst Simmel a year later, the institute lost its direct-from-Freud leadership, and the Los Angeles Society and Institute became an incident waiting to happen. Splits had taken place shortly before in New York-Columbia, in Baltimore-Washington, and in Philadelphia between the Society and the Association. 1950 turned out to be the year of "the big split" into the Los Angeles and the Southern California Societies.

From the theoretical point of view, the splits occurred over the contrasting views represented by Fenichel and Alexander. Fenichel's position at its core basically maintained the rationale and methodology of original Freudian theory: that the analyst aim to discern unconscious conflicts objectively, to transmit these to the patient, and to expect and respect the patient's ability and motivation, as well as his right, to execute freer choices of external action. Alexander's position, continuing the stream started by Ferenczi, aimed to learn where the patient's past life had been deficient, so that the analyst could correctively supply the missing emotional ingredients. In its essence, this was the theoretical dividing line in all of the splits around the turn of this decade. And it was in fact to be the basic dividing line for all future divisions between traditional and relational approaches. The two main leaders had been actually present in Los Angeles, although at different times, while other spokesmen represented the same polarities, with some variation, in other centers: Rado at Columbia representing Alexander against the dominant New York Psychoanalytic; English and Saul representing Alexander in Philadelphia; Waelder-Hall representing the classical in Baltimore; and Weigert and others the interpersonal in Washington. Was it to be the analytic attitude or assumed therapeutic roles; relentless analysis, or an effort to supply what had been missing in the patient's early life? The splits of the late forties, which culminated in L.A. in 1950, centered on the debate over whether the analyst should be objective and neutral, or whether he should assume a corrective emotional position according to the patient's particular needs and particular history of deprivation or trauma.

But ideas alone do not cause splits; these are brought about by ideas and people. People who get along can tolerate ideas that differ, and people who don't like each other personally can make accommodation when they are not divided by theoretical schisms. Divergences in thinking exist in all groups, psychoanalytic and others; so do personal differences. These are not incompatible with coexistence. But both together make for problems. Ideas and people both gave rise to these institutional analytic splits: divergent theories, and the human advocates associated with them who eventually chose to live and work apart. We are talking about a time, remember, when analysts who could not get along with each other separated; this has not always remained the case. In Los Angeles, feelings of all kinds were running high; friendships, groupings, aspirations, and social linkages were strong and compelling. The group atmosphere was electric. Patients were many, yet there was intense competition for them. Society meetings were rarely missed; papers and the ensuing debates were savored. The defenders of Alexander and Fenichel and Simmel—and their opponents—were passionate in their opinions. And analysts and candidates were lining up on both sides of the division.

The graduation paper I gave in 1950 was the last paper before the split. As I have said, candidates at that time had to present a paper before they could graduate; this requirement felt to me not like an obstacle, but like an invitation and opportunity. Since then, competition, pressure, and the conflict between training and increasingly complex lives have gradually whittled away at this requirement, which has since been discontinued. While this has eased the path to completion, I feel that something was lost. Analysts depend in their daily work on speaking, formulating, and presenting—to the patient. Yet young and old analysts alike meet demands for presentation of their work with severe inhibitions and resistance. While reasons of principle are often expressed, these are, I believe, secondary to anxiety. I suspect this is a factor in the recent strong opposition to certification by the American.

Several of the struggles I have observed in my analytic life—for example, the seemingly widespread inhibitions about spontaneous discussions, and the reluctance, or even refusal, to engage in written or other demonstration of clinical methods—have given me to wonder whether analysis somehow *produces* such obstacles to communication, notwithstanding its ostensible reverse goal of facilitating it. Or is there something in our institutional group life that brings on such resistance? This is certainly not the case in the supervisory situation, which can actually be used to counter such trends. No doubt the analytic function, to look into unconscious motives, cannot easily be separated from normal social intercourse in formal analytic group settings, and so it may be especially difficult to find the right position between the two within the analytic family, where the wish and fear of exhibitionism may lead to a social phobia of exposure. It is no accident that an energetic study group, called by some the "shameniks," has had an ongoing discussion group on this subject at the American for many years.

In 1950, however, I gave my graduation paper to the last combined meeting before the great split. I remember that the audience was sitting horizontally across a wide room at the Beverly-Wilshire hotel, divided along the lines that would soon divide two societies; I found myself speaking from left to right, as if I were watching a tennis match. My paper was called "The Analysis of a Doll Phobia" (Rangell 1952b). On a whim I later submitted it to a contest that I had seen announced in the *International Journal*, and was startled when it won the International Clinical Essay Prize of the British Psychoanalytic Society for that year. That experience may have imprinted the word "international" in me for the first time. And the imprinting was underscored when, exhilarated by that first award, I submitted another paper two years later and to my even greater surprise was awarded the same prize a second time. This paper was "The Psychology of Poise, with a Special Elaboration on the Psychic Significance of the Snout or Perioral Region" (1954c). This was the first time anyone had won the prize twice, and I think that the experience widened the scope of my view and orientation. I was left with an exuberant optimism, both about the solidity of my new science/profession, and my new sense of having a strong root in it. The second paper, incidentally, dealt directly with the affect of shame. It also brought in anatomy, neurophysiology, and embryology, all of which were related to the psychological subject I studied. Even in my early efforts I looked to bridge and to unify.

The big split, which in 1950 divided the Los Angeles psychoanalytic community into two major, separate groups, was essentially between the "neo-Freudians" around the views of Alexander, and the "classical" Freudians who followed the principles of Fenichel. The former were led, among others, by Marmor, Romm, Norman Levy, and Grotjahn, and the latter by Greenson and such representatives of the older generation as Simmel, Deri, Brunswick, and Lewy. The "old" classical group retained the name of the Los Angeles Psychoanalytic Society, and its roughly pyramidal structure, with charisma and authority concentrated at the top, and a relatively passive and inhibited rank and file. The new Southern California Society was more democratically oriented and established itself more rectangularly; it was less hierarchical in its structure, and there was a less dominant leadership. There was more striving and more stridency in the classical group.

I went with the Los Angeles Society (LAPSI) on the basis of my theoretical convictions and gut feelings. It was not because I liked the people more—I had friends on both sides—but because I felt that the psychoanalyst had a specific task to do, and that this called for an objective stance and consistent course that could be learned and adhered to. Nothing had convinced me that this was incompatible with being empathic and human. I felt that the humanistic concerns of the new Southern California Psychoanalytic Society—which attracted many—were important, but that these were intrinsic to the traditional method also, and that an exaggerated adherence to them would gradually confuse and diminish psychoanalysis.

I was one of only three candidates who at the time of the split did not join the side to which his training analyst adhered. I was already developing the strong belief that it was necessary to keep one's cognitive convictions and one's social, that is, affective, bonds separate. The choice we all had to make about Society affiliation at the time of the split was a multiply determined test of convictions and values. That it was so often made routinely in alliance with one's analyst has implications about the acquisition (or not) of autonomy in psychoanalytic theory and in training. I addressed this subject later in my paper (1982a) on "transference to theory."

Today, fifty years later, reviewers and historians looking back at the splits make opposing statements: that the splits were only over theories, or that they were all due to personalities. Even in the years immediately surrounding the split in L.A., I remember, a number of the senior analysts in the classical group denied any affective involvement. Some of the most unequivocally classical training analysts, including some who were generally quite fair, such as David Brunswick, stated in a rather complacent way that of course the split was only over theory, denying the contempt in which they held more "liberal" analysts, which made harmony much less likely. I remember how conscious I was before the split of the denial among this classical group of its hostility and open scorn toward some of the more vociferous members of the opposition. Deri referred to May Romm as "the May Company," while Greenson could never abide the strength or directness of a Marmor or Levy. I also heard it said half jokingly at the time that Greenson and Norman Reider, forceful rivals within LAPSI and both disciples of Fenichel, could not share the same city—so Reider took San Francisco and Romi L.A., and everyone was happy.

But affects, those ephemeral manifestations, grew dim and indistinct as the years passed, and both groups went their own self-satisfied ways. The theoretical differences began to fade too, as both groups were later to find common ground in overlapping "modern" theories. A leading analyst of the Southern California Society, Peter Loewenberg, who had a strong social footing in both groups, stated in an interview in 1990 that the split had all been due to personalities. "The differences were not theoretical; they were personality differences among some people who could not tolerate each other" (p. 11). The same opinion was held at the same time by a number of new leaders of LAPSI who, in keeping with the times, had become strongly eclectic in their views. The big split, they voiced now as they espoused fusion of the two groups, had been due to people not getting along. Each wrote history in accord with his current views and identity.

But people have as much to do with the course of theory as the disembodied ideas that they represent and further. This has been true from the beginning of psychoanalysis, and it is true today. Theoretical differences may separate advocates of opposing ideas, but the influence of theoretical differences merges imperceptibly into the influence of identifications, alliances, and transferences. Richards (1999) has pointed to this aspect of the etiology of schism at the time of A. A. Brill and his original American colleagues, a brief period of psychoanalytic history during which such factors have not been generally noted. While it has always been considered ungentlemanly to bring people or personalities into theoretical discussion, ad hominem (and ad feminam) factors, which are always present, are omitted at the expense of completeness. It is ironic that these elements, which are the subject matter of psychoanalysis, should so often be considered off-limits in studies of psychoanalytic history itself.

THE FIFTIES

While all this was happening, psychoanalysis was studying the ego, digging into it and absorbing it as the center of its theoretical and technical corpus. Hartmann was followed, and accompanied, by David Rapaport, the inspiring figurehead at the Menninger Clinic in Topeka. Rapaport was the author of monumental works on thinking (1950b, 1951b) and on affects (1950a, 1953), the two major areas of ego functioning. He also (1951a, 1958) extended the understanding of autonomy begun by Hartmann in 1950. Rapaport came to Los Angeles a few times. I first saw him from the audience as he spoke to the Society, or to the "nursery school" psychoanalytic study group that was a breeding ground of future analysts in Los Angeles. Rapaport was an awesome and mesmerizing speaker who could convey great complexity of thought with ease, and he walked from side to side at the front of the room, speaking slowly, deliberately, without a note, unselfconsciously constructing a complicated line of reasoning in simple, logical terms.

I actually met Rapaport in 1952, when, shortly after my graduation from the Institute, I was the reporter of my first American panel, "The Psychoanalytic Theory of Affects." It was Greenson who, during a thaw in our rocky relations, had been responsible for my invitation to take this role in the panel, which he chaired. That was the first meeting of the American where anyone other than Ernst Kris summarized a panel; he had done this routinely and expectedly at every Sunday morning wrap-up of every meeting of the American until then. This meeting in Atlantic City was a sort of breakthrough. Two younger analysts, hardly yet known, were assigned to present reports of two new panels: Arlow (1952) the one on perversions, and I (1952a) the one on affects. This innovation symbolized for many the passing of responsibility from one generation to another. When I finished delivering my panel report to the summary plenary session that Sunday morning in Atlantic City, David Rapaport, whom I did not know personally but who was already an intellectual hero to me, bounded up from the audience, shook my hand, and said, "Now I know vot I haf said!" This gave me a big lift and another boost forward.

What David Rapaport had "said" was a classic paper on affects. Titled "An Attempt to Systematize the Fragments of the Psychoanalytic Theory of Affects" (1952b), it was the first summary paper on this central but still unclarified subject, and it was regarded as nuclear and overdue. And systematize it he did; Rapaport did for affects what Fenichel had recently done for the psychoanalytic theory of his time. Rapaport was the ideal theoretician to do it then, combining as he did a scholarly grasp of cognitive, academic, and experimental psychology with a thorough knowledge of the history of psychoanalytic theory. Another classic paper presented on that panel was Edith Jacobson's (1952, 1953) "The Speed-Pace in Psychic Discharge Processes and Its Influence on the Pleasure–Unpleasure Qualities of Affects." These were not the easiest papers to follow or discuss, but to me they were informative as well as abstruse. To hear and process them required, even evoked, a kind of deep playful abstraction that each author applied with the skill and grace of a dancer. No doubt this concentrated experience laid the groundwork for my lifelong interest and fascination with the subject of affects in psychoanalysis.

A year later I was invited to be the reporter at another panel (things went fast in the American at that time for young analysts who were seen as able—and willing—to present). Encouraged by my experience with the doll phobia paper, and by my steady inclination to form and express my own opinions as well as to coordinate and report those of others, I volunteered to present a paper (1954a) at this panel too. The panel subject was "Psychoanalysis and Dynamic Psychotherapy: Similarities and Differences" (1954b). With the strong diffusion of analytic thinking into medicine and into the culture at large, this differentiation had quickly become a heated subject. For the cohesive classical group, one major emphasis was on defining psychoanalysis and preserving its borders. From a wider general viewpoint, the interest was on how to extend the borders without losing the center.

Thus it was always a question—usually a divisive one—as to how psychoanalysis could be separated from its derivative therapies. The two 1954 panels on this question called for definitions of psychoanalysis by any who would assay them, as a base for wider discussion. Only two of us tried our hands at this task, Merton Gill and I. Gill's (1954) definition was more succinct than mine: analysis of the transference neurosis by a neutral analyst by interpretation alone. At the time I felt some awe toward Gill's definition, and almost preferred it to my own (1954a); it was elegant and spare, without an extra word. I had known Merton in medical school, where he was a year behind me. There had been occasions then on which he had displayed a prodigious and to me intimidating knowledge, and an authoritative voice—clearly he still had both.

But looking back on the way psychoanalytic theories have changed over the years, I am satisfied with my own more cumbersome definition. Analysis, I said, aimed at "a resolution of that neurosis (transference *and* infantile)"—that is, not *just* the transference neurosis, but also the neurosis for which the patient came to analysis in the first place. For Gill, it was the transference neurosis only, and the treatment was by interpretation alone; it seems to me now that Gill was always for one thing only, but that that thing changed a number of times. I tried always to be inclusive, to seek a unitary theory that embraced all. I believe that my way has stood the test of time, and survived the vagaries of various less inclusive styles of thought. The here-and-now *and* the past, transference *and* reconstruction are still all necessary; one or the other alone is not enough.

On what I felt as "my" side of the debate at this first panel, there were Edward Bibring (he was ill, and his classic paper [Bibring 1954] was read by his wife Grete, who would follow me as president of the American a decade later) and Merton Gill (1954), and on the accompanying panel, the indomitable Leo Stone (1954). On the other side of the panel discussions at that time were the formidable Franz Alexander (1954) and the very appealing Frieda Fromm-Reichmann (1954). It was a heady experience.

Every discussion has its sequelae. This one had many for me. For one thing, I became a regular at subsequent meetings and panels on what I began to call "P and P 1,2,3,4, etc."—that is, the subject of psychoanalysis versus psychotherapy as it appeared periodically at local, national, and international Congresses. One of the most memorable of these was the regional meeting of the Southeast Psychoanalytic Societies "P and P 25 years later," which was held in Atlanta in 1979 (Panel 1979), with three of the original 1954 contributors participating, Stone (1979), Gill (1979b), and I (1981c). It was interesting to see the developments in the interval. Gill especially had gone through several significant changes; at that time of the 1979 panel, he saw no line of separation be-

tween psychoanalysis and analytic psychotherapy, with the transference as the sole or major identifying feature of both. Stone and
I had both expanded our original descriptions, but their basic
characteristics still stood.

It was good training and good discipline—and good fortune—
that I had to consider this basic question several times in close
succession, because the same theoretical problems and puzzles
came up, and the same basic differences in orientation, that had
given rise to the splits shortly before. The underlying question
was: What is psychoanalysis?

I have recapitulated many times since then my focus in the
1954 panel: unconscious intrapsychic conflicts in the etiology of
psychopathology, and an objective stance in the clinical process
with the aim of reconstruction and insight. The opposing view at
that time looked to external, cultural experiences as bearing more
weight in pathogenesis than the intrapsychic processing of these
experiences. There was also a greater emphasis on active intervention and corrective role playing on the part of the analyst to
bring about insight and change. While differing theoretical orientations around such basic questions separated local groups in
the four or five split institutes of that period, they all still remained
under the national umbrella of the American Psychoanalytic Association, and organizational togetherness endured. But the unified
theoretical view that had heretofore prevailed by consensus within
the American was not being maintained without strain. Within a
few more years, in fact, the division in basic thinking, and the
affects it aroused, had effected the splitting off of a rival national
organization, the Academy of Psychoanalysis, which separated
from the American in 1956. The groups that had split away from
the American earlier, following Horney, Sullivan, White, and so
on, readily became members of the new Academy. Any analysts
not committed to the Freudian mainstream were welcome. The
small existing Adlerian groups were eligible, and so were those
after Stekel, Rank, and certainly Ferenczi, who was the theoretical forerunner of Alexander. But this time, unlike the times of the
earlier splits, members of the new Academy could and did remain

active in both organizations. Those who were already members of the American mostly remained within it, with its consent. The American therefore to that extent at least bridged the splits, and thus became the overseer of at least two points of view, which now had to be scientifically and administratively amalgamated.

In the meantime, however, the American was maintaining its dominance, and it was still guardian of the continuously developing total (my word) Freudian theory. Despite the ideational differences that gave rise to the splits of the forties and fifties, including the establishment of the Academy, the divisions that the American bridged were now essentially over technique, not theory—over analytic attitude, not metapsychology. There was still an unspoken sharing of the most important theoretical principle, the basic sine qua non, that allowed the various groups to remain under one scientific roof: unconscious intrapsychic conflict. Fenichel's idea of many treatments but one understanding was still accurate.

But other things were going on in the rest of the world. In Great Britain the well-known theoretical splits into Freudian, Kleinian, and "middle-group" object-relations theory (and the differences in therapeutic practice that were automatically assumed to follow theory) had profoundly affected the analytic population, and three different and separate training arrangements were now living under one administrative roof. The dissension in England spread from there to Europe, South America, and even Australia; the I.P.A., in increasing contrast with the American, thus came to represent theoretical diversity. During the turmoil just before the war, when the divisive arrangements were going on in England, the American demanded, and gained, from the International, autonomy over scientific principles, training standards, and criteria for admission to training. This gave the American the only separate regional status in the International. It is essential for any reader who wishes to appreciate fully the complexity that followed to keep these various issues of domain and autonomy clear and separate.

Max Gitelson was president of the American in 1955 and of the International from 1963 to his death in 1965. He was intensely opposed to the views of Alexander and very close to Anna Freud, who was equally against the inroads, both intellectual and affective, being made by Melanie Klein. Gitelson and Anna Freud were in unison in their support of the American's independence with respect to its theoretical stance, which did not embrace either Alexander or Klein. The Freudian center of the American Psychoanalytic—which eventually became synonymous with (wrongly named) ego psychology—was critical of both the Alexandrian views about the corrective role of the analyst and the focus in Kleinian etiology on early infantile life. American psychoanalysis was thus both indigenous and European in the roots of its theoretical position. While there was no administrative cleavage between European and American psychoanalysis (both were in the I.P.A.), there was an intellectual split between Freudian and other on each side of the Atlantic: with Alexander (neo-Freudian) in the United States, and with Klein (Kleinian Freudian) in the rest of the world, although regional characteristics and group formations on these divisive issues would change in later years. It is also important to keep separate the issues of scientific orientation versus those of admission for training. On the latter too Gitelson and Anna Freud shared a deep partnership, this time *against* the American and its stance against lay analysis (both had been in favor of the American for its position on Freudian ego psychology). The American had thus established a vertical split, championing Freudian theory, but opposing the Freuds as to who could be an analyst. Things were to change on both these scores as well.

A REFLECTION ON THE SIXTIES

The sixties were a biphasic decade; they started out golden and rose steeply to what proved to be the pinnacle of the psychoanalytic century, and then fell off to end in a gathering of threatening clouds.

After the splits of the forties, psychoanalysis settled down to a long era of peaceful application of the theoretical extensions that were being carved out and accumulated. Psychoanalysts enjoyed golden years of peaceful life and practice, and even theoretical harmony within the central scientific core. Nowhere was this period of steady work, progress, and exhilaration more visible and enjoyable than in Beverly Hills and West Los Angeles, where I was living and working.

Two areas of psychoanalytic theory and development, the intrapsychic *and* the sociocultural, coexisted at this time as the American remained the "main" body, both organizationally and in relation to the Freudian legacy. This remained stable over a significant period of time, through the fifties and into the sixties, as what had become known as "ego psychology" steadily strengthened and advanced. This short-cut expression was really a misnomer, a colloquial condensation in use (or misuse) for Freud's total metapsychology. It consisted of Freud's five converging psychological "points of view," along with a sixth, the adaptive, that had been added by Hartmann (1939) and by Rapaport and Gill (1959); "ego psychology" meant all of these together. Of these six points of view, it was only the economic and topographic that would be widely questioned, inside as well as outside of the Freudian school.

Scientific panels at meetings of the American established the theoretical ramifications of the functioning of the ego and their relevance to the theory of technique. The analyst positioned himself alongside the forces active in the patient's unconscious conflicts, in keeping with Anna Freud's (1936) recommendation of a position of equidistance among the conflicting streams of psychic motivations. With the help of a therapeutic alliance between the analytic function of the analyst and the rational aspects of the patient's ego, the analyst, in an ongoing, conjoint, mutual effort with the patient, sought, and aimed to analyze, the unconscious conflicts of the patient, thus enlarging the capacity of the patient's ego to manage and resolve psychic pressures from both the internal and external worlds. It should be noted, as a counter to later arguments for revision, that affect and subjectivity were central within this classical, structured view.

The ascendancy of this theoretical and technical vision, however, made the American, and the psychoanalysis it represented and furthered, the main target of anti-psychoanalytic bias and criticism, as it accrued to itself the resistance and opposition of the nonanalytic world along with the ambivalences from within the field as well. Although there had always been detractors and competitive theories, the dominant theoretical stance from the forties through the mid-sixties—for the entire third quarter of the psychoanalytic century—prized an objective, neutral, scientific stance that was considered rigid or prejudiced in the minds of its detractors. I consider the second half of the sixties the turning point, the time when explanatory theories and controversies of a nature qualitatively different from any seen before began to dominate the field. Gradually these alternative theories acquired a pervasive and imperious quality, and began to be adopted by large and enthusiastic numbers of disciples with a strong interest in persuading others to join them and in establishing a position of theoretical "superiority" or greater validity. Competitive theories began to appear with regularity, so that within a decade a multiplicity of theories and theorists was flourishing, each vying for adherents and for dominance.

There were foci of initiative for these developments in a number of localities, where they coalesced and then began to percolate outward to the national community, and ultimately to the international as well, in a common soil of receptivity. Constellations of individual leaders, each with a small group of activist supporters and a larger group of more passive ones, changed both the quality and the quantity of the dissenting voices. There has never been a lack of frustration in any analytic population—it is an endemic condition, I believe, following upon the normal unfinished state of many analyses. (I believe that after any analysis, some dissatisfaction with psychoanalysis coexists overtly or latently with the analysand's satisfaction. In the psychoanalytic family, a myriad of personal reactions may also lead to a displaced disaffection with theory, making for a rich pool of reactive, critical, and rebellious feelings, all of which are, at times, acted out.)

Things were different now, however, from before. Now the adherents of new or alternative theories, however major their differences on basic issues, were increasingly motivated to remain connected to the main theoretical system organizationally, political and material considerations having become as strongly determining as scientific issues. Social connectedness and fraternal feelings were such, and the main body was important and powerful and desirable enough, that simply leaving the tent was no longer the automatic response that it had been in the culturalist and interpersonal separations from the thirties to the fifties. The wish to remain connected to the American Psychoanalytic Association in spite of significant theoretical differences had come with the increased recognition of that organization as the standard for Freudian psychoanalysis, and so the locus of official authority and power.

The first demonstration of that newly achieved position came after the splits of the forties and fifties, when both sides sought to remain within the embrace of the national organization. The Academy of Psychoanalysis included many analysts who retained their membership in the American, as well as the many who were not eligible to join it. This was indeed a compromise-formation, a testament to the strength and dominance of the American's position as the locus and protector of evolving main Freudian theory. Rebellion and protest against the Freudian view could no longer automatically cause one to leave the American, or allow one to ignore its status as leader.

I attribute this acceptance of the status of the American to a widespread (unconscious) knowledge of, and inner conviction about, the role of unconscious intrapsychic conflicts and their centrality in the psychoanalytic understanding of the human mind. It reminds me of the political slogan "In your heart, you know he's right" that Barry Goldwater used in his presidential campaign against Lyndon Johnson. Many may challenge the correctness of this slogan in the original political context, but nonetheless it describes a recognizable psychological experience. No one can argue with his entire being against goals of rationality, objectivity, and fairness, however inadequately we may meet them.

The alternative theories and divisions, both scientific and interpersonal, that took root locally from the late sixties percolated upward from the local to the regional and then to the national levels. The various locales were all different, but they shared a common receptivity, each with its distinctive combination of leaders, shapers, and listeners, people with power and favors to bestow, and other people who wished to receive them, sometimes at the price of their own independence. As division spread, the national ambience of American psychoanalysis became increasingly split and theoretically fragmented. This gradually and inevitably led to complex reactive changes in attitudes among individual psychoanalysts, and in organizational and educational structures. These changes in the theoretical and interpersonal ecology of the field will occupy me for the remainder of this book.

THE PRESIDENCIES

I am raising my voice on this charged subject because during the period when the sea change in psychoanalysis was beginning, I was in the middle of it all. From the sixties on I occupied positions of administrative leadership: in the American from the beginning of the decade, and from the end of the sixties in the wider organizational life of the International. I was intimately involved in the changing times, although in a paradoxical way—mostly as an adversary to change, or as a corrective force. I was president of the American Psychoanalytic Association in 1961–1962, and again five years later, in 1966–1967. In 1967 I was elected vice president of the International, and then served two terms as president, from 1969 to 1971, and from 1971 to 1973. In between, in 1964–1965, I was called back for a third term as president of my local society, because of a growing crisis there.

During that decade of presidencies, I was frequently introduced, with some jocularity, as the "President of Everything."

This was not an unalloyed compliment, nor was it a pleasure to hear; I relate it because my occupation of positions of leadership during those times was not only connected with theoretical and organizational events, but was sometimes a target around which these were aimed. Conditions in Los Angeles psychoanalysis in the mid and late sixties, for a number of existing ecological and interpersonal reasons, made that city a starting point and a focus for the theoretical disruption and splintering that spread across the country in the years following. This was no coincidence, and the effects of these developments locally are still present thirty-five years later in derivative forms, including the isolation of individuals, the splintering and regrouping of previous friendships, a multiplicity of separate analytic societies in one city, and a pall on individual creativity. Many of these unproductive and unhappy outcomes appear to have become permanent.

The sixties in Los Angeles were a dramatic time in a turbulent place. Much of what has followed in American psychoanalysis since then was influenced, directly or indirectly, by innovations and disturbances that took place then and there. The analytic issues and directions of the sixties determined the problems of the seventies and of the three decades after them. And from theoretical beachheads established in Los Angeles, changes advanced across the rest of the country that altered the map of American psychoanalysis. Of course, if conditions had not been receptive elsewhere, this instability could not have spread and grown as it did; Southern California never cornered the market on analytic discontent. But there does seem to have been something under the surface of the analytic culture, an especially malignant substrate, that Kirsner (2000) described as "fear and loathing in L.A."

Although I have on many occasions expressed my views about these happenings both as they influenced abstract theory and as they explain a succession of group events, I am not satisfied that I have ever summarized my experiences among these conflicting forces in sufficient detail to make fully clear how those views developed. As a figure in an active leading role during this tumultuous and decisive decade, I was often in the eye of the storm, and too involved in charged ongoing events to be able to record this history with the completeness or detachment it deserved.

I aim to correct that gap in this presentation. To do so requires substantive descriptions not only of the contents of the numerous controversies but also the personal issues that impinged upon them. Only by means of such an exposition of the development of the conflicts and the repetitious threads that run through them can I present my own vision of resolution, and my view of what I (1983) have called "the enduring armature of psychoanalytic theory."

It would be incomplete to claim such centrality for events in Los Angeles without acknowledging the special spotlight of interest focused on this location by virtue of its central "industry," and the visibility of the people who are therefore involved. As the main source of the entertainment viewed by the world, the embrace of psychoanalysis by "Hollywood" in the fifties and sixties brought into the American home an extra intense look at the new and now-successful discipline. This was a mixed development, not without risk of distorted judgments and a certain unlikelihood of reliable assessment. Just after my first presidency of the American, while I was preparing a next move in my professional and personal odyssey, a hugely public event that pointed directly to Los Angeles and psychoanalysis hit the front pages of every newspaper in this country and many abroad. On August 5, 1962, the most famous movie star in the world, the sex goddess whose image virtually spawned an industry, committed suicide. Marilyn Monroe had been a patient of Ralph Greenson, and the news of her death included detailed accounts of her last days in psychoanalysis. Numerous troubling circumstances surrounded this event, which became the focus of much public distortion, but which also brought up issues of boundaries and the handling of transference, even, or particularly, in cases in which deep disturbances were considered to exist. The nuances of analytic and therapeutic decisions, and the ease with which well-intentioned moves to supply deep needs for safety can boomerang, were hardly topics for the general press to address, but the film capital, where patients were also glamorous people, invested such issues with a special intensity.

STANFORD: THE THINK TANK

Before I delve deeper into this period of upheaval, however, I want to describe a respite, a hiatus from the intensity of my life as a psychoanalyst to which I treated myself after finishing that first term as president in May, 1962. Deciding that academicians had a good thing going that clinical practitioners never thought of, I granted myself a year's sabbatical, and accepted a fellowship of the Ford Foundation to live, work, and think at the Center for Advanced Study in the Behavioral Sciences at Stanford University for the academic year 1962–1963. We rented our house in Los Angeles, and I faced the challenges and lessons of arranging for my patients during my year's absence. Then my wife, children, and I moved to Palo Alto, where we learned how it felt to direct our lives out of familiar currents and into new channels. Active ego decision-making was developing as a theoretical interest for me at that time, and now it captured my attention as a process with which to live a life.

The results were exhilarating and invigorating. Fifty scholars in the social sciences converge at the Center each year: historians, political scientists, economists, psychologists, mathematicians, artists, diplomats, writers, perhaps a future cabinet member or two. My year saw two psychoanalysts among the fifty, Erik Erikson and me, and Carl Rogers was there from psychology. Erik was just back from his study of Gandhi in India. It was, to say the least, a stimulating experience. No one had any tasks or subjects except their own individual goals, and there were no impediments toward achieving them. Crossfertilization was the point, and the possibility of exchange on the role of the unconscious across this wide spectrum of thinkers was an opportunity that I never had before or after. My interest in intrapsychic conflict that year led to an invitation to hold a seminar in the department of political science at Stanford (1963), where a project on international conflict resolution was in process. Whatever the outcomes of future conflicts would turn out to be, I would not forget the stimulating exchange of expertise on conflict resolution on all levels from the intrapsychic to the international.

My own output during that year was not what I wish it had been. I probably took too much time to relate and to play, but some papers did develop, consistent with my ongoing scientific interests. One of these was an effort to trace and expose the microscopic sequences of the "intrapsychic process" (Rangell 1963b), which led eventually to attention to the multiple *active* functions of the unconscious ego. Another, stimulated by the intellectual environment at the Center, was to work out the line of delineation between psychoanalysis and the other social sciences. This theoretical task of separation continued my previous attempts to define psychoanalysis so as to differentiate it from the contiguous analytic and dynamic psychotherapies. I delivered a paper (Rangell 1967) on the relationship between psychoanalysis and the behavioral sciences a year later as the Franz Alexander Lecture of the Chicago Psychoanalytic Institute (Alexander had been the first psychoanalyst at the Center a few years previously). It was the last Alexander Lecture presented during the lifetime of the honoree. Focusing on the unconscious intrapsychic operations around anxiety as a signal, I also described in this paper how affects and "the human core" were the center of the analytic quest. A number of subjects were born that became trademarks of my theoretical interest for years to come. Mostly these hovered around unconscious processes as the background from which the action phases of intrapsychic activity derived. The active unconscious ego was becoming a main heading of interest. During the Stanford year I also brought the Presidential Address I had delivered to the American the year before, "On Friendship" (1963a), up to a form to be published.

During that year away, I continued to nourish my Los Angeles roots. I went back a few times to give lectures or seminars, was visited up north by a number of colleagues, and even a patient or two made the trip for an occasional emergency hour. It was a new enterprise, to conduct such isolated hours in my study on the hill, but these spread-apart clinical encounters added yet another dimension to my cumulative experience. I also remember that a colleague on the Educational Committee, Carel Van der Heide, with whom I had not been very close before, took the time to visit, to inform me of ominous (as he saw them) developments back home, and to ask me to vote by proxy on certain pressing issues. My interest in what was going on at home was keen, and I kept myself informed.

Toward the end of that reflective and experimental year, I did feel some conflict about where to go next. The temptation to remain on "the peninsula," as the Stanford area was called, was strong. But it was not strong enough. My waiting practice, the positive aspects of the analytic milieu, and the old L.A. pull—the Southern California landscape and ambience—won out. I returned to my clinical life and all the related activities I was used to. Almost all of my patients resumed their interrupted analyses. We discussed the interval as one would ordinarily face and analyze a weekend between sessions.

On my return I found the general psychoanalytic atmosphere to be as I had left it, only more so. You could still feel the mixture of the good, solid times of the fifties along with the beginnings of social and professional problems ahead. Friendships were strong, intellectual interests sustained, patients available. But there were also the beginnings of rigid stratification of the hierarchic social structure, and the upward curve of heretofore limitless expectations and optimism seemed finally to be leveling off. Anxieties, hostilities, and frustrated aspirations were on the advance, and theoretical excitement and intellectual enjoyment were flattening out. The middle band of members of the Society (my generation now, a decade and a half older), were jockeying for position and feeling professional frustration, stresses which clouded the specialness of Southern California.

6

THE 1960S CONTINUE;
PLATFORM TO THE 1970S:
THE STAGES OF DECLINE
OF A UNIFIED THEORY

THE CREST OF THE WAVE AND
THE DOWNWARD TURN

After the crest of the mid- to late sixties, there was a curious downward turn in the curve of theory development, with the questioning (and in my view gradual erosion) of the central trunk of the Freudian theoretical tree. Theoretical challenges, as I will elaborate shortly, were coming not only from outside the mainstream of psychoanalysis but also from competing alternative schools within psychoanalysis. Theoretical dissatisfaction now focused on the intrapsychic view of the psychic apparatus and its functioning, as these had been delineated in the Freudian line of thought.

The Gabbards in *Psychiatry and the Cinema* (1999) come to a similar timetable from another direction. Contemplating the influence of psychoanalytic thinking on American films, they consider 1957 through 1963 as the "golden age," and that the "fall from grace," which they believe persists to this day, began almost immediately after that. It is noteworthy, from my point of view, that Glen Gabbard has been long identified with Topeka and the Menninger Clinic, and that the film industry, which (at least in some way) also reflects American life, centers in Los Angeles. From my own personal history in the field, I have come to recognize these cities, Topeka and Los Angeles, as two of the crucial foci of theoretical change on the American psychoanalytic scene. The others were London, where Klein's influence had long been felt but whence it was imported to Los Angeles during this later period, and Rome and Chicago, where Heinz Kohut's story developed.

THE CRACKS NOW WITHIN

Up until this point in the history of psychoanalysis, theoretical divisions had made for animated discussions and a few alternative groups as competitive theories of etiology and neurosogenesis split off from the main body. The early dissidents Horney and Sullivan, for example, led their followers away from the psychoanalysis of internal states, and focused instead on the roles of external influences and of frustrating outer experiences in their search for a psychoanalytic explanation of the neuroses—whether in patients or, as Horney (1937) wrote, in "the neurotic personality of our time." But while clusters of analysts who shared these views did separate themselves into discrete and identifiable groups, some of which even developed their own organizational structures, none of these bodies of thought were forceful enough or sufficiently compelling to effect any significant division within the main trunk of psychoanalytic theory.

The 1960s brought another movement, however—a questioning of the mainstream "Freudian" center itself. Critical theorists were no longer objecting to existing theory in favor of environmental or cultural determinants; they were expressing a fundamental dissatisfaction with the intrapsychic view of the psychic apparatus and its functioning as it had developed from Freud through his almost official theoretical successors, Anna Freud, Heinz Hartmann, and David Rapaport.

There were two challenges to the traditional view of intrapsychic activity, and two different modes of questioning it. One route of opposition, the one spearheaded by Melanie Klein, had begun earlier in Europe, although it established inroads on this continent during the sixties through a window in Los Angeles. The Kleinians postulated an earlier time of onset of neurotic psychopathology than the Freudians did, and the existence of a complex body of thought and conflicts at this early stage of life. "Kleinian theory," which had taken firm root in England before the war, had not been amalgamated into the Freudian mainstream as a complement to it, but had come instead to be seen as a viable *alternative* to it. The relation between this theoretical turn of events and the struggle between the leaders of the opposing factions, Anna Freud and Melanie Klein, has long been recognized and discussed, and accords with the theme that I am illustrating in this book: that psychoanalytic theory has been formed by the interaction of scientific (substantive) and interpersonal (affective) issues.

The other challenge to traditional intrapsychic dynamics was not a phenomenologic or developmental one but a fundamental theoretical disagreement, and it contested the observational basis and adequacy of Freud's metapsychological and biopsychological theories. This major reappraisal was introduced in this country by a second Klein, George, under whose leadership it developed in a group identified with the psychoanalytic center at the Menninger Clinic in Topeka. Although Klein's influential paper "Two Theories or One?" did not appear until its posthumous publication in the *Bulletin of the Menninger Clinic* in 1973, the ideas had germinated earlier, in the mid-sixties (a version of the paper had been presented to the "Psychoanalysts of the Southwest" in 1966), and had gained strength rapidly. The small but important Menninger Clinic had sponsored decades of research and close psychoanalytic thinking by a serious and close-knit group of faculty and trainees under David Rapaport, and had been an influential center in the development of Freudian theory. Now there arose in this group an articulate and scholarly new nucleus that began to argue strongly and persuasively, as in Gill's introduction to Klein's (1973) paper, that Freud's abstract theorizing was not effectively connected to observed clinical data. These views attracted serious study and dichotomized the psychoanalytic theorists in this country—not as profoundly as Melanie Klein had divided theorists in London, but still cleaving the unified psychoanalytic theory in the United States that had survived both the neo-Freudian splits by culturalists like Horney and Sullivan, and the therapeutic correctivists of the Alexander school.

LOS ANGELES: THE SIXTIES

After my year with the American in 1961–1962 and the succeeding year of rest and writing at Stanford, I went in the summer of 1963 to the Stockholm International Congress. From there a congenial group of analyst-friends visited Russia together, particularly Moscow and then-Leningrad (this was during Khruschev's regime), with interesting tours of some of their psychiatric facilities. From Moscow, my wife and I went to Vienna for the first time. I settled down in Los Angeles, back to my full psychoanalytic life, in the fall of 1963.

Only a decade after its separation from the Southern California Society in the big split of 1950, the Los Angeles Psychoanalytic Society and Institute was again showing signs of unrest and instability. There were visible indications of internal strain: growing factionalism, group rivalries and stratifications, and individual frustrations and resentments. While there were no theoretical divisions as yet, general dissatisfaction with organized psychoanalysis, and its dominant theory along with it, was reaching a crescendo. The frustrations and complaints, I would say, paralleled the economic concept of "distributing the wealth"; there was concern about the distribution of the favors, the recognition, and the honors, intellectual and administrative, that in the psychoanalytic culture made for power and self-esteem. While similar conflicts were occurring throughout the psychoanalytic world, the locale most likely to result in action, in my view probably as a result of its specific interpersonal composition, was the Los Angeles Society.

Events began to unfold that turned out to be crucial for the course of psychoanalytic history. I had not been back long when a nominating committee, concerned about a serious crisis in cohesion and morale within the Los Angeles Society, asked me to accept the presidency of the Society once more, beginning in 1964, for what would be a third term. The challenge was to bring some order and leadership to a society where discontent was brewing and where the membership was seething over a widespread frustration over advancement—mostly to training analyst status, but to other teaching and leadership positions as well. I accepted the invitation against the warnings of my wife, who feared that in an atmosphere already rife with dissatisfaction, the envy of analysts disappointed in their wishes for advance would make a difficult job harder for anyone perceived to have been more fortunate than they.

The initial congratulatory excitement we had experienced (probably mostly from a nucleus of unambivalent friends) following my election to the presidency of the American had gradually been replaced, I felt, by a rather sullen resentment by a large number of colleagues who had not received the signs of special recognition that they coveted. However, I did take on the appointment in L.A., and during my tenure that year the Board did succeed in bringing about some improvement in the conditions responsible for the low morale. We set in motion plans for reorganization, which would help members move along in their progression in the Society and in their advance toward training and faculty positions in the Institute.

I had long felt that too much importance was attached to the status of training analyst. While I respected the need for the best in education, I always had doubts about giving such prominence to training analysts, many of whom were quite passive and uncreative in scientific affairs, and sometimes inhibitory of the work of others. I felt similarly that the Board on Professional Standards of the American had too much prestige, and too autocratic a stance toward the Executive Council. That is why, when I finished my first term as president of the American in 1962, I declined the invitation to run for chairman of the Board. Ironically, in recent times, there has been a swell of protest from the membership of the American against the special power of the Board, and a strong move to empower the membership with voting rights on all matters, including education. This subject is a complex and important one, and there are cogent arguments on both sides. While it is necessary to protect the maintenance of standards, it is equally important to keep them from becoming rigid. The Los Angeles Society-Institute shared these conflicts. My life in the local Society, and now in the American, had made me supportive of a greater voice for members who were working steadily and creatively at the level of daily clinical work, yet who may not have had much interest in training functions.

But an incident during that 1964–1965 term destroyed the improvements in equanimity and cohesion that we had achieved. It had an enormous affective effect on the membership, inflaming passions and adding to the hostile divisiveness. Although the incident was finally "closed," it was never resolved, and it had a permanent scarring effect.

A patient called the Society to complain that her analyst had struck her, and as I was president, she was referred to me. It was a delicate situation, and there was no machinery in place at that time for dealing with such ethical issues. After seeing the patient and hearing her complaint, I felt that the next move should be determined in consultation and I referred the matter to the officers of the Executive Board; they would act as a preliminary "ethics committee," and decide whether and how the issue should be explored further. The other four officers of the Board, without me, interviewed the patient, and voted unanimously that the case did have to be explored. In the course of the two interviews, however, the patient had reported that Ralph Greenson, who happened to be close with the involved analyst, had come into the waiting room and witnessed the altercation. The entire Board therefore decided to interview Greenson before deciding how to proceed, the thought being that if he did not confirm her statement, the matter could probably be dropped there. Greenson passed no judgment, but he did confirm the incident. He also informed the patient's analyst of the proceedings. The analyst felt that action had been taken unjustifiably, and that he should have been notified before anything was done. I felt that this was an understandable objection, but at the time there was no procedural precedent, and we had acted in good faith in the belief that the case might end there. The matter came to a head when the analyst appeared at the next Society meeting and accused the Board of acting without jurisdiction and from personal malice. Attention was deflected from the original complaint, and a motion was carried to investigate the motives and methods of the Board instead. The appointed investigating committee, after a painful inquiry, ruled that the Board had acted properly, and the officers were exonerated. But pursuit of the original grievance was dropped as well. Group spirits and confidence never recovered from this incident, which led to further polarization and permanent, although largely hidden, divisions within the Los Angeles Society.

Theoretical developments were afoot as well, influencing and meshing with the political ones. A quiet movement had been growing during these years whose effects would eventually be felt at the heart of the psychoanalytic movement. The earliest manifestation was a very quiet one. Ivan Maguire, a training analyst—something of a loner, respected for his literary scholarship but not part of the gregarious in-group of the Education Committee—had been meeting with a group of colleagues to introduce them to Kleinian, and also to Fairbairnian, theories. His group was a mixed one; some members were interested for primarily intellectual reasons, but others were disaffected with the main body and seeking other avenues of expression. I learned about this group only later; at the time I had no idea of its existence.

The next related happening was in January, 1969. I was in London for a meeting of the Australian Site Committee of the I.P.A., and I had been invited to deliver a paper to the British Society; I was a possible candidate for the next presidency of the International, and they wanted to become acquainted.[1] While I was there,

---

1. The paper I gave to the British Society on January 8, 1969 was on the theory of anxiety. I remember that Anna Freud, whom I had met with earlier that week, did not attend, but I was told that she had sent Ernst Freud, to report to her about it. I did not make much of this at the time, although it was a subject that I had thought would interest her, in that I was working on unifying her father's two theories of anxiety. Later, however, as I studied her correspondence of that time with Heinz Kohut about the coming election, I came to feel that her absence might have been more meaningful.

some colleagues asked me, "Who is Dr. Brandchaft, who is here talking with Hanna Segal?" The Londoners were curious because he was unknown to them; I was taken aback because I knew he was discontented at home, and because I knew of no official scientific activities that might account for his being there. Bernard Brandchaft and I had a long relationship dating back to our days at the University of Chicago, when he was an undergraduate and I was in medical school. His decision to come to Los Angeles had been influenced by my being there. I had contributed a great deal to his professional start in the city. But he had become increasingly discontent with his career path and rivalrous with me, and our relationship had over a number of years become correspondingly distant. He was part of the ongoing Kleinian study group in L.A., and his visit had to do with this, as I was soon to find out.

I put this uneasy incident out of my mind until a series of events, stemming from Brandchaft's presence in England, exploded. A procession of Kleinian analysts (and later Wilfred Bion) were invited to Los Angeles. These visits were their first to the United States, and they were fueled by and embedded in a contagious group excitement that would not only stamp the seventies, but affect analytic training through the eighties and nineties as well. This influx began exactly around that personally important year of 1969, in which I became president of the International—with it a new era was ushered in that permanently altered the harmony and theoretical commonality of the society in which I lived and worked. And it made the seventies and eighties the most turbulent period in the history of that society. The Kleinian analysts—Hanna Segal, Herbert Rosenfeld, the Meltzers, Betty Joseph, and others—came to Los Angeles, some repeatedly, to lecture, teach, and conduct private supervisions, both individual and group, to an increasing number of enthusiastic supporters, eager to absorb the new language and insights. Wilfred Bion, also recruited by Brandchaft and a few other activists who by then had joined with him, came to settle in Los Angeles. He was greeted with the same excitement, almost hero worship. While these activities were brought about by society members, they remained studiedly unofficial and outside of the Society-Institute, and therefore not subject to policies or votes. The general membership of the Society registered no protest, and was divided in its attitudes toward this new theoretical invasion.

By this time, Brandchaft had become close to Greenson, who had not initiated the move to bring the British analysts to Los Angeles, but who had lent his interest and support after the fact. Brandchaft and Greenson had both made clear their rivalrous feelings toward me, but the link between them was intellectual as well as affective, as was evidenced by the fact that Greenson participated actively in the new scientific atmosphere, and was known to have sent a member of his family to Brandchaft for analysis. This gave the Kleinian connection an ironic aspect, since Greenson at the same time was enjoying and making widely known a special closeness to Anna Freud.

This was the time of Greenson's (1969) paper "The Origin and Fate of New Ideas in Psychoanalysis"—a well-known paper with a double aspect. Greenson, writing at the time of the new local excitement about Klein, made a plea for openness to new ideas, but he urged also that these should be allowed to coexist with old, enduring ones. This message was congruent with my own feelings about how new and old ideas in psychoanalysis should ideally be related, with my desire for integration, and with my attempts at synthesis and a unified theory. It was also compatible with classical theory as exemplified by Freud, Anna Freud, and subsequent further classical development. In the context of that time, however, Greenson's paper, which was taken as support of the Kleinian activities in the society, has an interesting subtext. In making his intriguing differentiation between the classical and the orthodox, he enabled his message to be read in two ways. On the one hand, his attribution of rigidity to orthodoxy, while sparing the classical, allowed him to link himself with the ambient criticism of the traditional while at the same time preserving his connection with Anna Freud. Neither pole, Greenson said—dismissing the new or discarding the old—is defensible. I agree. But while Greenson warned appropriately against rigidity, he also said that "Classical analysts . . . dare not contend with the valuable ideas of those they consider to be outside of the mainstream of Freudian psychoanalysis." This set up a complex situation. The paper had been written as an ostensible call for scientific objectivity, yet in that context it was taken as a pro-Kleinian statement. The solace it gave the protesters allowed Greenson, a classical analyst, to make common cause with them, and so indirectly to undermine his rivals in his own school. Thus the curious theoretical alliance between Greenson and Brandchaft.

There was a day of reckoning for this double role of Greenson's, however, and it came at the London Congress in 1975. By then the Kleinian sweep of Los Angeles had tapered off, and Greenson argued publicly against Segal at the Congress, now from firsthand data and quoting clinical experiences in which he had participated as one of the cooperating hosts during the L.A. Kleinian period. When Segal registered strong objections to what she now felt had been a duplicitous double-agent role, Greenson, standing on this occasion for the views he truly believed, and in open association with Anna Freud, countered that he had joined the Kleinian sessions to see what the other side was doing.

It is very difficult at this distance to make clear the issues and the passions of that time, and their consequences. What was at stake was not really Kleinian or object-relations theory, or even openness to new ideas; it was the anti-classical frenzy to which the English visitors, in pursuit of their own purposes, had unwittingly lent themselves. In his 1980 review of a book on Klein by Hanna Segal, the even-handed William Gillespie stated that the issue with the Kleinian system in Great Britain "had to do not so much with the scientific status of the Kleinian school as with their allegedly unfair political and canvassing methods, and in particular with their alleged attempts to corner the training system and so eventually to achieve control of the [British] Society" (p. 86). Gillespie goes on to quote the opinion of Glover on "their illegitimate methods of advancing their cause." These descriptions could serve as well for what was happening in the Los Angeles Society among those emulating the British Kleinians. The chief impetus was the push against the classical. It was ironic that during their visits Hanna Segal, Herbert Rosenfeld, Betty Joseph, and the others—who were friends and colleagues of mine from my International activity—paid me personal visits, while their local hosts saw me as an outsider. Their original mentor Maguire had been displaced as well by those whose interest he himself had aroused, an indication of the diversion of interest from the theoretical and intellectual aspects of the debate to the political and personal.

The founders and the consumers of this bazaar of psychoanalytic styles in Los Angeles proved to be shifting and fickle. The invited British analysts, respected and established at home, found their reception in L.A. short-lived and unreliable, as those who sponsored them soon turned to other theorists who had in common with them mainly the fact that they provided an alternative to the classical mode. After Klein and Fairbairn and Bion, the dissidents turned first to Kohut and then to Stolorow, intersubjectivity, and enactment, following the trendy edge of innovation and change. For many analysts these labile group affiliations seemed to be more a function of group adhesion than of theoretical conviction. I remember asking one earnest member of this set where he was now. "I'm with Bernie," he replied (Bernard Brandchaft at that time was switching his allegiance from Klein to Kohut). Some did persevere in their beliefs, however, to form the nucleus of more cohesive groups, which led eventually to an array of formal separate groups of Kleinians, Kohutians, and intersubjectivists.

There is a saying that any long journey begins with a first step. This is as true in group affairs as it is in travel. No large movement occurs without a small beginning, even one that might seem trivial at first. I am reminded that the long and disruptive Watergate experience began when Frank Wills, the guard who noticed the taped office door lock on his second rounds of the night, put in a call to the police, and, to quote *The Nation*, "pushed the rock that tipped the boulders that started the avalanche that filled the valley" (Rangell 1980a, p. 55). So it was with the cataclysmic inundation that overran the Los Angeles psychoanalytic community. Kirsner (2000) quotes Mason, a Kleinian from England who came with to L.A. with the influx of Kleinians but who stayed to become a leader of the subsequent Kleinian Society: "Bernard Brandchaft was of seminal importance in the Kleinian development. Had he not lived in Los Angeles, the extensive interest in Klein would in all likelihood not have occurred" (p. 172). More likely, in the local professional milieu as in the national political one, the trigger event served only as a precipitant, as the day-residue is precipitant to a dream. A broader psychic readiness is always necessary and always present, and the nature of that psychic readiness determines in large part the final outcome. The psychic base of Watergate was such that without the precipitant of that specific individual—the spark that set off the conflagration—Nixon might very well have served out his term. But in psychoanalysis, movements of generalized conflict and discontent have always been endemic. They preceded the specific local conditions of the sixties, and even without the catalyst that Brandchaft and L.A. provided would in all likelihood have eventuated in the spread of the same theoretical conflicts, although perhaps in a different chronological and geographic sequence. Had there been on the L.A. psychoanalytic scene more of the clinical-experiential than the interpersonal, more a scientific than a group-arousing method, more of a sharing than an imposition of views, there would have been less of a divided society and more fused theoretical mixing into an inclusive whole.

If rivalry, frustrated ambition, and hostile envy were operating motives in the theoretical shifts, the resultant group life at least partially succeeded in addressing them. As a result of the expanding interest in the new theories, the traditional Freudian viewpoint—my own preferred viewpoint—was largely obliterated in Los Angeles (and found itself subsequently on the defensive in the American and largely in the International as well). Classical theory, the Oedipus complex, and the objective analytic technique became objects of antipathy, subject to deprecation and scorn on the analytic scene. With the theoretical differences in our locale also came some extraordinary breaches in the rules of collegiality. I personally experienced a good number of them. On several occasions I heard of patients having been told by a "modern" analyst that I was rigid and belonged to an old school that was now outmoded and becoming extinct. One analyst of the "new" thinking, upon learning that a patient had been referred to me by a New York analyst, telephoned the referring analyst across the country to inform him and set him straight—did he know the patient was referred to a rigid, old-fashioned analyst?

It is now four decades since the sixties, when the slow eruption began that eventually produced such a significant alteration in the fabric of American psychoanalysis. Some have seen in this sea-change a burst of renewed creativity, the first since Freud's original breakthrough, and a revitalizing plurality of theoretical positions; others have bemoaned it as a derailment of psychoanalytic development, based on disillusionment and a devaluing of the central assumptions of psychoanalytic theory. However one evaluates the results, from the history I have chronicled of the theoretical development of that time, envy, rivalry, and hostility played their parts in fueling these group movements. One leader with enormous charisma, a brilliant scientific life, and a strong and dependent following, uniting with another, disappointed and a social activist, against a common rival, can and did produce an irresistible series of historical events. (The phenomenon of the common rival may in fact be more widespread than the better-known common enemy.) In the case of one participant, envy and lack of gratitude were likely determinants of actions that led to a huge spread of the theory that made important contributions to the understanding of both these affective states. In the case of the other, the nature of the affective involvement covers a much longer period and reaches to deeper levels.

Thirty-five years later, as the new millennium began, these hugely disruptive controversies were revived and reinflamed. In *Unfree Associations: Inside Psychoanalytic Institutes*, historian-philosopher Douglas Kirsner (2000) studied the conflicts of that period in four prominent institutes in this country. In the chapter quite aptly entitled "Fear and Loathing in Los Angeles,"

Kirsner presented information and past and present attitudes about these doings from a series of interviews of individuals across the spectrum of the issues involved. Since that time, new archival research by Kirsner has permitted greater retrospective understanding and made old events newly comprehensible. Kirsner uncovered some letters in the Greenson manuscript archives at U.C.L.A. that illuminate the nature and depth of the motivations involved. Greenson, referring to the 1964 ethics investigation that I described above, wrote to Sam Guttman (chairman of the Program Committee of the American), "I feel very strongly about Rangell. . . . There may well be a big lawsuit . . . as well as proceedings for impeachment, because what he did was dastardly" (Greenson to Guttman, March 8, 1965). Writing to his friend Masud Khan, Greenson again expresses his fury over this incident, and chides Khan as having helped along "Rangell's megalomania" by inviting me to write an article in celebration of Heinz Hartmann's 70th birthday and publishing it as the lead article in the *International Journal* (Greenson to Khan, February 25, 1965). Khan replies that he had known me then only through my work, and that he would "hate to be the butt of Rangell's paranoid zeal" (Khan to Greenson, March 1, 1965). The next day Khan continues, "I was very dissatisfied with my letter to you yesterday," and urges Greenson to consider taking on the presidency of the American Psychoanalytic Association. His shirking that commitment, Khan says, "is partially responsible for Rangell being where he is and doing what he does." He goes on: "It is the judeo-christian cultural substratum of the analytic movement . . . that has left a bias for subversive and oblique manipulative social behavior among analysts and the latest trend is to find institutional coverage and rationale through setting up persecutory adjudicatory committees to execute this negative and intimidating manipulation of each other" (Khan to Greenson, March 2, 1965).[2]

---

2. Along with this picture of the psychoanalytic ambience in Los Angeles in the sixties, a striking precursor may be seen of Khan's anti-Semitism, which was exposed following his death thirty-five years later (Godley 2001).

Greenson replies, "I feel much closer to the International than to the American. I would rather be a Vice-President in the International than President of the American. If you can help get me a Vice Presidency, I would be delighted. Some day I would also want to be President of the American but that is enormously time consuming and also degrading" (Greenson to Khan, March 9, 1965). Khan replies, "I shall do all I can to prepare the atmosphere conducive to your nomination of Vice-President of the International. The first thing to bear in mind is to see to it that the right people propose your name. I think two very good people would be Dr. Robert Knight if he comes to Amsterdam and Pearl King. . . . Meanwhile I shall start spreading good-will about you all round the place so that we can muster enough votes. . . . One has to pull these things together slowly" (Khan to Greenson, March 17, 1965). This exchange did not occur in a vacuum. I had been elected president of the American for the second time, in 1965–1966, the first such reelection after a five-year interval that had ever taken place. Two years later, in 1967, I was elected vice president of the I.P.A. at the International Congress in Copenhagen from a list of nominees that included Greenson.

The Los Angeles conflicts reached Anna Freud as well. She sent Greenson a query: "People tell me there is a rift in the Los Angeles Society between you and Rangell. Is it true? And what is it about, personal or scientific?" (Anna Freud to Greenson, June 7, 1964). He replied, "The difficulty between Rangell and me goes way back to the War, when I selected him to work in our psychiatric program in Denver. Somehow he thought that meant I loved him and he has never forgiven me for not doing so. There is absolutely nothing scientific in our difficulties, and there never has been. . . . Masud Khan . . . could give you an insight into Rangell. . . . You might ask him about this situation" (Greenson to Anna Freud, July 2, 1964).

Remarkable revisions of history occur at all levels. That memory is largely narrative, and that historical truth faces a difficult struggle, is incontrovertible. Obviously Greenson and I had different memories of the circumstances of our meeting. About the time and the place we apparently agreed. As to the rest, however, it is a fact that he and I were both assigned, by orders from Washington and from different places, to the same Air Force post in Denver, to teach at the School of Aviation Psychiatry. Gaps in a twenty-year-old memory are certainly likely to be filled with one's own constructions, but Greenson's view of the subsequent events obliterates a significant and instructive aspect of them—the group process that led to the splitting and alienation that I have described at that post during that period. A building block of future history is removed.

Looking back on it after all these years, I think it is fair to say that Greenson was a subtle mixture of talents and flaws, intense and extreme in both directions. He was the most appealing and successful teacher in the Institute. He was an awesome public speaker. Many who went through training in Los Angeles, especially those who remained untouched by his negative affects or outbursts, would remember his lectures and presentations as a glowing and inspiring part of their analytic inheritance. And many who were accepted as part of his private entourage, who met celebrities and creative artists (including film-star patients) at his home, remain exhilarated by the experience, and bristle at any criticism. But it would be an oversight not to acknowledge also the economic factors at work. Greenson had a tremendous amount of referral power, and unprecedented access, as "analyst to the stars," to the enormous pool of well-known, glamorous, and wealthy patients indigenous to the culture of Los Angeles. His patronage was therefore highly desirable to some of his colleagues, and that made it correspondingly hard for them to disagree with him, either publicly or privately.

It should also be said that in the excitement of L.A.'s celebrity culture there were always temptations: it was not easy for some analysts to remain objective in their technique, or even to keep their analytic activities confidential. *Hollywood on the Couch*, written by two journalists (Farber and Green 1993), provided a chronicle of some of the practices and specific instances that resulted. This account contained some documented narratives, mostly of the misuse of transference or of the analytic situation, as well as anecdotal material felt by some to be gossip. Kirsner (2000), whom I have previously mentioned, also pointed critically to moral as well as morale problems. Although the analytic community for the most part paid the Farber and Green book little attention, and were divided in their reactions to Kirsner, both books were based on considerable research, and chronicled events and backgrounds with sufficient accuracy to warrant serious thought.

When used for the good, Greenson's attributes were of the highest value; in the service of aggression, however, their effects were devastating. He could turn against people unpredictably, humiliating his targets pitilessly. I saw him do this at a party to a physician who had become close to the analytic group, reducing him to a state of helpless embarrassment and physical weakness. Sometimes he apologized the next day—and sometimes the apology only set up the victim for a repeat round. It is hard to reconstruct such off-the-record episodes, and even if one could, the vigor and passion of his defenders would equal those of his detractors.

But an occasional skirmish is documented. In 1967 Lawrence Kubie gave a paper to the Los Angeles Society. Greenson was the discussant, and he mercilessly and needlessly attacked Kubie's presentation. Shortly afterward, Kubie sent me a copy of a letter he wrote to Greenson after the meeting. I had no personal relationship with Kubie; I knew and respected his name from a distance in my early New York candidate days. But he apparently felt that I should be the one to receive this unsolicited information, to represent the community he wished to address.

On March 1, 1967, from Sparks, MD, where he was on the staff of Sheppard Pratt, Kubie wrote:

> My dear Greenson,
> I reached home early on Friday morning the 24th. Your apology of the 21st reached me the following morning. A round dozen of our colleagues from both societies had anticipated you by phoning me, and by writing to me to apologize for your behavior, i.e. for its inaccuracy, for its exhibitionism, and for its confusing incoherence. Some said you were drunk. Some

said that you had done this often before, but never quite as rantingly. Therefore, although I appreciate the fact that you wrote, it is obvious that you addressed your apology to the wrong man. Rest assured that you had not, as you imagined, hurt my feelings. I felt neither hurt nor anger, but only chagrin that any analyst should so forget his responsibility to himself and to analysis. Therefore you owed your apology first of all to yourself, then to your Institute and your colleagues, and finally to analysis itself. But this is a debt that you cannot discharge merely by apologizing. You owe yourself the opportunity to lie down on the well-worn couch of some mature and unsparing colleague, in an all-out effort to find out what has happened to you over the years which could lead you to behave in this way. Clearly something destructive must have happened to you and I sincerely hope that you will go into full psychoanalytic therapy unsparingly.

I will add just one personal point. Once I have said my say about such an incident, I carry no trace of continuing resentment. You have damaged the image of yourself in my mind; but you can repair this by removing those causes which lie within yourself.

> Yours very truly,
> Lawrence S. Kubie, M.D.

I can only admire Kubie for this letter, which I wish I had had as a model much earlier. If I had been able to react as he did, instead of using my energy otherwise—resenting or being upset at the situation over the long period, staying out of Greenson's way, competing with him, trying to join him, always engaged with him and aware of his being there—perhaps much local, social, and professional trouble might have been avoided. But although I had sought a period of analysis with an older analyst respected by both of us, this did not solve the problem.

Some time after I returned from Stanford, during one of the thaws in our relationship—there were several—Greenson asked me to share the new penthouse office he was planning to open. This was clearly to be the office of the stars, and the opportunity to share it was a plum coveted by many. I knew of certain analysts who were quite put out at not being invited. As I look back on it, this was a bold and interesting move on Greenson's part; given the relationship between us it was an astonishing thing for him to have done. I felt that my independence would be at stake, however, and so declined his offer. This further darkened the air between us, and Greenson ended up sharing the office with Milton Wexler. For me it was a highly charged decision, one of those roads not taken that might have altered the course of the history that followed.

Greenson's personal qualities, both the charming and the disruptive ones, played a large part in defining the atmosphere at the L.A. Institute during the good and bad times of the postwar decades. But the complex and emotionally charged relationship between influential analysts was the background in this locality, where the definitive breakup of the more or less homogeneous American psychoanalytic theoretical structure began in a period of revolutionary change. And there was corresponding splitting and confusion among the membership at large, which was quite ready to absorb the opportunities afforded by the situation.

Let me say explicitly here that there is no doubt that the traditional Freudian group contributed its share to this entire series of separatist events, and that it continues to do so. It was in truth rigid and inflexible to some degree. This stemmed in part from the way theory was interpreted through the early years, in part from the personalities involved, and in part from the novelty and awkwardness of practice in a new profession. There were hierarchies, exclusivities, and power plays aplenty, and many of those who gradually became the senior Freudian analysts grew authoritarian and forbidding, thus setting themselves up for these group counterreactions.

TOPEKA

That is how it looked in Los Angeles at the end of the sixties. But there was another major critical reexamination and suggested modification of psychoanalytic theory in progress during the same period, independent of the developments in California and different in both motivation and scientific style.

The close-knit and exciting group of psychoanalytic researchers and clinicians that had worked under David Rapaport at the Menninger Clinic in Topeka starting in the forties had since dispersed around the country. Now in the late sixties and early seventies this group was rallying under George Klein in New York, to question and disagree with the very same central Freudian metapsychology that had been brilliantly developed and furthered by them years before. This theoretical turnaround by probably the most thoughtful and dedicated group of theoretical thinkers of the time, considered by many a delayed palace revolution, took place neither on the basis of further clinical observation and resulting new conclusions—that is, the scientific method of psychoanalysis—nor on any new methodology of data collection. It was based on the further thinking-through of the cumulative observations of a half-century of psychoanalytic practice the world over, observations gathered by the accepted psychoanalytic method, and it offered a new view of theory to better explain these data. Many in the group, including Rapaport and Klein, were not themselves practicing psychoanalysts, and Roy Schafer had begun training in psychoanalysis only after he had left Topeka.

Although the seminal paper that announced this revision, George Klein's "Two Theories or One?," did not appear until 1973, the work had been in progress for five years before that, interrupted by the untimely death of Klein in 1971 at the age of 53. A strong endorsement of the revised position was contained in an introduction to Klein's paper by Gill (1973) who, as coauthor and editor (1967a) of Rapaport's incisive *Collected Papers*, had been, with Rapaport, the foremost expositor of Freud's metapsychology through the forties and fifties. Also veering away from the Freudian explanatory theory they had formerly furthered were Holt (1972, 1973, 1976) and Schafer (1976), who wrote in strong opposition to aspects of theory that they now considered mechanistic and not applicable to the clinical process or to human psychology. Howard Shevrin (1976), part of the original group, remained conspicuously in favor of his previous positions, and was now conducting research at Ann Arbor, confirming experimentally in brain studies the speculative theories of Freud from a psychological and neurophysiologic perspective.

The revised reasoning of Klein and the group led them to propose two distinct psychoanalytic theories, not one. One was clinical, based on direct observation, and the other not apparently linked to the clinical situation. Clinical theory, experience-near and observable, was incontestable, while abstract theory, experience-distant and speculative, was open to major revision.

An earlier article by Robert Waelder (1962) had addressed this subject empirically. Waelder had pointed out that there is a hierarchy of theories, from clinical to abstract, and that all of these contain at all their stages more of the one and less of the other. Here too I believe that the argument of a complementary series is a very convincing one, in this instance against a definitive separation of the clinical from the abstract. It is characteristic, however, of many of the alternative claims made during refinements of theory that they remain impervious to rebuttal, however logical or persuasive. I have pointed out, for example, along the same line of thinking as Waelder's, that transference, which is a clinical concept, is also an abstract construction, while psychic structure and mental dynamics, more abstract concepts, rest on a clinical base. But the cognitive challenges raised to suggested new theories are often and characteristically allowed to remain without resolution, and so serve as magnets to those of successive generations who seek for whatever complex reasons further change. There is also again the issue of consequentiality. If Waelder's point is correct— and no argument against it has been mounted—how can the separation into the two suggested theories continue to apply?

This sophisticated nucleus of scientific researchers, as they explored and reconsidered important cognitive aspects of theory-building, took a leading role in what would become a rapidly intensifying movement of criticism of and opposition to standard accumulated theory, and in favor of a succession of alternative explanatory theoretical systems. Each of these as it gained group momentum would be accompanied by corresponding societal and administrative changes. While later experiences lead me to think that in all of these developments scientific issues were dominated and superseded by sociological ones, I was not directly privy in all local situations to the group relationships and affective inter-personal factors that accompanied, caused, or in some cases merely followed the theoretical, scientific changes. In the instance of this "Two theories or one?" question, two phenomena, the intellec-tual issue and the distancing of themselves from previous posi-tions, arose simultaneously in a number of dispersed individuals who had been together in a close bond years before, under their inspirational Moses (i.e., Rapaport) who, according to Gill, "dis-cussed abstract metapsychology with the fervor of a political orator and the thunder of a Hebrew prophet" (1967b, p. 5). Such a thunderous influence can have a biphasic effect on disciples, as analysts know. Both Gill and Schafer have had particularly roller-coaster theoretical histories since that time, although along dif-ferent paths.

PRELUDE TO ROME

I am not sure how the developments in Los Angeles—and per-haps in the more isolated Topeka—related to the wider social and political ferment of the sixties, in which authority and "the es-tablishment" in general were common targets, frequently rebelled against and sometimes overthrown. It is not impossible that they were related. This was the period of postmodern revisionism, which (across the board as well as in the arts) directed intellec-tual disciplines into new directions and styles. And whether by serendipity or inclusion or contiguity, the trends that were gain-ing momentum in society were doing so in psychoanalysis as well.

These two streams, the social and the psychoanalytic, con-verged for me in a personal experience in the streets of Rome at the time of the International Psychoanalytic Congress in 1969. The

Nominating Committee of the International, which met on Sunday, that evening posted a list of the candidates for office on the congressional bulletin board. That is when I found out that I was a nominee for the presidency of the I.P.A. It was the American's turn for the presidency, and all three of the American vice presidents—Jacob Arlow, Heinz Kohut and I—had been potential candidates for the office. But it was I who had been chosen. That same evening, and over the next few days, there were parades in the streets outside the halls of the Congress, protesting organized psychoanalysis as a manifestation of the establishment. This demonstration was of a kind not usually seen in medical or scientific circles; the marchers, mainly candidates of the psychoanalytic institutes in France, Switzerland, and Germany, shouted and carried placards denouncing the methods and agenda of the analysts attending the Congress. I learned later that this was but one vociferous part of the general student rebellion that was sweeping France that year, and that was supported by students from other central European countries as well. The psychoanalysts at the Congress had been targeted in a general movement against capitalists as dictators and oppressors. Placards using dollar signs instead of S's read "Down with the IP$AA." Science, economics, and politics were all mixed together in rebellion against money, authority, and the establishment. Protests against authority in psychoanalysis itself were rising too, and would reach a more formal form in the mid-nineties.

When I came to the Congress I was little prepared for this emotional storm. As my 14-year-old son and I walked in the streets the day before the election, we were loudly invited by the paraders to join the march. The next day, I told my son, it would be different. I would be a target, the symbol of the enemy.

These large movements had small local parallels. In the sociopolitical world at large, capitalism was the enemy. In the intellectual and academic world, as this convergence in Rome showed, it was psychoanalysis. Within psychoanalysis itself, it was the "Freudian," classical establishment that was the main offender. And in the groups like Los Angeles where this viewpoint held sway, it was the leaders, real or symbolic, of the classical caucus who represented the most objectionable authority of all, and who were rebelled against. Authority, power, material or hierarchic, knowledge and explanations, tools, even claims to these—all of them, the protestors insisted, were to be distributed evenly, not concentrated at the top.

ROME: KOHUT, 1969

At about the same time as the Kleinians were arriving in L.A. and the work in Topeka was coming to fruition, a third and equally important force was converging on psychoanalytic theory. This was the self psychology of Heinz Kohut, which came to full public expression in Kohut's first book of 1971, but which is considered by his followers and others (although for different reasons) to have had its origins around the Rome Congress of 1969. Self psychology achieved a momentum in the decades that followed that brought it closer to the status of a new psychoanalytic paradigm than any theoretical development up to that time. Self psychology aspires to a different understanding of *intrapsychic* processes, in contrast with other new systems that address more external, object-related phenomena. In essence, in this new way of thinking, the self in its multiple functions takes the place of the ego.

This major shift, like the other two, developed out of a mixture of science and politics; in this case, however, it was an individual rather than a group phenomenon. From direct personal experience and from an intimate vantage point, I can say that Heinz Kohut, who introduced this new psychological system, became a Kohutian on July 30, 1969, at about 10 A.M., at the Rome Congress of the International Psychoanalytic Association; I share this experience as an example of the effect of feelings on the course of theory. I have hesitated for a quarter of a century to report my view of this episode due to the delicacy of the subject, but its validity was unexpectedly confirmed for me, objectified, and even enlarged upon when a collection of Kohut's correspondence was published in Cocks's *The Curve of Life* in 1994. The inclusion in this volume of Kohut's letters leading up to the Rome Congress provided some important new insight. The distortions apparent in them aroused enough affect in me that I felt impelled to attempt to clarify the events as I knew them. From Cocks's book also came the suggestion that Mr. Z (Kohut 1979) was Kohut himself, and that Mr. Z's second analysis was a self-analysis—"Kohut never told anyone that he was Mr. Z, but both his wife and son became convinced that this was the case . . . and several of Kohut's colleagues and friends have intuited this relationship" (p. 20)—so raising some more general questions about the straightforwardness of Kohut's data.

Self-psychology *as a separate theoretical system* began around events at this Rome Congress. It was built, to be sure, upon previous substantive papers of Heinz Kohut (1966, 1968) on narcissism and empathy, which had been accepted as part of total analytic theory. Many have commented upon the suddenness of Kohut's departure from his position as a committed contributor to classical Freudian theory, and of the claim that his body of work constituted an independent theory of its own. A number of authors and commentators have offered explanations for this theoretical reversal, but I know from firsthand experience that these are not consistent with what took place. Here is a perhaps typical example of one such distorted, or at least erroneous, point of view. In an interview with Virginia Hunter on the careers of prominent analysts, Ernest Wolf (1994), a supporter of and contributor to self psychology, notes this change, of course, and volunteers an explanation for it. Wolf describes how Kohut, a member of an inner circle including Anna Freud, Marianne Kris, Jeanne Lampl de Groot, and a few others, arrived in Rome in 1969 expecting to become the next president of the International Psychoanalytic Association. By the time of his arrival, however, Wolf says, Kohut had developed basic new ideas about empathy and the self. When he made these known to this close circle of friends, Anna Freud and the others withdrew their support of his candidacy, costing him the election he had been prepared to expect.

The facts and the sequence, which I know from my own part in them, were quite different. It is true that while there were three possible candidates for the presidency, Kohut arrived at the Rome Congress in 1969 expecting to be elected. It was generally believed that he was the choice of Anna Freud. He arrived in Rome having already indicated his choice of a secretary, Brian Bird of Cleveland—it had not occurred to me to do this, nor had Arlow made any such move. Arlow and I had heard that there had been a party in anticipation of his expected election at the home of the Kurt Eisslers in New York during the preceding (December 1968) midwinter meeting of the American, and that some of his supporting group had been there.

It was I, however, who was chosen by the nominating committee and subsequently elected. At the Wednesday business meeting where the election took place, Kohut congratulated me, saying, "I don't know how anyone could want to be president. I am a scientist, not a politician." I remember how disappointed I felt, given what I knew to have been his own expectations, that he could be so patently insincere. I also remember deciding consciously that I would overlook this, and grant him the luxury of this uncivil and hypocritical reaction on the basis of a narcissistic hurt that I could well understand. We had been close friends, and we remained so. It is only since the recent revelations I mentioned above, which bring some of the preceding events to light for the first time, that the scale has tipped in favor of my revealing this episode in the service of scientific and interpersonal history.

Kohut's first book came out two years after this Congress, in 1971; at the time it seemed to me to define the path he had chosen immediately after, and as the result of, his loss of the presidency. I watched and understood his mood and his thinking in the period that followed, as he moved further and further away from the mainstream, and built an increasingly devoted following of his own, from which he received much more adulation than he ever would have as chief administrator of the International. Anna Freud had by no means turned away from Kohut in Rome, or even at the Vienna conference two years later; in fact she continued to back him after the publication of *The Analysis of the Self*. In the acknowledgments of his first book, Kohut thanks Anna Freud, who had read an early version and who "stimulated [him] in many important directions," and Marianne Kris, for the "unfailing support" she gave him in pursuing his investigations (Kohut 1971, p. xi). This is a far cry from their learning of these views for the first time in Rome, or from their turning away from him on this account. It was only after the publication of his second book in 1977 that Anna Freud ruefully commented that Kohut, "once a member of their circle, had become antipsychoanalytic" (Young-Bruehl 1988, p. 440). I myself did not go as far. In my outgoing address at the next Congress in Paris in 1973, I still accorded the new book a place within psychoanalysis. I was being hopeful, although I feared that my hope was misplaced. Still, it seems to me, Kohut thought of himself as "differently analytic," rather than "anti"—he came to favor his own brand of what was psychoanalytic.

From my vantage point, the new theoretical soil that Heinz Kohut chose to cultivate for the remainder of his life was not the cause of his failure to win the presidency of the International Psychoanalytic Association, as claimed by some. On the contrary; it was a sequel and consequence of that event. Years later, while I was still keeping quiet my views about this segment of self-psychological history, I was surprised when Lottie Newman, the editor of his first book, casually and spontaneously volunteered that "everyone knew" that Kohut had turned to his new theory because he was not elected president of the I.P.A. I had not heard that from anyone else, although it confirmed my own belief. It was quite a different explanation than the one given by Kohut's analysand and then colleague Ernest Wolf, which I had taken to be common opinion.

I continued to keep these thoughts private, however, until the posthumous publication of Kohut's correspondence revealed new and corroborative facts. This correspondence contained a flow of private letters between Kohut and Anna Freud over the eight months preceding the Rome Congress. This exposes a flurry of

activity around the impending election that belies the uninterest
Kohut asserted to me at the Congress, and it is relevant to the
subsequent history and direction of psychoanalytic theory.

One of the currents emerging from this flow of letters is Anna
Freud's encouragement and support of Kohut's candidacy. She
introduces the subject early, in a letter to Kohut of November 24,
1968, toward the end of the year before the election. "I have a
special reason for not hesitating any longer. Dr. Van der Leeuw
was in London over this weekend and we had long talks about
the international analytic situation, the future of psychoanalysis
(about which we were both worried) and the next Presidency for
the International. You probably know very well how the matter
stands. There are three possible candidates: you, Rangell and
Arlow. Van der Leeuw and I and a good many people of whom
we know want very definitely you—in case you are ready to
stand. . . . This is the right time for a decision now and you should
let your friends know" (Anna Freud to Heinz Kohut, Nov. 24,
1968). (Van der Leeuw, however, who was I.P.A. president at the
time, spontaneously and privately told my wife and me that he
hoped I would be elected. What this discrepancy means is unknown, but perhaps he was insincere with one of us. Such things
are not unknown in political circles. Another possibility is that
Anna Freud was not straightforward with Kohut.)

Another now documented fact is Kohut's attitude toward the
office. In contrast with what he said to me after the election,
Kohut replied to Anna Freud (Kohut to Anna Freud, Dec. 3, 1968)
as follows: "I am willing to be nominated for the presidency of
the International. . . . Your letter moved me deeply. [When I
decided similarly some years ago about the American] I was
prompted by deep concerns for the future of psychoanalysis in
the United States. . . . I could see things brewing . . . that no one
else saw as clearly, and I knew that I had a chance to prevent the
worst. . . . I feel very uneasy—increasingly so—about the two
most popular candidates. If analysis were not in danger there
would probably be little harm in having either one of them since
their influence would be countered by the resistance of the rank

and file. As it is, strong positive efforts in the right direction must be made . . . to cement the bond between those of the members (they are in the minority) who understand and love our science. . . . In a triple race, the Kleinians will first vote for Rangell and then, if Rangell gets the lowest number of votes, they will switch over to Arlow. A respectable number of Americans will of course vote for me, and so will many of the Europeans. . . . I know that you . . . will do what can be done . . . to increase my chances for election."

As to the idea that Kohut lost the office because of his heretical views, again his own words challenge it. On January 4, 1969, he wrote to Anna Freud, "It is foolish at this time to give thought to what I might do, should I become a leader of the I.P.A.—but the question occurred to me whether a future Congress program . . . might not be entitled 'Foci of Psychoanalytic Thought,' beginning with your work at Hampstead (perhaps Dr. Lustman as chairman of the program), followed by a Congress on ego psychology. Let me know some time what you think of the idea." His views up to the election were not only not heretical, they were aggressively, and with a promise into the future, supportive of Anna Freud.

On February 10, 1969, Anna Freud informs Kohut, "I had an upsetting letter from Van der Leeuw [that] he had met a number of the representatives of the European Societies and had found to his surprise that they have all made up their minds to vote for Rangell as their next president. I do not know why, neither does he, but it all seems an indisputable fact. This throws all our expectations into confusion. . . . You will encounter heavy opposition in the U.S. from supporters of Arlow and Rangell, but we had been confident that you would have the European votes. . . . And I do not think it would be a good thing to offer oneself for defeat. . . . I had a talk with Marianne and Dr. Eissler and I told them a bit about van der Leeuw's experiences. They were equally upset. . . . If you want to fight the election, we, as your friends and supporters, shall do our best. . . . Do let me know how you feel about it."

Responding on February 16, 1969, Kohut writes, "I agree . . . it is not a good thing to offer oneself for defeat. . . . But with all the feeling of relief, I will not deny that the disappointment was great." He goes on to look over the field. "By comparison with Arlow, Rangell is the lesser evil: for the simple reason that he is the weaker person . . . without strong convictions. . . . I have serious disagreements with the Arlow-Brenner approach. . . . Rangell's writings, on the other hand, seem on the face of it perfectly harmless. I find them polished, intelligent, very nicely put, but completely unoriginal. He is beloved by the South Americans. . . . If he gets elected, . . . he will probably do quite well as a peace-maker and compromiser. And strong pressures that would test his stamina and his devotion to analysis are not likely to arise."

But the doubt that had been introduced continued to have an effect. The same day, he writes to Ruth Eissler, "Once I had made up my mind to undertake the job . . . plans were beginning to form in me: about programs, about organizational moves, about addresses to be given—and to turn away from them now is not easy."

At that time, no more disparaging comment could have been made to Anna Freud about an analyst than Kohut's comment that the Kleinians liked me and that I am "beloved by the South Americans." Kohut's revelations were in a sense correct, although he twisted it and offered it to Anna Freud as a negative. But anyone familiar with the theoretical histories of the three candidates in that election year would be startled at this exchange. My theoretical views have always been unequivocally expressed, and stand on their own. I have no wish to disavow being liked by the Kleinians, or by any other group. The Kleinians do in fact like me (not the Los Angeles imitators of Kleinianism, but the Kleinians)—not as a co-Kleinian, but as one who listens to their views and presents his own. I had celebratory visits to South America during the sixties (while I was president of the American and vice president of the International) as one who had spearheaded the successful Pan-American Congresses in Mexico, Buenos Aires, and New York. I was a facilitator and conduit of "ego psychology" in South America, and I was warmed by the audiences there and by their pleasure in this equal treatment. I have an affective affinity with the group in Lima, Peru, from several visits there, where the analysts moved during our discussions from their Kleinian stance toward a more total theory. What makes it impossible for me to accept these letters of Kohut's in silence is not so much their inaccuracies but their mean-spiritedness—and this from a man who was my friend and my confidante about our shared and strongly held classical views.

On April 6, 1969, Kohut writes, "Concerning the I.P.A. I do not think that we should withdraw our interest from it. . . . The only thing that still stirs me from time to time is the arrival of expressions of support which I am still receiving from various quarters. I had, unfortunately, already started my 'campaign' before I received your fateful message, i.e., I had written more than 100 personal notes to people in all parts of the world who would, as I had reason to believe, support my candidacy in Rome. . . . I received many enthusiastic messages about my last paper which gives me heart to hope that my efforts are not in vain. Well, somewhere I must be an incorrigible optimist—perhaps because I too [that is, like Sigmund Freud] am the firstborn child of a young mother." (It is worth noting that there were no electioneering activities in those days, as there are now. Neither Arlow nor I had done anything of this nature regarding the election.)

I did not know any of this when Kohut spoke to me after the election in Rome. But my surmise that day was confirmed by the documentary history recorded—and later revealed—in his own letters. On September 9, 1969, five weeks after the election, he writes to Anna Freud, "I am sorry you should feel guilty about my reaction to the presidency affair. There is no reason for that whatever! . . . Now, I am unambivalently relieved that I am not burdened with this chore."

As a further postscript to this 1969 history, which continues to demonstrate the gulf between actuality and its psychic registration, the same record of Kohut's letters contains an indication as to how he himself retained this important event. In 1977, Kohut writes to Wallerstein to congratulate him on being elected a vice president of the I.P.A.: "It's a job that I filled for quite a number of years and found very rewarding. I could have stood for election to the presidency in 1969—as a matter of fact there was a good deal of pressure for me to do so. I have no doubt now that the writing of *The Analysis of the Self* and *The Restoration of the Self* was more fulfilling to me than an election to the presidency of the I.P.A. would have been. . . . Anyway, these are crossroads in life that each person has to face on his own" (Cocks 1994, pp. 356–357). We see here a common, if not universal, example of the eccentricities of human memory processing and storage.

Kohut's relationship to Anna Freud following the Rome Congress is documented in Young-Bruehl's (1988) biography of Anna Freud. While Anna Freud "viewed Kohut as one of the few genuinely creative minds among the world's psychoanalysts" (Young-Bruehl, p. 19), their closeness did diminish following the Rome Congress. Although there was no open scientific disagreement between them, "their contact diminished steadily after 1969, and became almost completely confined to personal, social and organizational matters." Yet even in 1972 she wrote "an appreciative note to him about how helpful his essay of that year on narcissistic rage had been in her thinking about one of her patients." By 1978 at the very latest, however, she had concluded that Kohut "had become antipsychoanalytic" (p. 440).

This account of some aspects of the genesis of self psychology, however much it belongs alongside Kohut's letters and other published accounts of his life and work, does not substitute for scientific evaluation of the claims and contents of his theoretical system itself. The issues and principles are the same as they are when one approaches the huge literature on the personal Freud. While such studies are of great interest, both as psychoanalytic history and as psychobiography, the science in each instance stands or falls on its merits. An account of the motivational or temporal history of a theory says nothing about its validity. The scientific standing of self psychology has been discussed at length over the years by supporters and detractors. My aim here is to set the historical record in perspective in terms of the influence of the personal and social milieu that surrounded the development of this particular theoretical system.

Some of the same principles I have been adducing as tests for suggested new theories have been used by other analysts (Curtis 1985, Rangell 1997a, Segel 1981, Stein 1979) to critique the scientific tenets of self psychology, with its emphasis on empathy in psychological development and in psychotherapy. Some of my own views on the substantive issues involved, consistent with my general tendency to add rather than to replace, are that empathy *is* included in the analytic attitude, that narcissism is as ubiquitous as anxiety in human psychological life and fully embedded within total Freudian theory, and that tragic man must indeed be added to guilty man, but may not replace him. The selfobject is another name for attachment (Bowlby 1969–1980), for figure-ground (Rangell 1955a), and for other concepts of togetherness that have been addressed in the main theoretical system and in some of the alternates. I have elaborated elsewhere on both the self (1982b) and the object (1985) in total Freudian psychoanalysis.

ANNA FREUD

The above saga involved Heinz Kohut as protagonist and Anna Freud as correspondent. But there was more to the chronology of events that I am recording, and more to the story of disturbing distortion that permeates this period of psychoanalytic history. I believe that this transitional period of the sixties and the seventies was the crucial one that determined the turbulent theoretical and organizational outcomes that followed it, and that served as the backdrop for the pluralism to come. There were events that led up to the Rome Congress and events that succeeded it, unknown previously or at least not articulated, that must be considered to have played a direct or indirect part in bringing subsequent developments to pass. I will therefore pursue this subject further, although it leads into difficult and sensitive terrain. When the light of historical inquiry shines upon them, surprising and saddening discrepancies can be seen between the theoretical stances espoused by individuals and their personal idiosyncratic reactions.

One such aspect of our history involves some puzzling attitudes and behavior of Anna Freud. I enter upon this sensitive topic with a reluctance barely overridden by the feeling that it is necessary if I am to clarify this murky period, which attests to the truth of the commonplace that sterling intellectual contributions and leadership can coexist with interpersonal judgment that is not as conducive as it might be to the advance of the group. I am not speaking of Miss Freud's active bolstering of Heinz Kohut for the presidency of the I.P.A.—that was a personal preference. But the segment I will address next does provide some new evidence related to the motivations that preceded and succeeded the events of the Rome Congress.

This next phase in this history of theory centers on the historic international Vienna Congress in 1971. This Congress marked Anna Freud's first return to the country her family had fled over thirty years before, and it was replete with poignancy, drama, and celebration. But subsequent writings reveal it to have had also a dark side, not much known until now, regarding psychoanalytic beliefs and the inner workings of psychoanalysts. Like my experience of the 1969 Rome Congress, about which I kept quiet for three decades, my interest in the Vienna Congress was also reactivated by newly published material, some of it reported in Elisabeth Young-Bruehl's (1988) biography of Anna Freud.

I will again proceed retrospectively from current phenomena to the background data that make them understandable. When Young-Bruehl's heralded work appeared in 1988, I eagerly acquired it, having been given enthusiastic advance notice of its publication by Lottie Newman, who as the executor of Anna Freud's literary estate had invited Young-Bruehl to write a definitive biography. Lottie had edited many of my own papers, was a friend and supporter of my analytic work, and was living for a period in Los Angeles, where she had come from Connecticut with her husband, Richard Newman. On the strength of Lottie's recommendation, I immediately bought several copies of the book, intended as gifts to close friends in London, who would devour such a biography of "their" Miss Freud. It was only a few days later, perusing the book hurriedly but with great anticipation, that I was shocked to see that I was included in this work exclusively in a chapter on how Anna Freud acted "In the Face of Enemy Forces."

That chapter turned out to revolve around the Vienna Congress of 1971, which followed the one at Rome where the matter of the I.P.A. presidency had been so central to Anna Freud's pre-Congress activities. In Vienna, as Young-Bruehl reports the events almost two decades later, the "enemies" in the chapter title were the I.P.A. in general, and me, its president, in particular. The key issue was the application of the Hampstead Child Therapy Clinic for component Society status within the I.P.A. The report of this more than twenty-five-year-old event described me as having scored a personal victory in the sequence of events that took place, having successfully imposed my own agenda (to impede and ultimately reject this application) first on the Council and then on the members, thus confirming the official hostility of the I.P.A. to child analysis and to the general advance of psychoanalysis as it could be enhanced by child analytic training and practice.

Young-Bruehl writes: "When Rangell announced to the open business meeting that 'the recommendation is for this report to be taken back by all members . . . for study, discussion and the rendering of an opinion in a leisurely way in the next period of time,' he was announcing his own victory at the Executive Council meeting preceding. '[The report] will also be open for discussion now,' he went on, and there was a dead silence. Anna Freud had decided to say nothing, just as she said nothing when Rangell announced that the Executive Council had accepted an application from the Hampstead Child Therapy Course and Clinic for 'study group' status. This application marked a deal of last resort [since] discussion of training and membership in the I.P.A. for child analysts was being so obviously blocked" (pp. 404–405).

The reason the Hampstead Clinic could not be accepted forthwith was simple and clear. There was consensus both within the

Council and among the membership that an analyst is not trained for any limited age period. A psychoanalyst is ready to accept and try to understand a person at any time across his or her life span. It is significant that no administration of the I.P.A., before or since Vienna, has initiated a move to admit Anna Freud's Hampstead Clinic, pride of the analytic field though it is, both scientifically and clinically. When Lampl de Groot and then Anna Freud wrote me on the eve of the Vienna Congress, asking why the International had not in twenty years formally recognized the Hampstead Clinic, I did not know how to answer her. In fact, none of us knew what deliberations had taken place in the past, or what political relations between the Hampstead, the British Society, and the I.P.A. had led to the isolation of the Hampstead Clinic from the British Society and therefore from the International. But the present Council had to confront that situation when the application was received. In much of what followed, the frustration and disappointment of two decades were displaced onto the new administration. A hint of some background ambivalence appears in a comment of Young-Bruehl's about "Anna Freud's desires for independence and affiliation" (p. 406). There may have been more of the former in the early years of the Clinic, and more wishes to affiliate only in later times.

When the Hampstead Clinic was first established, it had several reasons for embarking upon an independent course of development: postwar conditions, the growing bitterness of the Kleinian conflict, the strong affective and cognitive position of Klein within the British Society, and the resultant tensions between Anna Freud and the Society. Free of surrounding bureaucratic pressures, an independent Hampstead could better pursue its scientific Freudian program. An arrangement to this effect after the war also satisfied the British Society, which had not permitted the Clinic to add adult training to its program, seeing this as an indirect move toward a second Society in the city. This very agreement led to complications when Miss Freud made her proposal for Society status in the International. Miss Freud, describing herself as having been a peacemaker before, now declared herself as militant.

She came to the Congress with mixed emotions. Her return to Vienna, with all of its poignancy and drama and heartache, included also the challenging task of getting her Clinic accepted. I believe that this was an unfortunate mixture of agenda and affects for her, for the International, and for psychoanalysis. This history and reasoning, which long preceded the application in Vienna, is probably the answer to Lampl's and Anna Freud's inquiry about the status of Hampstead in its first two decades, and, I can add, since then as well. Yet Anna Freud had never turned her militancy or anger against any Executive Council or president before, nor did she later—her animus was directed only at the leadership in Vienna. As there are always several sides to such stories, I regret that her biographer did not give me the courtesy of an interview.

Young-Bruehl says that "discussion of training and membership in the I.P.A. for child analysts was being so obviously blocked." This was unknown to me. Blocked why? And by whom? By me? I fail to follow the reasoning behind this surmise. Any psychoanalyst might look to the past for an answer. Was Anna Freud still disconcerted over the results of the election in Rome? Did she perhaps think that her choice for president, Kohut, would have accepted her application, even though the Executive Council considered it not administratively feasible? Kohut himself was sitting on the Executive Council as a vice president; he had no objection to what was taking place, nor did he propose any better way of handling it. By changing her application to one for study group status, Anna Freud did not make "a deal," as Young-Bruehl calls it; that was routine procedure, and the only way for a group to start the process of entry into the I.P.A. We worked to facilitate this; that was a way of helping Miss Freud against the odds. I did not know that Anna Freud "had decided to say nothing" as some kind of strategy. She had made her position clear, and I do not remember feeling that there had been anything left unsaid. What did she keep silent about?

The tone and content of Young-Bruehl's Vienna report makes clear that Miss Freud carried a huge misunderstanding away from that Congress. This was not directly communicated at the time, but I now think that it became manifest later, in indirect behavior the reasons for which were not clear at the time. There was nothing sinister about either the announcement of the Hampstead application or its quiet reception by the members—it was all purely routine. I do not know what "dead silence" implies. Does Young-Bruehl now, or did Anna Freud then, imagine that the hundreds of members present were narcotized, or intimidated? The recommendation to carry the item over to the next Congress was in fact the Council's way of giving Miss Freud's application a better chance of acceptance, for at that time it was not considered administratively feasible, and if acted upon on the spot would for certain have been defeated. Child analysis was not being opposed or depreciated in any way; to the contrary, Anna Freud's passionate advocacy of child analysis and all that it has contributed to psychoanalysis were never questioned, and I know that all the members of the Executive Council appreciated them profoundly. It was unfortunate that an honest but reluctant decision made in accordance with the belief that training to be a psychoanalyst could not be limited to experience with children should have led to such ill will and division. Considering that the applicant was Anna Freud, it was not easy to make this decision, and the action of the Executive Council, rather than reflecting prejudice or hidden motive, might be seen instead to have required courage and character.

The facts behind the actual events concerning the Hampstead application in 1971 were actually quite different from Young-Bruehl's description, and so were my own motives and the motives of others to which I am privy. Before the Vienna Congress, on receipt of the Hampstead Clinic's application for component status within the I.P.A., I appointed Samuel Ritvo to chair the committee that would oversee Miss Freud's application. Ritvo was a child analyst well known as a strong and devoted supporter of Anna Freud's cause in every aspect of her life and work. This was perhaps recognized by Miss Freud; according to Young-Bruehl, one model for the Vienna Congress on aggression had been the

successful Amsterdam Congress of 1965 on obsessional neurosis. Young-Bruehl quoted Anna Freud as recognizing Ritvo's
prominent role in Amsterdam, where he had presented a much-
applauded case of a man analyzed as a child by Beata Bornstein.
What neither Anna Freud nor her biographer knew (or reported)
in connecting the two Congresses was that it was I who appointed
Ritvo to head the Committee in Vienna, precisely to give the
Hampstead application its strongest possible position. Perhaps a
time will come—perhaps it *has* come, now that psychoanalytic
training faces such severe logistical problems—in which this
issue of a limited age group will be seen differently. Thirty years
after the Vienna conference, Rosenblitt (1999), outgoing chairman
of the Board on Professional Standards of the American, suggested
that the time has come to consider dual training tracks for child
and adult analysis, and a task force has been set up by the Board
to explore the subject of "stand-alone child training." At the time
of the Vienna Congress, it is true, no such exploration was considered, nor was it considered by any of the other administrations
that intervened between mine and the year that Rosenblitt made
his comment.

As my history, writings, and career attest, when this issue
reached the agenda in Vienna, a friend of child analysis was at
the helm. I had worked and written both alone and with Mahler,
Spitz, and Ekstein on children and early psychic functioning, I
(1965c) introduced, chaired, and spoke at the first panels of the
American on the relations between child and adult analysis. I was
the adult analyst who founded the Los Angeles Society of Child
Analysis in the fifties, and was called at that time "a crypto child
analyst" (Van Dam 1988) by my child-analyst friends. The successful American Association for Child Analysis, which Miss Freud
called "Marianne Kris's organization" (p. 386), was started at my
impetus, during my first presidency of the American. Grete Bibring
who, Young-Bruehl writes (describing the view of Anna Freud),
"was chief among the American Psychoanalytic Association officers who wanted to meet the group halfway" (p. 385), came to
this issue as president in the next administration, in which she

succeeded me. This new association, a haven for child analysts ever since, had been set up to resolve the same problem between child analysis and the American as the field was now seeing between child analysis and the International, by forming a parallel organization that would encompass a more diversified group of child trainees than was possible in the American. This did not prevent child analytic training within the Institutes of the American, which continued to go on energetically. And, although the atmosphere of the Vienna Congress with regard to child analysis (as Young-Bruehl describes it) would lead to an opposite opinion, Marianne Kris and Jeanne Lampl de Groot, and many other child analysts everywhere, were good friends of mine—not opponents, then or since.

I came to the Vienna Congress with high emotions. It was a historic event, marking a pinnacle of achievement, a time of celebration, history, acknowledgment, and reparations, an opportunity for working through and rebirth after the worst nightmare of all time. It was both exhilarating and sobering to me that I had been instrumental in having this Congress held in this city, the first city of psychoanalysis, the city of its birth. The Hampstead application for admittance as a Society was in the wings, an obviously difficult and conflictful issue. But Frances Gitelson (then Secretary of the I.P.A.), the Executive Council, and I faced the issue with good will, and we were all determined to do what was right and best. We wished to give Anna Freud every opportunity, and bend whatever we could in her direction, although we knew there would be difficulties.

The largest Congress of the International ever assembled was in attendance at the Hapsburg Palace on the opening day, waiting for Miss Freud's entry into the Great Hall. I was on the platform, facing the back of the auditorium where Anna Freud would enter (to this day I do not know who set up that scenario). Miss Freud came through the door and walked down the length of the cavernous room on the left aisle. The audience was electrified. I received her on the podium, and introduced her. She began to speak—in German. The audience exploded in appreciation. She then settled into English, and delivered her scientific paper on aggression. It was actually an intuitive suggestion of my wife that had initiated the subject of aggression for the Congress, and all of us, the entire Program Committee, had immediately felt that topic to be exquisitely relevant to the place and circumstances of this Congress, as well as of unique theoretical importance to psychoanalysis itself.

Two personal honors were bestowed upon Miss Freud on this occasion. One was a medal of Pallas Athene, the Goddess of Wisdom. This was a specially crafted medallion of an old Roman coin with the head of Athena in the center. Two analysts in particular had done the heavy work for this one: Helen Tartakoff of Boston, who conceived the plan, and Eva Laible of Vienna, who had the medal crafted in that city in the short time available. The two labored frantically to execute the idea, which had been approved and set in motion unanimously and enthusiastically. There was a big mix-up and crisis when the original medal promptly corroded, and we had to get a new one in a hurry. The path was not smooth. The second honor bestowed upon Miss Freud was my doing: Heinz Hartmann, the second honorary president of the I.P.A., had died the previous May, and the position was now open. I felt that Anna Freud should now be made honorary president. Although her relationship to the International had been ambivalent, she had served as Secretary for three terms under Max Eitingon beginning in 1927, and for another under Ernest Jones in 1949, after the war. I felt that now, in Vienna at this moment, was the time to honor her in this way. The Council voted "yes" unanimously. Again there was a curious little faux pas. The printed agenda distributed at the business meeting omitted the item of the honorary presidency. I was fortunate to remember it suddenly, in exactly the right place, and so chaired the motion through into action at the right time.

The version of these events reported in Young-Bruehl's biography saddened as well as disappointed me. "[Anna Freud] was just bemused when the analysts encouraged the journalists in the mythmaking by piously presenting her with a medallion inset with an ancient Greek coin picturing Pallas Athene, the Goddess of Wisdom," Young-Bruehl writes. "'The whole thing was not as bad or as difficult as I expected it to be,' [Miss Freud] noted to Grete Bibring. . . . Naturally there was a feeling of estrangement about it all. . . . Most of the analysts who found the Vienna Congress so moving . . . had no idea that their Pallas Athene . . . felt personally betrayed" (Young-Bruehl, p. 404).

About the honorary presidency, I read with dismay that Anna Freud "never lost her bitterness or revised her attitude toward the I.P.A. She offered her resignation from the Executive Council, but was kept from making even this much of a public protest by Leo Rangell, who proposed instead that she allow herself to be nominated as the successor to Ernest Jones and Heinz Hartmann in the position of honorary president of the organization" (p. 406). The idea that I had proposed this honor to prevent a protest was new to me. That I could even have managed to prevent Anna Freud from making a protest was a surprising enough idea in itself, but the motive attributed to the action I had brought about to honor her I find impossible to understand.

For me, the Congress was very moving, very substantive, and without the undercurrents delineated in Young-Bruehl's book; I did not know that Miss Freud's mood had been dominated from the start by the sense of betrayal reported in her biography. At the opening ceremony, I went about my business, bestowing the Pallas Athene medal on Anna Freud to commemorate the occasion, with the deepest feeling of its historic meaning. On one side of a silver rim surrounding the coin was inscribed, "Auf Meine Treue Anna—Antigone Gestutzt. Sigmund Freud." On the other side was written, "With Gratitude to Anna Freud on her return to Vienna, 1971, PSA 27." Freud had on a number of occasions referred to his daughter as his Antigone—the daughter of Oedipus and Jocasta who remained loyal to her father under duress. Everyone who was party to the plan about the medal was buoyed up by the symbolic recognition that it represented. As for the honorary presidency bestowed on Miss Freud, here I take full responsibility. It was my idea, and I was proud of it. To me it was a natural event; I was glad I had thought of it where others had not. That I might have done this to prevent some protest by Miss Freud is an astonishing notion. I remember with what relief I caught the error in the program in time, and managed to restore the motion to just its proper place. The spirit around this event as it is written up in the biography eludes me completely.

Clearly a dark side emerged during the assemblage in Vienna alongside the celebratory occasion, and it was a challenge and task to keep the two separate while doing justice to each. There was a small but intensely charged interest group that was protecting, in its view, not only the Hampstead Clinic and Miss Freud, but also child analysis. Passions within and surrounding this group ran high. It was during a private caucus of this group that a member of the Hampstead, Lothar Rubinstein, collapsed and died of a heart attack. I do not know what conflicts or divisions existed within the group during this meeting, perhaps alternative views on how to consider and relate to the International—as friend or foe—but in that charged and passionate atmosphere this was one of the unfortunate outcomes.

Given the unusual and sensitive aspect of Miss Freud's request, and in view of its very special source, the officers and Executive Council conceived the idea of establishing an active liaison between the Hampstead Clinic and the British Society, for the purpose of opening channels through which the Hampstead students might pursue and complete full training. For the liaison person between the Hampstead and the British Society, we were able to enlist William Gillespie, who was acceptable to Miss Freud, the British Society, and the Executive Council of the I.P.A.—no easy diplomatic coup. This agreement eventuated in a track that permitted Hampstead trainees to expand their training by analyzing adults under the auspices of the British Society, an arrangement that has made for satisfactory total training from then until now.

So it was astonishing for me to read in her biography that Miss Freud, expressing relief and approval, attributed the favorable outcome of this very plan to the British middle group, rather than to the sympathetic efforts of the officers of the International who had been the mediators of this arrangement. Reporting the agreement to Greenson she writes, "The British Society has made its peace with the Hampstead Clinic now. Largely to avoid our becoming a second Psychoanalytical Society in London, they have made very sensible advances to us and together we have worked out a compromise according to which the Society accepts a Hampstead Training Course in child analysis as their second official training course. . . . A document referring to this has been signed last week by Dr. Gillespie and myself, and both the Society and the Clinic are pleased. Following it I have withdrawn my application for Study Group status with the International and, as you know, I never wanted to be a study group anyway" (Young-Bruehl, p. 405). No mention is made of the role of the I.P.A. in bringing this solution about. The British Society, with whom Miss Freud had done battle for three decades, had become the good guys, and this particular Executive Council, or its chief executive, the bad. Yet it was not by coincidence that the British Society, which had never before agreed to such a plan, should have approached Miss Freud at exactly that moment.

That Anna Freud could be more circumspect with her feelings under other influences and conditions can be seen in her handling of another matter. At one point she took issue with an International newsletter article that failed to mention her participation at the First Conference of English-speaking Psychoanalysts in London in 1970, in which she had agreed to participate even after the British Society had manifested a condescending attitude toward Hampstead. Although Miss Freud's feelings turned "from cool to icy" (Young-Bruehl, p. 396) at the oversight, she wrote sympathetically to Frances Gitelson, Secretary of the I.P.A., who had actually written the article, exempting her from responsibility. Frances, along with her husband Max Gitelson, had had a warm and trusting relationship with Anna Freud from the past. To her, Miss Freud wrote, "Of course I knew that it was the report from London which was responsible [for the slight]" (p. 196).

Young-Bruehl's biography, which so reveals Anna Freud's feelings and attitudes, helped me understand much that had felt unexplained during the Vienna Congress, and in the years before and since. My wife Anita and I had been aware for many years of a real distance from Miss Freud, but had never been able to locate the reasons behind it. This coolness—almost to the point of rudeness—seemed appropriate neither to the position I held nor to the occasions at which we met. When at Maresfield Gardens she showed Anita, who loved art, psychoanalysis, and Freud, in to see the desk collection of her father, she uncharacteristically did not remain in the room with her. We certainly learned what it was to be with her when she was being "from cool to icy."

This points to another area of limited psychoanalytic vision on the part of Anna Freud that caused me personal dissatisfaction and at times distress, and that kept her from effective leadership, even in her efforts to further the theory she loved so much. My immersion in psychoanalytic theory made me feel this lack quite acutely at times, but I made myself overlook it, because I was never certain of what was going on, and because my tendency at such times is to resort to self-criticism. In this retrospective account, however, in accord with my wish to demonstrate how interpersonal factors influence theory as much as scientific ones, I am now moved to point out that Anna Freud's negative feelings over what she perceived as my lack of administrative support kept her from recognizing that we shared many important—and endangered—ideas about psychoanalytic theory, and prevented her from making common cause with me in support of views we both held dear. While this was disappointing, I wonder now whether the three decades after the conference might have turned out differently if her personal feelings had not so obscured our theoretical kinship that no effective alliance could be made between us.

I will mention here only a few (to me) pivotal occasions. One I have already described above: my presentation of a unitary theory of anxiety to the British Society earlier in the year of the Rome Congress. I have no evidence that Miss Freud's absence from the meeting of the British Society—I was with her elsewhere that same week—was meaningful, but I must now place it in the context that has unfolded since then. At the time I had been surprised at her absence, believing that the subject was close to her affectively as well as cognitively, being so central to the core Freudian theoretical structure.

At the Vienna Congress itself, Miss Freud, sharing the platform with me at the opening session, was conspicuously dismissive of my presidential address, which had been built upon a very central, affectively imbued Freudian theme. My subject, "Aggression, Oedipus, and Historical Perspective" (1972), might under normal circumstances have been expected to elicit at least her interest, if not her enthusiasm and public support. In my attention to the reciprocity between Freud's two instinctual drives, and in stressing the mutual enhancement between child and adult analysis, I expanded on two subjects dear to Anna Freud. Regrettably, however, she did not recognize the commonality of our views, and was rather ungenerous in her failure even to acknowledge the relevance of this effort to the theoretical body of Freudian thought. This is especially striking because, as Young-Bruehl points out, Miss Freud in her own plenary address, which was delivered side by side with my opening paper, "made it plain to those who could hear that adult analysis had contributed nothing in nearly thirty years to the explorations of the central questions she had posed after the war about how the aggressive and sexual instinctual drives interact, fusing and defusing" (p. 390). In a glaring omission, she took no notice of the immediate exception that had just come independently and supportively from the same platform. This incongruity was noticed and commented upon at the time by a number of significant colleagues and scientists, such as William Gillespie.

There were similar reactions from Miss Freud, affective responses on issues ranging from the personal to the scientific, in evidence over the three successive Congresses in Rome, Vienna, and finally Paris. At the Paris Congress in 1973, I announced Anna Freud's election as honorary president in her absence (which Young-Bruehl ascribes to her displeasure over the preceding Congress), and gave an outgoing address on a kind of behavior new to psychoanalytic theory. The address was received with a reaction of interest and excitement, but further confirmation of Miss Freud's idiosyncratic registration of events came to my attention from a surprising and unexpected source. In a book describing his own history and experiences, Jeffrey Masson (1990) tells of a conversation with Anna Freud. In response to her complaints about the declining course and fate of analysis, he brought up as an intended antidote his having met a number of analysts who respected her father. He was especially pleased, he went on to tell her, with my presidential address to the I.P.A. (1974a) on "the syndrome of the compromise of integrity," which he had just heard delivered at the Paris Congress. No sooner had he mentioned this than he felt, from Anna Freud's reaction, that he had "touched a hornet's nest." "You are completely wrong," she countered. "The good old days are gone. And the battles that many of the senior people in the International are fighting have to do with attempts to prevent my child study center from incorporating as an institute in the International Psychoanalytical Association." Then she extended her hand in farewell. "I fully expected never to see her again," Masson writes (pp. 156–157). It was apparent that prior events still defined her attitude, and superseded scientific issues.

The Congress after Paris, in London in 1975, offers another demonstration of how individualistically history is recorded, and in what subjectively fashioned forms events from the past trickle up to the present. At that Congress, there was an opening plenary session debate between André Green and myself on changes in psychoanalytic theory and practice (in which my defense of the Freudian position against trends in other directions elicited a good deal of animosity, which was often directed at me personally). Anna Freud was the official discussant. In a personal letter to me while we were arranging the program, she had expressed her complete agreement with my position, but she largely demurred from confirming this in her public discussion. In a subsequent letter to Harold Blum, joining with him in criticism of that Congress, she complained of "a definite tendency to destroy the gains and advances which have been made already, and to substitute for them something less valuable" (Young-Bruehl, p. 426). She made no exception of my paper (1975b), and failed entirely to recognize the similarity of her views with those of mine that she had read and discussed.

A reference to this same debate appeared unexpectedly twenty-eight years later, in quite an extended form. This was an interesting demonstration of how events not experienced firsthand can be interpreted retrospectively. Writing in a celebration of the work of André Green, Martin Bergmann (1999) refers to this debate as a landmark in the history of psychoanalysis, placing it in a series with earlier debates—on Ferenczi's active technique and Wilhelm Reich's character analysis, the Marienbad symposium, and the controversial discussions between the proponents of Melanie Klein and Anna Freud. Including our debate in this illustrious series a quarter-century later, Bergmann came to his own conclusions about the nature of the interchange. He summarized the contents of the two major papers: mine, he said, named the oedipal, phallic, castration phase as a hub of psychoanalytic interest and insight, and emphasized the gradual evolution of theory, with openness to continuous change but retaining repression and the unconscious core as "permanent psychic attributes of man"; Green's added new dramatic crises and creative changes, and was laced with the spirit and contributions of Lacan, Bion, and Winnicott. Bergmann then went on to the discussion by Anna Freud, who "lent her enormous prestige as the daughter and heir to Sigmund Freud in support of Rangell's position. Her participation in the conference meant that the controversy would not be seen as taking place between Rangell and Green, but between Anna Freud and Green.

"In the debate itself, Rangell and Anna Freud carried the day," Bergmann says, but he goes on to suggest that "the era they represented had already passed." He notes approvingly Green's creative work on the negative, on psychic space and the dead mother, on the move from ego defenses toward object relations, and on "the deadly power of decathexis as a fundamental alternative to repression." Bergmann also states that the restriction of psychoanalysis to the treatment of neuroses by Anna Freud's suggestion of an optimum scope "contributed to the demise of the Hartmann era, even in the United States" (p. 199). Indeed, Bergmann reports, this debate occurred just as psychoanalytic theory exploded from a fairly uniform system to a cluster of competing theories. The analytic center, "so eloquently defended by Rangell and Anna Freud, could not turn back the tide of change that André Green had represented."

Bergmann, from this distance, and I, from my memory of participation, have interesting overlaps and differences. That my position and Anna Freud's were cognitively kin is confirmed. That Anna Freud lent her support to my position was hardly in evidence—at least not to me. The view that the debate was seen as one between Anna Freud and Green has merit. I was glad to hear the opinion that "Anna Freud and Rangell carried the day" (cognitively) from someone other than myself. That Green's position carried more strength affectively, however, is borne out by the fact that the debate failed to stem the tide encroaching on the core of Freudian theory and pushing us toward the pluralism that followed. Bergmann and I differ about the value of these changes. I doubt that Anna Freud would agree that her suggestion of an optimum scope for psychoanalysis, restricting it to the treatment of the neuroses, led to any diminution of Hartmann's work on adaptation. I also do not think it likely that Anna Freud would concur about the "demise" of the Hartmann era, in spite of the current widespread criticism of Hartmann (Bergmann 1999a, 1999b). It was a lively day in London.

The affects that arose around the Vienna Congress continued to be felt in displacement long after the Congress was over. Young-Bruehl describes Miss Freud's new scientific initiatives at the Hampstead following her disappointment in Vienna and writes, referring to a memorial address I gave for her in San Diego in 1983, twelve years later, "Colleagues like Leo Rangell did not fail to register the critique her self-sufficiency implied, but they were never able to acknowledge it without disparagement. His public statements never disguised his attitude: 'At one Hampstead Symposium,' he noted, 'Anna Freud stated, with somewhat less than complete objectivity, that the I.P.A. and other organizations concentrate in their scientific programs on what is already known, while the Hampstead Clinic centers on the advance edge into the unknown'" (p. 407). This time the interpretation is clearly that of the biographer, not a quotation from Anna Freud herself, although I am not sure it would not have been shared. However, the statement about Miss Freud that Young-Bruehl quotes and interprets was not disparaging. The scientific programs of the Hampstead, the I.P.A., and the American, all three, pursued scientific work intended both to fill in the known *and* to advance the edge into the unknown. My assertion that Miss Freud's statement was affective, not factual, stands. So does the admiration for Miss Freud that runs through the contents and spirit of the entire address. I would hardly have made remarks so disrespectful of the eulogized under such circumstances, nor is it likely that a condescending address would have been published in the *Psychoanalytic Study of the Child*, where it appeared (Rangell 1984b). As to the author's statements that I am "never able to acknowledge [Anna Freud's self-sufficiency] without disparagement," and that my "public statements never disguised this attitude," I am left to wonder what other "public statements" she has in mind to add to the list, and how much she omits to the contrary from the body of my writings? I believe that Sigmund Freud would have admitted the possibility that disagreement and appreciation can coexist. However, the opinions registered in this biography made clear to me why my invitations to the Hampstead scientific symposia in the years since Vienna were so irregular and so unpredictable. I was welcomed as a major participant when I was there, but I was never sure I would be there again.

This stream of negative feelings that I am describing was revealed to me little by little, first by my experiences in Rome and Vienna, then in the Kohut–Anna Freud correspondence, and finally in the published biography of Anna Freud. Many of these feelings can be seen to have preceded Miss Freud's deep personal disappointment at the Vienna Congress. Harbingers appear in Kohut's letters even before my election in Rome, and therefore long before the Hampstead Clinic made its application to the International. To trace the stream to its source, which appears to be necessary, I must look to an antecedent in the more distant past, years before I came onto the international scene, which may have planted the seed from which this tree of distrust sprang. The happenings in Rome and Vienna in fact closed a long chronological circle, and it is hardly a coincidence that Miss Freud's complaints and feelings about the Congresses are written in a series of letters to Romi Greenson, her close friend and confidante in Los Angeles. "You did not hear everything that went on in Vienna between me and the Board of the International. But if you knew you would not be surprised that I have had enough of them" (Anna Freud to Greenson, cited in Young-Bruehl, p. 406). This is odd, since Greenson was present in Vienna, and he was at the business meeting where the issue was discussed and voted upon. I remember him sitting in the first row with Max Schur, where he did nothing to influence the open proceedings, or to object to the course they took. What went on at the council meeting, which Greenson did not hear, was straight and honest talk about the issue being discussed.

Many of the opinions and feelings cited by Anna Freud's biographer came from letters to Greenson, which makes my self-imposed task of studying the interplay here between theory and affect a difficult one. I must discriminate carefully (between Miss Freud, her biographer, and various other complex sources) in attributing authorship, and I must bear in mind that I am not an impartial observer, but have my own axe to grind. Yet there is a need for the clarifications I feel I must make. The issues raised, and the individuals involved, are too important to the history and fate of psychoanalysis to allow the received interpretation to go unchallenged by alternative viewpoints. We do not have Greenson's side of the correspondence, but Miss Freud's partner in this exchange was an analyst who had been engaged in an ambivalent and destructive relationship with me for twenty years. Sometimes this was overt and more often covert, but it was generally known in the community and, I found, also spoken about nationally.

The relationship between Anna Freud and myself, which would not have been any relationship at all had it not been for my positions in the I.P.A., was to me at first a source of anticipated pleasure, but over the long period a sad experience. Anna Freud and I had a brief personal encounter long before Kohut/Vienna, of which she may not even have been aware. At the time of her first visit to Los Angeles in 1959—a much-heralded scientific and social event—I, a young analyst, was assigned to discuss her paper on "The Nature of the Therapeutic Process." This came about because the Education Committee had not been able to find a more senior analyst who was both able and willing to undertake the role. Greenson, then chairing the Education Committee, continued to look for other discussants, going so far as to postpone the decision until the next meeting of the Education Committee and ask members of the Committee to think in the interim about who might be able to undertake the role. But no senior analyst volunteered or could be appointed, and the assignment was then left for me. This was a special occasion to the analytic community, very exciting and scientifically challenging in the extreme.

Anna Freud never sent me an advance copy of her manuscript. Greenson held a reception for her at his home the night before the meeting, to which I was significantly not invited. When I had to phone that night to ask her for the paper (she was staying at his house), he asked me effusively to come over, which I declined to do. I never did receive a paper from which to prepare my discussion, and I had to compose it on the spot from what I heard the next day. So although the introduction of Los Angeles to Anna Freud was quite spectacular, at the same time for me it was flawed, clouded by the intervention of an ambivalent intermediary and whatever portents that had for future relations. I risk the appearance of pettiness here for two reasons: first, the whole saga made, and continues to make, me sad. And second, I think it is important to raise the possibility that the conclusions Anna Freud came to years later in Vienna developed through the filter of many exchanges with Greenson. It is hard not to imagine that her early exposure to his animus, triggered again and confirmed by her feelings about the

Princeton meeting, 1959. All names are noted from left to right. Bottom row: Max Gitelson, Muriel Gardiner, Elizabeth Zetzel, Anna Freud. Middle row: Rudolph Loewenstein, Phyllis Greenacre, Robert Waelder. Top row: Emanuel Windholz, Leo Rangell, Samuel Guttman, Eleanor Galenson. This meeting was followed by a steering committee, comprised of Samuel Guttman, Brian Bird, Victor Calef, Leo Rangell, and Martin Stein, who established the Center for Advanced Psychoanalytic Studies, which is still in operation in Princeton and Aspen

Anna Freud and Rangell in Los Angeles during Ms. Freud's first visit to California, 1959

Dr. Sergius Pankejeff (Freud's Wolf Man) with Muriel Gardiner and Anita Rangell in Vienna, 1963. (Photo taken by Leo Rangell)

Pan-American Congress, Mexico City, 1964. Joseph Michaels, Rebe Grinberg, Leo Rangell, Elizabeth Zetzel, Leon Grinberg, Louis Zetzel, Anita Rangell, Heinz Kohut, and Helen Fischer, Administrative Secretary of the APA

Elisabeth Garma, Rangell, Gilou Garcia Reynoso, and Angel Garma in Buenos Aires, 1968

Front center: Anita Rangell, Adam Limentani, Rangell, and Janet Nield, with the Australian Study Group in Sydney, 1968

Reception for Rangell's election as President of the IPA, Los Angeles, October 19, 1969

Rangell presenting Anna Freud the "Mein Treue Anna—Antigone" medal in Vienna, 1971

Group gathered around a statue to Freud at his birthplace in Pribor, Czechoslovakia, 1971. In the front, center, are the then Mayor of Pribor, Rangell, Harry Trosman, and Frances Gitelson

Rangell with Serge Lebovici and Paul Castaigne, Dean of the Medical School at Salpêtrière, at the dedication of the Charcot Library at the Salpêtrière, Paris IPA Conference, July, 1973

Executive Council of the IPA, meeting at the Freud Home in London, 1975. Kenneth Calder, Frances Gitelson, Irene Auletta, the Administrative Secretary of the IPA, Guillermo Teruel, Rangell, Serge Lebovici, Daniel Widlöcher, Wolfgang Loch, and Ed Joseph

At a celebration upon the publication of Rangell's work, *The Mind of Watergate*, Los Angeles, 1980

Joseph and Anne-Marie Sandler with Anita and Leo Rangell in Beverly Hills, California, 1981

Ruth and Serge Lebovici, Rangell, and Harold Blum at the Buenos Aires Congress, 1991

Anita Rangell, Leo Rangell, and Daniel Widlöcher at the Amsterdam Congress, 1993

Jack Arlow and Leo Rangell in Berkeley, California, 1995

Horatio Etchegoyen and Leo Rangell at the Executive Council in London, 1996

General Francisco Morales Bermudez, former President of Peru, Rangell, Saul Peña, Beatriz Boza, and Otto Kernberg, Lima, 1998

I.P.A., might account for the otherwise incomprehensible attitudes and reactions that surfaced years later in Rome, Vienna, and Paris. Her choice of Greenson as confidante about the hurts in Vienna would seem to confirm these connections.

As my role in the International grew, so did these tensions. Arthur Valenstein, a friend and associate on many projects both within and apart from the I.P.A., was close to Miss Freud and cognizant of these interpersonal problems and their complications; eventually he undertook to address the situation with her, as it was constantly affecting programs and other issues. But he told me, during a summer he spent with the Anna Freud group in Walberswick on the coast of England, that he could get nowhere with this discussion.

There were two active roads between London and Los Angeles; Melanie Klein and Anna Freud stood at their London ends, and it is ironic that neither connection served to strengthen Freudian theory in this country, but instead helped to disperse it. Was there a chance that it might have been otherwise? Bergmann, as we have seen, concluded that in the debate with André Green, Miss Freud and I "carried the day." But as I am trying to show, theory progresses by affect as much as by cognition, and in "real" psychoanalytic life, no team could "turn back the tide of change that André Green had represented."

With regard to Bergmann's support of Green, incidentally, I believe that to pit decathexis against repression is a misleading lure away from logical progress. There *is* "decathexis"; it is one of the older terms, and one I believe is worth recathecting. But to bring it back to the fore as "a fundamental alternative to repression" is a vivid example of one of the fallacies I have been stressing.

REFLECTIONS ON THEORY FROM THE VIENNA CONGRESS

Unexpected digressions such as this last one into the details of the Vienna Congress are not necessarily deflections from our study of the history of psychoanalytic theory. In fact they not only bring some order into a twisted maze of affects, but may add to theoretical clarity as well. The issues raised at the charged Vienna Congress, and their affective and scientific ramifications, offer us the possibility of looking a little further back to untangle some thorny knots in the development of theory: namely, the Freudian versus Kleinian struggles, the relationship between child and adult analysis, and the debate over psychoanalysis versus psychotherapy. The affective and theoretical issues that came up at the Congress can both be seen to have played direct and not insignificant roles in these polarities, all of which have been prominent in the course of theoretical history.

The affective storms that raged in Vienna energized these divisive issues, and exerted pressure toward their solution. The Hampstead application touched upon them all. Moreover, the three theoretical polarities I have just named, all of universal analytic significance, can be seen to be related to the goings on in the British Society from the twenties through the decades in which psychoanalysis consolidated and then spread the world over. Freud's discoveries were first introduced to the English-speaking world by Ernest Jones in London. This led to the formation of the British Psychoanalytic Society, which quickly became a locus not only of prolific creativity but also of the most significant theoretical debate to divide the young science.

When Melanie Klein established roots in London beginning in 1925, the psychoanalytic body experienced its first major sustained split in theoretical orientation. This became the subject of much scientific debate and many high feelings, and eventually it led to a solution that would have widespread effects and influence. Looking back, the well-known "arrangement" of three theoretical and educational tracks under one administrative umbrella may well have served as a prelude—possibly even a model—for the later theoretical pluralism that flourished in opposition to a unification of theory that could never be achieved after that first internal division. The effect of this on the psychoanalytic body was different from the earlier disagreements that had led the first serious dissenters to find a home outside of the psychoanalytic field rather than within it. Modern studies by King and Steiner (1991) and Baudry (1994) have documented both the efforts made toward a meeting of the minds and the obstacles that prevented this, as the leading theoreticians in London sought for a common understanding while the bombs fell on their city. The series of Extraordinary Business Meetings and Controversial Discussions attest to the earnestness, intensity, and devotion of this Society. That theoretical integration and a resulting unification could not be achieved is a testament to the fierce individuality of its creative members, as well as to the strength of the drives, and the tenacity and power of formed human personalities.

In addition to the three-way theoretical split and the associated tri-chambered environment that came to characterize British psychoanalysis, there was another structural result of the crises of those times, which included the war raging overhead—the establishment of the Freudian child analytic center outside the Society. As a result of agreements among various leaders in the Society and in the field at large, the Hampstead Clinic, as it evolved from the inspiring and world-famous Hampstead War Nurseries into its postwar form, pursued an independent course as the recognized center of child analytic treatment, training, and research. But this independence, preferred by Anna Freud in part because of the Kleinian pressures within the Society, was not without cost. Once the Clinic had become the unequivocal center of the Freudian position, child analysis within the British Society was left to the influence of Melanie Klein. From that point of entry, *general* Kleinian theory expanded within the Society and over much of organized psychoanalysis, while the authentic voice of *Freudian* theory remained outside the official psychoanalytic bodies.

At the same time, the Hampstead was not a full psychoanalytic training center but a specialty center limited to a specific age group, the very fact that led to the confrontation at the Vienna Congress. Another outcome of the subtle side-position of Anna Freud's activities, and one with which she had to agree, however reluctantly, was that the Hampstead was officially named "The

Hampstead Child *Therapy* Course and Clinic." It was not an analytic training center, and its graduates were child therapists, not
psychoanalysts. Again, this led directly to Anna Freud's later application to become an analytic Society member in the International.

That this administrative solution—to leave the most important center for Freudian child analysis outside of official borders—
had a long-term effect on the course of theory can be seen in the
ensuing theoretical debates. These weighed ever more heavily
against the continued dominance of the Freudian view. Once
Melanie Klein had been left to dominate the section of the British
Society that oversaw training in child analysis, it was but a step
to a wider general application of Kleinian theory, just as it has been
a natural progression for all psychoanalytic theory, Freudian or
any other, to progress from the specific to the general. Many
unusual and heartfelt discussions were held by the Society to resolve theoretical divisions, including the aforementioned Extraordinary Business Meetings and Controversial Discussions, but the
ultimate outcome, and within it the fate of Freudian theory (which
eventually held the smallest of the three divisions), may have been
significantly facilitated by the fact that the standard-bearer of the
Freudian position had come to reside outside of the official administrative body of psychoanalysis, and had in addition become
associated mainly with the specialty of child analysis at the expense of psychoanalysis as a whole. To the degree that Anna Freud
focused her energy, force, and contributions on her affectively
driven championship of only one branch of psychoanalysis, the
field as a whole was denied her effective leadership.

From my theoretical viewpoint, these developments in British
psychoanalysis, and the resulting compromise solutions, served as
a regrettable precedent, and squandered an opportunity to develop
a unified theory. The establishment by the British Society of a divided rather than a unified approach to psychoanalytic theory was
a step toward the present pluralism against which I am arguing
as a long-term solution for our field. The theoretical polarities I
have listed above—psychoanalysis and psychotherapy, Freudian
and Kleinian psychoanalysis, and child and adult analysis—still

need clarification and integration. All three, whatever their areas of separation and overlap, share a common identity that require assimilation into one coherent theory.

In my opinion, Anna Freud's view of the child analytic patient—that the still-active presence of the parents influences the transference such that child analysis must be combined with ongoing parental input—is more tenable than Melanie Klein's seemingly purer contention that the transference is as strong and all-embracing in children as it is with adult patients. The parameters and modifications normally required by the developmental limitations of child patients mean that the analysis of children has characteristics in some ways more akin to psychotherapy than to the unmodified analytic method used for adults. However, Klein's greater presence within organized psychoanalysis in the active and influential British Society helped the Kleinian position dominate, first in child analysis and gradually for all age groups—at first locally, then through exportation to a great portion of the rest of the world.

Ironically, the humanistic emphasis and the active new relationship practiced by Anna Freud, to my mind rationally indicated for child analysands, would have fitted in effortlessly with the emphasis on empathy and intersubjectivity that have gradually infiltrated modern adult analysis as well. Matters, however, got crisscrossed. Where Anna Freud's humanistic attitude toward the child might have radiated upward to soften the analysis of adults where necessary, the "neutral" position applicable to adults was moved downward by Klein to harden inappropriately the analytic stance toward children. Conversely, the humanistic position that should have permeated all of psychoanalysis became confined to Freudian child analysis, while the neutrality appropriate to adult analysis was applied across the board. This was an unfortunate reversal. The rigid and exaggerated positions of Kleinian psychoanalysis, with its excessive focus on transference, its exaggeration of the role of the earliest years, its minimizing of reality, its interpretations below the defenses, and its concretization of metaphor, were extended not only from child analysis to the analysis of adults, but also geographically across the world to other continents. Of the three working groups within the British Society, the Freudian branch was quickly relegated to third place.

This was hardly a favorable outcome for the expansion and advance of the total body of Freudian thought. Actually, Anna Freud's classic contribution of the equidistant position between the psychic structures internally and between the internal and external worlds should be the standard for all ages—always in alliance with the ego, and always taking into account whatever parameters are necessary. Where the child's undeveloped ego requires a more educative stand, the child analyst acts as an auxiliary ego; so does the analyst of so-called "borderline" adults in whom the ego is also insufficient. A mutuality of this kind between child and adult analysis might have encouraged the field to develop in a natural harmony with the humanism that has come to the fore recently (but not harmoniously). But psychoanalysis in Britain and the continent was strongly influenced in another direction. With the Kleinians' zeal for certainty, their focus on the deep intrapsychic, and their dismissal of external reality, a large part of psychoanalysis was losing touch with the real world.

It was not by accident that America became the stronghold of Freudian psychoanalysis in the decades after World War II. With every major center in the United States benefiting from the emigration of noted European Freudians, and given the indigenous practicality that made America less susceptible to fanciful Kleinian ideas and more susceptible to the appeal of a rational ego, wild theoretical views were held in check here for a long time. But within the British Society conflicts continued, and they did not favor Freudian theory. After the new arrangement that followed the Vienna Congress, Miss Freud is said to have felt that as a corollary of this move, her own group would no longer "be torn internally by disagreements between those with sole loyalty to Hampstead and those with close ties with the British Society" (Young-Bruehl, p. 406). This is exactly the kind of conflict that had been taking place in the years before the Vienna Congress, while many of the most productive Freudian analysts were at the Hampstead, and

naturally enjoying social and fraternal relations on a wider collegial basis than in the Clinic alone. I knew many analysts during
this period who were theoretically Freudian but affectively close
to the "middle groupers" and sometimes even the Kleinians, which
made for the divided loyalties Miss Freud noted. The history of
subsequent theoretical development, however, shows that her
hopes were not realized. The less conflictful traffic with the other
British groups did not enhance Freudian loyalty, but mostly the
opposite. The social determinants of cognitive beliefs are far from
insignificant, and even the new official interchange could not overcome the influence of the social split in the analytic environment.
The most active Freudian leaders were widely known theoretically,
and were therefore motivated to extend their social relations beyond confining theoretical borders. It was no surprise that soon
after Miss Freud's death, the split she had noted within many of
her crucial supporters eventuated in fusions of what once had been
separate, even polarized, theoretical positions. Once Miss Freud's
influence was no longer there, leading Freudian theoreticians were
able to write actively on projective identification, for example,
which before had been a taboo subject on the Freudian side.

In 1984, two years after Anna Freud died, Joseph Sandler
chaired the first Conference of the Sigmund Freud Center of the
Hebrew University on projective identification, and edited a
book (1987b) on the conference. With the same thoroughness
with which he had revisited *The Ego and the Mechanisms of Defense*
with Anna Freud at the end of her life (Sandler with Anna Freud
1985), Sandler established a symposium featuring an articulate and
diverse group, and examined projection, identification, and projective identification from both the clinical and theoretical stand-
points. This concept had once been associated with Klein, Bion,
and object-relationists, but now Sandler, Kernberg, and others,
discussing in-depth clinical material of Betty Joseph and others,
admitted this popular mechanism into the fold of Freudian and
general explanatory theory. This was accomplished partly by
separating projective identification from the rest of Kleinian
theory, and stressing its applicability to regressed patients and

its importance in the transference. But there was a contributing development from the other direction, too. While the concept had been introduced by Melanie Klein in 1946, Sandler suggested that an antecedent and precursor went back to 1936, when "Anna Freud had introduced a number of defense mechanisms which involved the idea of transpositions of self and object" (p. 161). There was general approval in the audience for this extension of the previous Kleinian mechanism into traditional Freud; only Meissner at the end objected to this distinction between the clinical material and the theoretical labels applied to it, calling it "psychobabble" (Sandler 1987b, p. 196). To which Sandler responded that "quite clearly our honeymoon about projective identification came to an end just before our proceedings did" (p. 196), and concluded the conference. While Sandler also wrote later (1993) that "not everything is projective identification," retreating a bit from the previous acceptance, a distinct rapprochement between theories had come about.

Other theoretical developments also veered rapidly away from the influence of Anna Freud and what she stood for. The increased loyalty to Freudian theory that she had envisaged came instead to the opposite, as more recent developments show clearly. Robert Wallerstein was not a Britisher, but one who during their stimulating years had routinely and elegantly summarized the Hampstead symposia—a series that Miss Freud initiated as an antidote to her disappointment in Vienna (Young-Bruehl 1988, p. 441). He announced his position of "many theories" rather than one in 1988, five years after Miss Freud's death, officially ushering in the era of theoretical pluralism. Sandler's earlier significant contributions, such as the background of safety (1960), the inner representational world (Sandler and Rosenblatt 1962), and countertransference and role-responsiveness (1976), were followed by his differentiation (J. Sandler and A.-M. Sandler 1984, 1987) between past and (closer-to-the-surface) present unconscious, making for a greater emphasis on here-and-now analysis and less of a quest for repressed memories and reconstruction. Fonagy (1999), Sandler's successor to the Freud Memorial Chair in London, wrote in favor of the new relationship over insight, and explicitly against the process of reconstruction and the pursuit of recovered memories, declaring such methods harmful to the patient. None of these innovations would have pleased Anna Freud, nor are these new preferred views in keeping with previously held psychoanalytic methods or goals.

If there is anything to be concluded from this section on the Vienna Congress, which has become longer than I hoped but which seems to me to have been a pivotal event in the history of theory, it relates to a panel I chaired on "Leaders and Led" at the International Congress in Helsinki in 1981. Exploring this subject in relation to psychoanalytic group life (1981d), I proposed that it was the charisma of ideas, not of personality, that electrified the world when Freud came on the scene a century ago. It was significantly not the personality of Sigmund Freud that made an impact—indeed, this would not have been a dependable foundation upon which to build an enduring scientific discipline. I would say now from personal observation and experience that this same holds for all the true leaders of this psychoanalytic century, as much of Anna Freud as of her father. Freud is said not to have been a particularly adept *menschenkenner*; this cannot be convincingly verified, although many feel that letters and history point that way. I think that the same may be true of his daughter, which likelihood I infer from direct observations. The statement by Young-Bruehl that "For leadership positions, she [Anna Freud] never favored the brilliant but self-important or exhibitionistic types over the team players" (p. 155) is open to dispute in a number of instances. In her writings, Anna Freud has indeed been "the true daughter of an immortal sire," as Ernest Jones (1953–1957) characterized her. In her clarity, consistency, and originality, she inspired me throughout my scientific life, where she has always had a special place alongside of Freud, Hartmann, and Fenichel. But I have also felt over many decades that like her father she sometimes placed her trust in analysts who turned out not to be reliable or enduring conduits of the Freudian legacy she loved so much.

The person she hoped would rescue the science from its declining state as president of the International in 1969 she herself had concluded by 1978 to have become "antipsychoanalytic." This she wrote in her last letter to Greenson. A year later, in a eulogy after Greenson's death, she said, "we have not yet discovered the secret of how to raise the real followers of people like Romi Greenson" (Young-Bruehl 1988, p. 440). Many would agree strongly with this sentiment, while others would question it. Loyalty was a strong and laudable trait of Anna Freud's, but it may have obscured other recognitions. When Greenson's most famous patient committed suicide under conditions that gave concern to many psychoanalysts, Miss Freud sent him her sympathy "by return mail" (Young-Bruehl, p. 412). However, I have the impression that in some instances she was able to make more reliable assessments. While affects at times interfered with her embrace of those who supported the theory she held dear, and led her to place her trust in others, in her later years Anna Freud told Arlow that she admired his work (Arlow 2000, personal communication), and I have reason to believe that she also came to feel warmly toward Charles and Irma Brenner. Yet under the influence of Kohut, she had once considered both of these even greater "evils" than me.

This history of vulnerability combined with great strength is not intended to replace but rather to modify and supplement Young-Bruehl's comprehensive account of the life of her brilliant and multifaceted subject. While Miss Freud was superlative at hewing to the line established by her father and advancing the theories set forth by him, some of her affective reactions and interpersonal judgments, and the actions she took on their account, subverted her efforts. In the limited overlap of my life with hers, I found her to be in her finely honed scientific-psychological sense an admirable successor to her father, but I found too that her social judgments often misled her. Anna Freud was exposed to many brilliant and charismatic individuals during her creative and privileged life; perhaps her experiences of the circle around her compelling father—the Stekels, the Ranks, the Reichs, or even the Ferenczis—opened her to this vulnerability, especially when the capacity to charm is used to impress. A cartoon in the *New Yorker* from the Watergate days showed a bar, and one drinker saying to another, "Let's face it, if the people wanted a sincere Nixon, he'd give them a sincere Nixon." Some people, even analysts, are good at this.

THE SPREAD AND RADIATION: RECEPTIVE SOIL

One cannot ascribe to the actions of one or a few individuals an overriding importance and influence, at least not without taking into full account the input of the supporting mass, the receptive group. In all such group events and movements, it is the reciprocal roles of the tip and the base of the population pyramid— and those in-between, and the reciprocal interactions between all of them—that give historical trends their shape (Rangell 1981d). This is as much the case in a scientific society as it is in political movements or in a nation.

I predicted in Los Angeles as the seventies began that the new factions would find self psychology after Klein and Bion had run their course, that these two ways of psychoanalytic thought could not occupy the same space. That came to pass. The still-raw new Kleinians in Los Angeles became Kohutians almost en masse as soon as self psychology arrived; it was avidly embraced by the same leaders and the same followers, for the same reasons of group psychology and the maintenance of self- and group cohesion. Just as envy and (lack of) gratitude were instrumental in the furor for Klein, I have no doubt that issues of the self played roles in the pull to self psychology, however much such interpretations of group behavior cannot be based on verifiable methodology. Although there were certainly analysts who familiarized themselves thoroughly with the new systems before embracing them, in both cases it appears to me that it was the superficial promises rather than knowledge in depth that attracted the large numbers of followers. The claim that choice of theory followed a period of thoughtful observation does not stand up in the face of the series of rapid conversions among such different explanatory systems.

Kleinian theory in Los Angeles had peaked and was already on the wane when self psychology came along and easily superseded it. This new theory, as is well known, "took" equally easily in the wider analytic world, and became a major challenger to the Freudian edifice, a modern counterpart of some of the quickly spreading divergent schools in earlier phases of psychoanalytic development. While this time its adherents chose to remain within the field of mainstream psychoanalysis and to debate its position within the American, the simultaneous claim of a supraordinate position was visible in a series of local and regional meetings and Congresses on self psychology, as well as in the ambitious formation soon of a separate International Association for Self Psychology. These movements were consonant with Kohut's rejection of numerous attempts (by his supporters as well as by parallel theoreticians) to link his views with those of other analytic thinkers, such as Mahler, Winnicott, Alexander, and even Jung and Freud. Kohut was not in the mood for inclusion; he felt, for example, that Freud's "guilty man" could now be replaced by the psychological-philosophic summary concept of "tragic man."

The ready absorption of Kohut's new psychology can be compared to the history of the Jungian corpus, or to the excitement and widespread familiarity generated by Erikson (1950, 1956) (although Erikson's psychosocial extensions were not considered separatist), or to Franz Alexander's (1950) influences—on medicine with his theories of psychosomatic specificity, and on analysts with his suggestions of therapeutic role-playing.

Since the beginnings of psychoanalysis, any deviation that promises a new paradigm has found a large nucleus of ready and expectant receptors. This is not surprising to any psychoanalytic clinician, who is ever aware of the irregular course of individual analyses with their built-in push and pull of conflict, as impulse and defense and their myriad derivatives occupy the analytic space. Individual dynamics, coalescing in the group psychology of the analytic milieu, bring a similar irregular, conflict-laden course to the life of the group. The inevitable deprivations, the delays in the fulfillment of ambitions, the failures to satisfy narcissistic needs all fuel a slow but ever present fire of frustration and resentment, directed not only at the objects felt to be responsible for the disappointments but also at the theoretical ground of the whole enterprise. It takes but a spark to ignite the flame of group action, which, in the analytic society we are describing, is characterized by the quick embrace of alternative theories. When charismatic or seductive leaders offer a simplified theory that promises more satisfaction than a more complex composite one, the chemistry between leader and led, between theory and adherents, is catalyzed, and a reaction of acceptance and excitement follows.

MY PARALLEL WORK ON THE EVOLVING
MAINSTREAM: THE INTRAPSYCHIC PROCESS

For me personally, the sixties had a double thrust. Parallel to the intense and invigorating administrative work that absorbed much of my psychoanalytic activity and identity ran a never-flagging interest and participation in the theoretical issues and challenges of that time, and a personal motivation to solidify and advance them. It was in fact the intellectual thrill of being part of this discovery team that motivated me and gave me the wherewithal to pay the personal price of the leadership positions that came my way. As well as immersion in the organizational and administrative life of the psychoanalytic movement, the sixties gave me a fruitful decade of theoretical contributions.

I was occupied during this period with a series of writings that attempted in incremental steps a microscopic examination of the mental activities that take place in the unconscious from original stimulus to final psychic outcome. The stage for this had been set by a pair of studies, some years apart, that dealt with Freud's two theories of anxiety and their unsettled conclusion. In these two studies I developed a unitary theory of anxiety, which combined

Freud's first theory of direct transformation or actual-neuroses (1895) with his second signal theory of anxiety (1926). Freud's first theory was essentially a somatic formulation, while the second, the more universally accepted, was his psychological explanation of anxiety as the signal of danger. Freud is considered never to have given up his first theory, even as the second became the standard formulation; the fused theory I described combined the two, containing the nuclei of both within one running process. In the first paper, I described how the tension or traumatic state of the first theory also contained the psychological signal of danger from the second theory; in the second, I pointed out that the intrapsychic process leading to the signal of danger is also always preceded by the microscopic, trial-traumatic state (Freud's tension or actual-neurosis) from the first theory. To Freud's "non liquet" ("it does not flow"), with which he had characterized his continuing struggle over the unresolved state of the two theories, my two papers enabled me to offer "now liquet." Perhaps this fusion was an early signifier of my own penchant for unification. It was also, in a small way, an attempt to join the physiological, Freud's first theory, with the psychological, his second, which I felt could not be other than together.

The fusion of the two theories of anxiety adventitiously effected another unification, this one between psyche and soma. My work had been an elaboration, a microscopic dissection, of the signal process that Freud had proposed of testing for the presence or absence of anxiety. In pursuing the unconscious sequence between the initiation of an impulse to the experience of anxiety or of its absence, I began to describe in detail the steps of a ubiquitous, ongoing, and continuous intrapsychic process. Tracing the successive stages by which the ego undertakes to test for the signal of anxiety, I outlined a sequence of events in which the ego first initiates a "trial action" of the intended discharge, then samples the expected reactions of the superego and the external world to the partial experimental act. The result of this test run is the receipt of a signal of anxiety or of safety, and the ego then determines its further course depending upon which signal it receives.

While I was embarked upon the two anxiety papers, a panel of the American on "The Significance of Intrapsychic Conflict" (1962) serendipitously concentrated me upon the remainder of this intrapsychic process, from the moment of receipt of the anxiety/ safety signal through the ensuing activity of the directing unconscious ego. The panel led to another pair of papers, this time on intrapsychic conflict, which extended the examination of the intrapsychic process to the stages *following* the receipt of the signal about whether or not the coast is clear to proceed toward intended acts. If there is anxiety, conflict is the next step. One paper on "the scope" (1963b), and another on the "structural problems" (1963c), of intrapsychic conflict focused closely upon some fourteen steps, from the initiation of the process to the final outward pathways into external behavior.

During the same period, I wrote "Psychoanalysis, Affects, and the 'Human Core'" (1967), in which I aimed to trace the relationship and the line of demarcation between psychoanalysis and the behavioral sciences (a subject stimulated by my year at Stanford). I proposed that it was this nuclear human area of unconscious intrapsychic conflict that demarcated the region of psychoanalytic expertise, and differentiated psychoanalysis from the other social sciences. Shortly afterward, in a paper (1969a) called "The Intrapsychic Process and Its Analysis: A Recent Line of Thought and Its Current Implications," in deference to the previous works of Hartmann (1939) on adaptation and the conflict-free sphere and of Rapaport (1951a, 1958) on autonomy, I expanded "intrapsychic *conflict*" to the more inclusive term "intrapsychic *process*." Since trial action can result in conflict or its absence, I suggested that the center of psychoanalytic interest be expanded from "intrapsychic conflict" to the wider "intrapsychic *process*," which can run its course with or without conflict ensuing as it reaches to achieve adaptive outcomes. The ego, in its trial, signal function, can meet the signal of safety as well as anxiety. This dovetails with Sandler's (1960) paper on the background of safety.

These studies became for me the platform for a new focus of interest, the active moves of the unconscious ego *after* it receives its trial signal, which are part of the unconscious decision-making function of the ego. Continuing my examination of the intrapsychic process, to the ego's psychological activities after it receives the signal of danger, I began to attend to the still-unconscious phase in which the ego must decide whether or not to institute defense or some other measure to deal with the anxiety and the danger it presages. At this point on the intrapsychic arc, the conventional conceptualization leads directly to the move to repression or some other defense, thus producing the traditional type of oppositional ego/id conflict, or from there to symptom formation by the usual compromise formation. At this juncture of the continuing unconscious process, however, I proposed a new type of intrapsychic conflict, conflicts about what to "do" next, which I called "choice-dilemma" conflicts (Rangell 1969b). These are brought to bear when the unconscious ego, faced with a choice between the branches of a conflict, must "decide" what to do next. Defense is one outcome, compromise formation another. But another common yet overlooked alternative, seemingly obvious but routinely bypassed in our theoretical framework, is a choice of one arm of the conflict over the other: that is, the choice of the instinctual impulse or the superego edict. While Brenner has defined one major psychic outcome in his work on compromise formation, this does not include all possibilities. Not every outcome of conflict is, or necessitates, or even can be a compromise.

7

THE 1970s AND 1980s: DIVERGENCES

MORE OF THE CUMULATIVE THEORY;
THE UNCONSCIOUS DECISION-MAKING
FUNCTION OF THE EGO; THE PSYCHOANALYTIC
THEORY OF ACTION

This work led to what became the center of my theoretical line of thought: the ego as agent, as "psychic brain," as decider and director as a person navigates through life in the external surround. In the early seventies I added "the unconscious decision-making function of the ego" (1971a) to the inventory of ego functions.

This topic—of the *active* unconscious ego—has been conspicuously underattended as a subject of major interest; it has been pointed to, however, though briefly, by many analysts from Freud on. To Freud (1923), analysis sets out "to give the patient's ego freedom to *decide* one way or the other" between conflicting motives (p. 50, italics mine). And in his "Outline" (1940), the ego performs its task "by learning to bring about expedient changes in the external world to its own advantage (through activity)" (p. 145), . . . [and] as regards *internal* [emphasis Freud's] events by gaining control over the demands of the instincts, by *deciding* [emphasis mine] whether they are to be allowed satisfaction" (p. 146). Bibring (1954), in his classic article differentiating psychoanalysis and dynamic psychotherapy, points out very simply that "the main goal of analysis . . . consists—to put it briefly—in . . . establishing the ego's *freedom of choice"* (p. 766, emphasis added). And Waelder (1960), who refers to the ego specifically, quoting confirmation by Freud, as "a *problem-solving agent"* (p. 169, emphasis Waelder's), states that psychoanalysis works by "offering its patients a possibility of working out a viable, non-neurotic, solution" (p. 46). Quoting Freud quoting George Bernard Shaw, Waelder continues, the goal is "to be able to choose the line of greatest advantage instead of yielding to the direction of least resistance" (p. 168).

Hendrick (1942) had come to the same point in his theory of ego mastery, and a direct connecting thread can be seen from this to the "task-solving" functions that Waelder (1960, p. 177) sees as the center of the ego's activities. Going forward from there, while most authors neglected the active role of the ego in the face of anxiety, there have been two exceptions: Anton Kris, and Joseph Weiss and Harold Sampson. Kris offered a series of papers (1977, 1984, 1985) in which he described two kinds of conflicts— either/or conflicts and convergent and divergent conflicts— within the intrapsychic sphere, and the central role of these in human mentation. Weiss and Sampson (1982, 1986) built upon these same concepts in their mastery theory and their view of the unconscious planning functions of the ego. While interest in this view proliferated for a time, Weiss and Sampson's work has regrettably become split off from the main trunk of Freudian theory; it has attracted a separate group of practitioners who concentrate on mastery alone, as Weiss left understated the roles of drives, the superego, and the other more complex functions of the ego. This is another example of an advance unfortunately accompanied by an unnecessary hypertrophy of one aspect and atrophy of others.

In a different vein, Paul Gray and Fred Busch also explored one aspect of this general area of detailed ego functioning, Gray in his (1973) focus on the active unconscious role of the ego as ally in the therapeutic situation and then in his (1994) elaboration of close ego analysis, and Busch (1992, 1995b) in his extension of Gray's emphasis on close analysis of the ego and its resistances as the center of technique. Yet while both these authors focus closely and constructively on the ego's operations around anxiety and the web of *defensive* operations, they fail to give proper place to the ego's *adaptive* functions, and to articulate at similarly close range its functions of directing decisions and action. The concept of "developmental lag," as Gray (1982) used it with regard to the delay of the field to acknowledge and absorb the implications of ego psychology for psychoanalytic technique, applies as well to the slowness to highlight and integrate the active, decisive, prospective role of the ego as director in intrapsychic dynamics.

I continued to extend the theme of the active unconscious ego into the eighties. In "The Executive Functions of the Ego" (Rangell 1986), I elaborated on the exercise of "unconscious ego will" as one of the executive functions of the unconscious ego in the intrapsychic process. "Free will" and psychic determinism are both relative rather than absolute; they are in fact another complementary pair. Freud's discovery of psychic determinism was a revolutionary innovation, but "will" still remained: Freud did not automatically eliminate what had come before. However, psychoanalysis understands that old concept in new ways. One is its derivation from the instinctual wish. The other is unconscious ego will, the active, directing, executive function of the unconscious ego that shapes intention and creates action. Waelder (1934, 1963) also recognized and made room for the coexistence of determinism and freedom. In a summary formulation of these investigations, I wrote, "Human history, individual and collective, results from a combination of determinism, random occurrences and the guided event" (1986, p. 30).

Both Hartmann and Rapaport stopped short of continuing their major work on adaptation and autonomy into the logical next step of a psychoanalytic theory of action. While Rapaport felt activity/passivity to be "at the very heart of an adequate conceptualization of the human psyche" (Gill, 1967c, p. 531), he felt unable to pursue the subject to its solution, according to Gill, and left the question unfinished. Hartmann (1947), in his paper on rational and irrational action, stated that "a theory of action based upon the knowledge of the structural aspects of the personality . . .

is the most important contribution psychoanalysis will one day be able to make in this field" (p. 38). He felt, however, that there was as yet no psychoanalytic theory of action. Schafer (1976) wrote of this missing aspect of behavior, action, in a much quoted work, but from outside the structural view. In keeping with his linkages to George Klein's work, Schafer considered the person, rather than the ego, as agent. It seems to me, however, that this was a reversion to a preanalytic view of action, and that the widespread interest in Schafer's formulation was in keeping with the general turn—at its peak at that time—against Freud's metapsychology and the structural view. In contrast, I retain action (along with intention and decision) within ego theory, and thus within the structural and total metapsychological points of view. This extension, in my view, completes in the direction of external action the line of thinking of Freud and his major followers, which had been—and still is—conspicuously underplayed in the psychoanalytic literature; it also rounds out the series of papers in which I developed this line of thought (Rangell 1955b, 1963b,c, 1968a,b, 1969a,b, 1971a, 1974b, 1986, 1989a).

THE COMPROMISE OF INTEGRITY

In my outgoing presidential address at the International Congress in Paris in 1973 I introduced a new diagnostic entity into psychoanalytic nosology, the syndrome of the compromise of integrity (Rangell 1974a). Although the phenomenology to which this referred had always been built into interstructural dynamics and the intrapsychic process, this aspect of human behavior had remained inconspicuous within psychoanalysis until I lifted it out and pointed to it explicitly.

My interest in this behavioral phenomenon came from several sources. I already had a profound interest in affective group life, including its large-scale manifestations in national politics. I had always tried to integrate my analytic observations of psychosociopolitical life with ongoing clinical and life experiences. A specific instance of questionable integrity in national life had recently acquired special intensity. Twenty-five years as a Nixon-watcher had come to a head during the Watergate crisis of 1972. I was riveted by the dramatic events, convinced we were seeing history in the making, and began to conduct a study in depth of unfolding events. During the July that preceded the Paris Congress, the Ervin Committee was convening in Washington to begin to investigate the break-in of the year before.

But another stream of observation and experience had also been impinging upon my consciousness for a long time, one that at first I was loathe to admit. My personal experiences, direct and intense, with affective group life during many years of national and international office in my own professional discipline struck me as being not too different in quality from what I was seeing in national or even local politics, and in social life as well. People in group life are not what they are when they enter an analyst's office—and people do live and behave in groups. Freud (1921) extrapolated his insights from individual depth studies to the psychology of groups, with a resulting great expansion of our understanding of mass behavior. I found, and suggested as a generalization, that the opposite also holds: that studies and interpretations of group actions can help penetrate to new levels of individual psychopathology. As analytic studies of the individual cast light on group behavior, analytically informed observations of group behavior can prove equally instructive about individual reactions.

These two situations left me thinking that a psychoanalytic understanding of psychopathology embraced a much wider span of behavior than just the psychoneuroses and more disturbed syndromes that analysts were used to dealing with in clinical practice. I felt that this unfolding national drama, and the psychological issues and problems that it brought to our attention, operative in all individuals living in groups, constituted a qualitatively new dimension, and that this applied as much to individuals as to groups.

My observational data from both of these areas, the sociopolitical and the analytic-institutional, were reinforced by clinical practice and life experience, and led to formulations that address everyday ongoing aspects of human life. Integrity involves integration of the superego; intellectually we accept this readily, but our actions are not always in keeping with our intellects. Clinically and observationally, integrity includes a necessary willingness to live by superego values.

Besides naming the syndrome in my presidential address in Paris of 1973, my studies culminated first in a paper (Rangell 1976), and later a book, on "the mind of Watergate" (1980a). The subject of this work was not Richard Nixon himself, but the people who elected as their president a man whose nickname for twenty-five years had been "Tricky Dick." The object of my study was not the man, but the nation. While the president as an individual was out of bounds for analytic study, everything in the public domain was open to attempts at understanding, and groups of all sizes came under my scrutiny. Twenty-nine of the thirty "men under Nixon," all of them high achievers, went along with the break-in knowingly. I extrapolated from this to the general population: where ego interests are high enough, the effectiveness of superego controls lessens. This obtains in politics, business, academia, science, and also in psychoanalysis. I could not avoid this observation. It had pressed itself upon me as a critical aspect of my many years of direct experience.

In my work on Watergate, I postulated that C of I (my shorthand for "the syndrome of the compromise of integrity") is as ubiquitous as neurosis in human affairs. As neurosis arises from conflict between the ego and the id, C of I is the outcome of conflict between the ego and the superego. Such conflicts, and the more ego-syntonic forms of their compromise solutions, are as built into ordinary human conduct and interchange as the subclinical neuroses, and together with them comprise the psychopathology of everyday life. C of I is to sociopathy and crime as neurosis is to psychosis. These two sets of dynamics are not mutually exclusive, nor is either excluded from general intrapsychic dynamics. Interestingly, Kohut stated that he came to his new theoretical emphasis on narcissism from his experiences as president of the American

Psychoanalytic Association. "In what was perhaps more than a throwaway line, Kohut often . . . said that he had learned all he knew about narcissism from his service as president of the American" (Strozier 2001, p. 140). My complementary idea relating to problems of integrity came from similar experiences as a president, from local through national to the International Association. Actually, our two sets of observations are related, each of us seeing the outcomes from the opposite pole: while Kohut saw narcissism from too strong an id, I described moral breaches from too weak a superego. Both can lead to a common result, a narcissistic compromise of integrity. In my clinical-theoretical description, I wrote, "Narcissism unbridled is the enemy of integrity" (1980a, p. 23).

No one who has served as leader of a group of thousands can avoid being a target of transference affects, the irrationality of which are striking in both their positive and negative aspects. Inappropriate behavior, from obsequious flattery to malignant criticism, may derive from the conventional dynamics of neurosis or from the syndrome of C of I. Either the id or the superego can be compromised. A good deal of the behavior in a living group is a subtle combination of neurotic and corrupt group interactions, both horizontal and vertical, acted out both hierarchically and laterally. An unconscious substrate of ego–superego conflicts, aiming toward narcissistic satisfaction at the expense of superego regulation, results in compromises of integrity. The intensity of these maladaptive outcomes is in direct proportion to the reward wished for or expected, whether it be recognition, promotion, or praise. The underlying bases of such behavior can come from various topographic levels, much as the neuroses, with their roots in the unconscious, percolate upward through the preconscious and conscious into external action.

It was not difficult to incorporate these new observations into the cumulative structure of psychoanalytic theory. The tripartite structural divisions were there to explain them. In the face of personal experiences of my own, I remembered how Freud had turned the observation of difficult and troubling obstructions into a positive path. I always regarded Freud's method of turning obstacles into insight as one of the most remarkable aspects of his character, as well as of his intellectual genius. Coming upon resistances and opposition did not turn him away from analysis; instead, once he recognized them as data, they led him to the discovery of defense. My expanded formulations, which moved from an exclusive focus on compromises of the id to the recognition of equally common compromises of the superego, attempted to do for group life what the psychoanalytic method had done for the individual—first to understand, and later, perhaps, to treat.

From the beginning my clinical work has been the platform upon which my life as a psychoanalyst stands, and from which my theoretical opinions and guidelines are derived. In my clinical work I have been in agreement with Hartmann's (1960) inspiring monograph on moral conflicts, which established the rationale for the analyst's neutral and nonjudgmental position. Analysts are nonjudgmental, an observational stance backed by Waelder (1960). But my work on the compromise of integrity led me to the realization (also shared by Waelder) that the "neutral" stance is itself part of a complementary series, and yet another example of an all-or-none prescription that would be better left gray. In the practical world in which scientists, including psychoanalysts, live and work, there are limits to a morally noninvolved stance. We may be neutral as long as it is safe, for society and the individual, and within the basic rules under which human beings agree to conduct their lives. The psychoanalytic vantage point is not without a moral position, nor should it be one of neutrality without limits.

Ambition, power, and opportunism, "the three horsemen" of compromise of integrity (1980a, p. 23), are excessive in this syndrome, but in their normal form they are aims built into ordinary life. We wish our children to be ambitious, to acquire power via skill and mastery, and to develop the capacity to take advantage of opportunities. But any of these traits can hypertrophy to the point of malignancy. John Dean, who had been one of Nixon's inner group but who later recanted and blew the whistle that led to a president's downfall, wrote a book called *Blind Ambition* (1976). And exaggerated opportunism—the pursuit of one's own aims at any cost to others, a prominent trait of Richard Nixon's throughout his political career, is a negative character trait as well. Power unchecked leads to human suffering, from schoolyard bullying up to the horror that took place in Germany in our own century. As normal behavior lies at only a short remove from neurosis, the distance from mastery as success to mastery as abuse can also be a short span.

This line of thought—from anxiety, to active unconscious decision-making, to breaches of integrity among varied external outcomes—brings with it the question of responsibility and accountability. Freud could not discover everything, and he left many discoveries to the future. Hartmann and Rapaport elaborated autonomy and action, but they too eventually had to leave it to others to develop these further; both are important subjects of analytic study, on a par with, parallel to, and not excluding psychic determinism. Many analysts today, as the century closes, are thoughtfully stating (in e-mail, the new medium for public opinion, through which large numbers may speak spontaneously without the formality or thoroughness necessary for publication) that psychoanalysis *is* a moral discipline. In their comments, many analysts are moved to make this observation as an antidote to their fellows who confuse current neuroscientific discoveries of the brain activity that accompanies psychological behavior with the *causes* of that behavior. It is now necessary to recognize that the brain does not "do" things aside from the person, who acts through the mind that comes from the brain, via, I add, the system ego within his mind. As may be seen in the sequence I have traced of unconscious intrapsychic activity, the ego is the specific agency, responsible for the specific incursions of the individual into the outer world, rational or irrational. The agent is the same in life as in the analytic process, where it is the rational ego that is the ally of the analyst.

The field has been slow in granting these expanded views of active unconscious ego processes their place. While the individual concepts in isolation are in some cases applauded (or at least not opposed), they are not easily absorbed. Yet without this expanded theoretical vista—if analytic interest limits itself to the preparatory phases of human motor behavior, or to the mechanisms around anxiety or defense, without an equal alertness to unconscious purposes and intentions and their execution in actions into the outer world—psychoanalysis merits the criticism of Rollo May (1969), who sees psychoanalysis as "an exercise in indecision." Psychoanalytic contributions have their own timetable and social fates when it comes to acceptance, which are established in accord with the surrounding cultural ambience. New ideas in psychoanalysis, which have their own fates, as Greenson (1969) has pointed out, also have their own timetables. Because man did not want to know that he acts without knowing why, he first resisted the discovery of psychic determinism, which was a threat to his narcissism. With the extension of psychoanalytic knowledge into unconscious *action*, the question of responsibility comes complexly into play. "Man not only does not know why he acts; he also does not always know *that* he acts" (Rangell 1989a, p. 200). Now man does not want to know that he might be *more* responsible than he knows; this arouses guilt as well as anxiety. Man is both less responsible and more responsible than he thinks. Psychoanalysis has always exposed contradictions.

LOS ANGELES FROM THE SEVENTIES

I have been summarizing my own continuous line of scientific interest during the period between 1960 and 1990; this represented in my thinking additions to the main trunk, accretions upon an expanding unitary theory of psychoanalysis that is never static but constantly evolving. But such examples of cumulative theory-building were the exception, not the rule. This gradual development of the central theory has in fact been very much a minority stream, paralleled by and much overshadowed by a different trend, one toward multiplication of theories. From its roots in the two-theory developments in Topeka, through the establishment of the three British schools, to the wide receptiveness of analysts on this continent (for a variety of internal reasons) to diversity, a qualitative scientific alteration had begun to gain momentum.

When, beginning in the seventies, the progression of theory began to take off, Los Angeles, one of the places in which the change began, was an example of the general trend. Through the seventies and into the eighties, the atmosphere and the theoretical ambience of psychoanalysis in Los Angeles changed drastically. While specific events were initiated by only one of the then two official existing Societies in the city, the shifting emphases ended up affecting both groups equally. The Los Angeles and Southern California Societies had split over the "classical" approach twenty years before, but there was now an energetic new spirit of shared mutual interest. Klein, Bion, Fairbairn, self psychology, intersubjectivity and therapeutic immersion, all now united the two groups, where once the "old" analysis had divided them. They had united in pluralism before this became a movement. In its spirit of openness to new ideas, the Southern California group moved effortlessly from an Alexandrian postoedipal center of etiology to a receptive interest in Kleinian preoedipality. The skipping over the Oedipus complex from both directions, that is, first from the cultural, postoedipal focus and then from the preoedipal and infancy periods, was not articulated, but it was accomplished in action as part of the atmospheric change in the analytic community. In "Transference to Theory" (1982a), I described how certain new "eclectic" groups leapfrog the oedipal, at first championing cultural, environmental, and postoedipal conflicts, and then leaping with equal vigor to the postnatal period and preoedipal infancy as the period most determining periods for future life and character. Skipped over and blotted out is the oedipal period itself, with its sexual conflicts and castration complex—the etiologic bed for the neuroses mainly reconstructed in psychoanalysis.

A new era had arrived. There was no longer one new theory at issue but instead a succession of theories and theorists, attesting to the unstable base upon which these developments were taking place. Each new theory attracted more passion than scientific rigor. The atmosphere was conducive to excitement, but not to scholarship or even fidelity. At no point could the claim be reasonably made that any of the changing theories were based on a new set of observations followed by alternative explanations consistent with them. The theoretical preferences that bound groups together were based not on new observations, but on interpersonal allegiances and friendships that shifted rapidly and gave rise to the quick swells and regular alternations of new explanatory theories.

Nor could the rapidly changing theories have been based rationally on therapeutic results. I remember a small group of analysts explaining to me on successive occasions that it was analytic results that lay behind their quickly changing theoretical affinities. "It works for us," they said very sincerely, as they were enthusiastically changing from Klein to the newer self psychology. They had said the same thing at the time of their previous switch from Freud to Klein, however, and they said it again later, when they became, all together, advocates for intersubjectivity. None of these allegiances to a new school, however, lasted long enough for any authentic psychoanalysis to have been conducted. This group shared a leader with whom they moved from one theory to another, and the leader and the movement strengthened their social unity and their pleasure in being together. This cohesive group demonstrated, almost as a social biopsy, a phenomenon usually more visible in large groups: that while *what* is politically correct may change, "political correctness" itself remains consistently operative in group life.

These reflections on certain negative aspects of group behavior are not to be taken as a rejection of the positive aspects of socialization and group life, intrinsic as these are to the human condition and human survival. In psychoanalysis, "the impossible profession," as in all other civilized pursuits, social bonds and friendship groups may be highly felicitous and of great value to practitioners. They may enhance the stability and security of their participants, and they stimulate creativity where in a solitary life there might have been none. Friendships are the commonest of all object relationships, and the ones that have received the least attention (see Rangell 1963a, for a discussion of the dynamics, the motivations, and the pitfalls and complications of the human proclivity for this most important type of affiliation). Baum (1981), who could have spoken for many others, described the usefulness throughout his professional life of a small psychoanalytic group. I have known small groups of analysts, together since candidate days, whose members have blossomed into leading scientific contributors over the years. But for every group like these, large and small, there is one of the kind that tend to inhibit their members, perhaps holding them in thrall to a charismatic leader who progresses at the expense of followers who willingly suspend achievement, and even independent opinion.

The reorganization of the Los Angeles Society continued into the seventies as a major concern of the several local administrations that followed the upheavals. One aspect of the continuing turbulence during this period took the form of an intense antagonism toward the American, which expressed misgivings about new standards and rapidly changing activities that had been introduced at LAPSI. At one point, in reaction to widespread dissatisfaction and as an attempted solution to the confrontations between the Society and the American, a bloc of fourteen new training analysts was approved by the Education Committee; this was an unprecedented mass appointment which, in an effort at theoretical parity, included appointees from across the spectrum of theoretical leanings. In my opinion, this gesture produced neither stability nor cohesion. On the contrary, this turbulent period in the history of the L.A. society, and the various vicissitudes and realignments that resulted from it, have left an indelible mark. One derivative of the original upheaval was the spawning over time of a number of separate societies. As LAPSI itself turned from one new direction to another, each time rejecting the previously espoused theory, those members with newly acquired but more enduring theoretical convictions organized into new societies that represented their respective views—the (Kleinian) Psychoanalytic Center of California, for example, and later the Institute of Contemporary Psychoanalysis (self psychology). Strategically, however, in accordance with the style of the times, and in hopes of attracting members and candidates, all of these groups came to call themselves "eclectic," as now do the two original parent societies in the city as well. While LAPSI, to distinguish itself from the others, retained the official aura of the most "classical," it too now presents itself to candidates and to the public as eclectic, as does its sister society of the American, the Southern California Society. (Two others, the Los Angeles Institute for Psychoanalytic Studies, mostly but not exclusively for clinical social workers, and PCC, are in the I.P.A. but not the APsaA, while ICP at this time eschews both larger organizations.)

A new theoretical culture was prevailing, one of pluralism, polymorphism, and multiplicity of theories. "Eclectic" and "open-minded" have been the passwords to acceptability, in the ears of the public and of most of the analytic population. It is no longer possible to present an educational program without presenting an equivalence of all analytic theories. An institute with a commitment to one psychoanalytic theory alone cannot expect an incoming class. Even those groups known to be Kleinian or Kohutian officially declare themselves as teaching and representing all theories. Every theory seems to be acceptable except, strangely, the Jungian. While Jungian psychoanalysis has a significant number of adherents and practitioners, it has been considered taboo in the "Freudian" Societies, as all the separate groups still wish to call themselves. But even with regard to Jung, and the growing interest in Lacan, I have recently noted winds of change.

Thirty-plus years after these developments, and, I consider, derivative of them, the more-than-middle-aged members of a long-standing, influential study group within the Los Angeles Society asked themselves a question: Why, they wondered, did their group—perhaps their whole generation—many of whom were individually quite accomplished and successful, not seem to be leaving any legacy of work or leadership to psychoanalysis or to the society? And why are they never quoted as to opinions or principles in ongoing theoretical debates? This discussion was reported to me by a member of the group. My own belief is that when groups commit their allegiance, in however subtle or passive a way, to strong charismatic leaders, they risk becoming too bound and conflicted to speak with their own voices. Contradictory but inhibiting identifications take their toll, permanently stunting independence and creativity. By way of historical contrast, this is not always so; certain analysts who defected with Horney in the thirties, for example, were later able to separate themselves successfully from her, and return to the main body to do creditable work.

History can record events in distorted forms. One example of an innocent misinterpretation recorded as history appeared in the *Southern California Psychiatrist*, the newsletter of the Southern California Psychiatric Association, in 1998. The new president of the Southern California Psychiatric Association, a young analyst, wrote in an editorial (Gales 1998), apropos "the hottest controversies in psychoanalysis" today, that such intense theoretical differences are as old as psychoanalysis. Citing "the struggle between Greenson and Rangell in the 60s," Gales went on, Greenson represented the liberal, open position and Rangell the conservative, closed one. It is not difficult to see, if one looks back rather simplistically into the past, that such a distorted generalization can be arrived at with no particular deeper background intentions, but from misinformation, by history simply wearing thin. The fact was that Greenson and I, whatever our personal antipathies, were united in our theoretical beliefs, and were of the same psychoanalytic school of thought. It was actions and attitudes, not theories, that separated us. In the tangled area of transference, for example, I essentially agreed with Greenson's theoretical writings on the therapeutic alliance, called by him the working alliance (1965), and on the real relationship that he and Wexler (1969) described about the same time. We separated on the question of how to act upon those concepts.

The Novicks (1998), on the other hand, were referring accurately to the personal struggle between Greenson and me when, setting out to resurrect the concept of the therapeutic alliance, they pointed to its misuse. They viewed its decline as due to practices employed on its account by Greenson and Wexler in the treatment of famous film star patients. This is an example of what I earlier, in my discussion of flaws and fallacies, called *consequentiality*—the behavior that follows upon alleged beliefs. Well used in the context of an analytic attitude and the neutral stance that makes transference (and the transference neurosis) possible, the "real relationship" is a valid concept, but its interpretation and realization are subject to misuse.

A NEW ORDER: THE AMERICAN AS TARGET

From the 1970s on, as first a few, then a gradually proliferating greater number of divergent theories established a new pluralistic ambience, the scientific background of psychoanalysis changed qualitatively, and a new type of restlessness followed, along with widespread theoretical diffusion. Influences from the top—from training analysts, respected teachers, and administrative leaders—set the tone and established the theories in vogue in each institute or society. Often promulgated by widely read and charismatic authors and opinion-makers, these in-vogue theories of the moment could be absorbed, enhanced, and rendered contagious by the cumulative pressures of repetition and group approval, thus increasingly being applied to clinical work, and identified with by small or large groups within the society as their current systems of belief.

The unconscious resentment against established theory now had many channels for discharge, all promising to be more ego-syntonic and more successful than those available before in producing stable states of positive self-esteem. New theoretical systems could be espoused, each of which selectively eliminated unwelcome or anxiety-producing elements of the previous total theory. Each new theory eliminated or effectively downplayed specific resistance-arousing formulations: in one, drives in favor of objects; in another, conflict in favor of defects; in yet others, oedipal etiology in favor of preoedipal or inborn factors. A modern and more global version of this mechanism can be seen in the swell of opinion today in favor of the genetic origin of all mental disease, to the exclusion of psychological etiologic factors.

Again, theoretical divisions, as other splits, are a function of both ideas and the people who hold them; cognitive beliefs and affective or subjective factors mix and fuse, resulting in contiguous groups of divergent identifications. There are always present in the culture of psychoanalysis some discontents; therefore the soil is always in readiness for change, whether evolutionary change or the more sudden changes of protest. This average expectable substrate of frustration is a mixture of residual dissatisfaction with personal analysis, and disappointments about failure to advance in whatever desired way in the analytic community. Admixed with these, increasingly in current times, are economic anxieties. These factors intermingle in varying degrees, consciously or not, and encourage the fusion of the theoretical and personal. The first, the always-important affective background established by dissatisfaction in one's own personal psychoanalyses, I can attest to from my own wide-based experience. In moments of relaxed intimacy, it is quite general to hear from even prominent analysts of disappointment with their own analyses, however it may have been understood and adjusted to. As in the occasional written records to that effect, such as the self-described history of Ernest Wolf cited above, such experiences are heard verbally quite endemically.

Our theories automatically pervade all aspects of psychoanalytic life, from science and education to the derivative applied aspects of analytic activities. Psychoanalytic science, organizational administrative developments, and training and education have always been inextricably mixed and reciprocally interrelated. This current period of increasing theoretical ferment is no exception, which but demonstrates the phenomenon more energetically. Theoretical divisiveness within institutes has affected the training process, which has influenced the kind of graduates emerging from these new educational experiences and exposures. While some came to consider themselves as belonging to one school or another—Kleinian, self psychology, object relations, and so on—others felt divided or confused, straddling fences and borders. Some adhered to one or another appealing or intellectually charismatic person or set of ideas: Winnicott; Bion; in one instance that I know of, Balint; and in one institute, "mastery theory." All this is reminiscent of how groups or populations in earlier times became Adlerians, Jungians, or Rankians. Only a minority, in my opinion and experience, have embarked on the road toward a cohesive, consistent, total, organized theoretical vision, and those have usually been analysts who began their training before this period of fragmentation took hold.

In addition to its influences on the training process, this period of divided theory has had organizational effects as well. The inevitable conflicts and confusions in their training, and the stunting of the development of the Freudian theoretical system, resulted in the graduation of candidates increasingly ill-equipped to fulfill the requirements for membership in the American. Disappointment and resentment have mounted, leaving the American the scapegoat and the target of fierce hostility. The slow pace of advance to membership and more prestigious training appointments led first to mounting vexation, and then to moves for administrative changes and reforms. As unfulfilled ambitions accumulated, calls for change built up. The changes demanded have not involved improved preparation from below, however, but only the relaxation of standards and requirements from above.

It is no accident that the movement to make certification separate from membership in the American was initiated in Southern California, where the conflict between the fact of increasing divergence and the desire of the central organization to maintain standards was at a maximum. As frustration spread and took root among those dissatisfied with the slow pace of advance, the push was born, and gradually gained momentum, to change the standards for membership. Local autonomy is a simultaneous quest;

graduation from an institute should be enough, it is argued, and should include automatic admission to the national organization. This is in keeping with policy in I.P.A., where theory has been historically less unified and more varied. Since the national standards and expectations were becoming increasingly unrealistic in the face of the new theoretical diffusion (to that extent justifying the growing label of rigidity applied to the American), these trends were becoming more ubiquitous and intense.

Following the huge theoretical disruptions that began in the late sixties, an inordinate percentage of applicants from both of the Southern California institutes failed to gain admittance to the American. Even more unsettling, unable to write up the required number of cases in a satisfactory manner, graduates desisted from applying. A significant number, to my first-hand knowledge, doctored their local and national case presentations, some in subtle and others in less subtle ways; typically oedipal emphases were presented, it being felt that this is what was expected and necessary. (In addition, I feel that students knew that they had in fact neglected this aspect in their cases, indoctrinated as they had been against "classical" thinking in their training and education.) In consequence of these developments, the American became regarded as conservative, authoritarian, and despotic by a large group of disaffected analysts, which belief in my opinion at times reached an almost paranoid level. "We know the American is against us" was an accepted statement in Southern California regional bulletins and newsletters. "The East is against the West," was the group response when a local candidate for national office was defeated in an election, or even with no apparent rationale whatever (this was reminiscent of Lyndon Johnson's resentment and envy of the Ivy League Kennedys, or of Nixon's earlier bristlings against a snobby Harvard-Yale elite in Washington). My description of the period and my surmises about its dynamic, I must preemptively assure my readers, does not mean that criticism of the American is always baseless; other attitudes and developments in that organization have properly led to criticisms and disappointments on rational grounds, and these must be voiced and dealt with. But the aspect of displaced disappointment should also not be overlooked. Also for the record, the American during this period upheld a unitary theory—not a monolithic, but a composite and coherent one.

MY CONTRASTING EXPERIENCES IN THE AMERICAN

These group sentiments made a stark contrast with the experiences I had had in the American since the early fifties; this was a saddening fact, and in my own locale it left me feeling a lone and isolated individual among these strong anti-American currents. The American had provided me with the most warming and uplifting experiences of my professional life. From the time of my first scientific participation as a young graduate, I could feel the solidity, fairness, and strength of psychoanalysis, as represented by the dedication and sincerity of its leaders at that time. As a young participant, I had been exhilarated by an ambience that I experienced as open, unbiased, and scientific. To be open-minded does not mean to be without theoretical opinions, convictions, and standards; nor does it mean rigid boundaries and autocratic limitations about what constitutes psychoanalysis. The pluralistic culture of today, however it extols openness to new ideas, still rejects certain groups and theories—the Jungian school, as I have commented before, for example—and not always for consistent reasons. The American itself in my opinion has not articulated sufficiently or clearly its right, scientifically and I believe even legally, to conduct its affairs with a defined set of scientific principles.

The American, which recently has been an automatic target for analysts who hold various competing views, stood during that firm middle period through the 1960s for a psychoanalysis based on a fundamental theoretical psychoanalytic core. It stood for a psychoanalytic understanding based on unconscious dynamics, on conflict (best explained by the opposing forces of the three postulated psychic systems), and, developmentally, on the major nodal point at the conflicts of the oedipal period, yet without denigrating preceding or succeeding developmental stages. The definitive and ideal mode for transmitting this understanding, in the therapeutic philosophy of the time, was to establish and maintain the "analytic attitude" as the fulcrum of psychoanalytic methodology. The oedipal was understood as the center of the neurosis, but psychopathology could arise from any other level as well, or from other causes, psychic or organic. And the ideal technical attitude that made for the specific analytic relationship was a blend of objective and subjective, neutral and empathic. The self-congratulations about the new order apparent today are based on regrettable distortion; much of what is correctly said about the subjective participation of the analyst today was already there in past practice. A good deal of what is attributed to "the old American," and referred to with derision by many in the "new" one, I can say from direct experience, is false history.

While my first exposures to the American were as a scientific participant, my early beginning positions in administration included periods on the Program Committee under the then-young Charles Brenner, the Membership Committee under Gerhart Piers (not much heard from in later years), the Committee on Institutes, and the Committee on New Training Facilities. These experiences uniformly filled me with satisfaction and feelings of pride in my peers. Their spirit, open-mindedness, sincerity, and devotion to principle, their rejection of all meanness or pettiness, served as a welcome antidote to the interpersonal haggling and demeaning attitudes that I was increasingly living with locally. Perhaps this was an inevitable consequence of the difference between intimate living within a group and operating with equal intensity from a more distant and less personally involved perspective.

I experienced this same sense of personal expansion and scientific confirmation at every official participation or informal collegial exchange in my work on the national, and later on the international, levels. Similar feelings, unexpected at first, were reported in later years by local analysts who ventured into or were appointed to national administrative positions for the first time. The same feeling of surprised pleasure and confidence prevailed in the scientific arena, too, when they presented papers, or served on panels, or even participated in study groups. Most often, the new activists would report that the American had changed and had become more democratic, open, and accessible. This seems to me an exact counterpart of the child finding new respect for (and identification with) the parent when he grows up. I remember sitting next to a newly elected representative from a local group who was taking part nationally for the first time. He had been particularly virulent against the American in the past, but now he exclaimed as the proceedings went on, "Gee, there are gentlemen here!"

I was reassured, in my early years of participation and wider exposure, about the power and validity of psychoanalysis as it was demonstrated in the character, motivations, and authenticity of its leaders. This sense of security in my colleagues was confirmed during the years I held office myself. Joan Fleming, chairman of the Board on Professional Standards during my first term as president, was close to Franz Alexander yet a Freudian, and relentless in her integrity and incorruptibility. So was Martin Stein in the same position during my second presidency. Integrity is not defined by theoretical beliefs. I remained astonished at the objectivity and forthrightness of Council and Board leaders, at the courage they displayed in trying practical and moral situations. There was no rigidity, coldness, or inflexibility; if anything there was perhaps too much tolerance of questionable local practices, in the spirit of avoiding any taint of authoritarianism. Altogether this demonstrated to me the analytic attitude we aim for toward our patients: fair, interested, objective, and flexible. I was later to experience the same characteristics among the leaders of the I.P.A. as they oversaw an even more dispersed and uneven domain. All of this service—never sufficiently recognized—came at a cost of considerable time, money, and self-sacrifice, and it was compensated only by satisfaction in the tasks performed.

MULTIPLE AND RECIPROCAL CHANGES

Starting in the 1970s, the changes began to gain momentum, carrying us toward unknown destinations. A lot was brewing; there were many issues in transition both scientifically and administratively, having to do with the identity of psychoanalysis and its practitioners. The new developments and conceptual modifications were still ideational and affective; they had not yet been written into official rules or guidelines, or into any binding codes or procedures. Group ecologies throughout the American psychoanalytic world were now evolving in idiosyncratic directions, different in different localities, in size, in history, in the influence of charismatic leaders and the quality of their disciples, in creativity, in group energy, and the like. There were common bonds and shared frustrations, fusions of interests and of historical developments that bound psychoanalytic populations in centers around the country to each other in the pursuit of common goals and in their drift into parallel group and organizational arrangements. But it was neither surprising nor illogical, against this background of rapid change, that small splits were breaking off from main psychoanalytic bodies, some organizing into recognized groups, some remaining informal clusters of individuals, and some, comprised of individuals of independent thought and intention, veering off into solitary reflection and idiosyncratic activity.

The break-offs took place in various ways. Sometimes new thinking led some members to leave an old group; sometimes, where the group as a whole had changed its orientation drastically, a number of remaining traditionalists might separate from the now-altered main body. Thus, in some cases groups with more traditional leanings and values split from more radically changing parent Societies, as happened in the formation of PINE in New England, and sometimes a small, more classical group formed, remaining within a larger Society, as occurred in Washington. In some Societies the whole group divided, as in Southern California, where self, Kleinian, object-relational, and classical divisions were established. There was a wide and general claim of eclecticism. Even those Societies that saw fit to continue to regard themselves as classical, such as the Los Angeles Psychoanalytic Society after its official "reorganization," needed to present themselves as eclectic and pluralistic, in the service of attracting candidates.

TOWARD PLURALISM

This theoretical tendency toward multiplicity strengthened further, into the eclecticism and pluralism that have become the watchword of American psychoanalysis today. Divisions set in motion in specific locales, as I have described, deepened and spread geographically until such divisions became first widespread and then dominant. All of them eventually coalesced into a national movement that spoke with a new voice at the American, which as a consequence of the new demands and challenges has undergone a series of metamorphoses. During the fifties and sixties, the American represented (what were considered to be) the central and indispensable elements of Freudian psychoanalytic theory. The period of multiple theories that unfolded after that represented a direct contrast with this unified view of theory. It was the adherence of the American to the traditional theory—separate from the Kleinian view prominent in Great Britain and Europe—that led in the forties to its quest to attain regional status within the International, and so to maintain its own scientific and training standards. But in the new culture, in response to the ascent of pluralism and the evolving multipronged sensibility, the scientific ambience and programs of the American also began to change in direction and content. The American came to resemble the International in the new variation in its theoretical fabric.

LAY ANALYSIS

While the theoretical developments were escalating, an old problem was beginning to demand solution. This was the long-smoldering question of lay analysis. Practicing lay analysts, who had smarted under feelings of exclusion since the institution of the American's medical requirement, began to cohere into independent study groups and societies. They had Freud's strong convictions to support them, and had typically been engaged energetically for many years in serious scholarly studies that paralleled the courses of study and training in the American; in many instances they were taught by the same individuals.

In my scientific and educational capacities I addressed many such predominantly lay psychoanalytic groups during those years. I was struck by how much the scientific course of these parallel groups and institutions had come to resemble that of the main bodies. Sharing as they did the same profession, the same literature, and the same clinical data, it is not surprising that the history and development of their theoretical views should have overlapped. Lay and medical psychoanalysis seemed to have progressed along parallel paths, influencing each other in their intellectual preferences and beliefs, and reflecting the same processes of partly retaining classical concepts and partly replacing them with multiple schools of theoretical dissension.

These nonmedical groups proliferated and grew, sometimes in cities where societies had existed before and sometimes in smaller ones where the new groups were the first psychoanalytic organizations. Clinical and theoretical discussions centered increasingly on new theorists, and there was a correspondingly skeptical stance toward "classical" Freudian concepts. Kohut, Kernberg, Klein, Bion, Fairbairn, Winnicott, and Lacan elicited intense attention, while Freud, and the accompanying emphasis on drives, defenses, ego, and metapsychology, received a polite but reserved reception.

The divisions among practicing American psychoanalysts—of all kinds—during this time were complex and attended by strong affects. One major division was around the question of *who* should practice psychoanalysis, the other about *what* to practice. One dividing line was ideational, scientific, theoretical: "What is psychoanalysis?"; the other was personal-cultural-affective, relating to social issues and group processes: "To whom does psychoanalysis belong?" Those two questions had to be resolved, both separately and together. But these two issues that split psychoanalysis—the scientific and the philosophic-administrative—were not always kept sufficiently separate as to allow for optimum clarification and development. There were overlapping areas of conflict, in that both of these issues were influenced by divisions between "insider" and "outsider," as described by Richards (1999) in his paper on the politics of exclusion. Richards considers this issue with regard to the question of lay analysis; I would extend it to include the scientific arena as well as the administrative one. Within the institutes of the American, as well as in the institutes that had been kept outside, increasing resentment was felt by those who were "out" toward those who they felt were "in," but the object of resentment was different in the two situations. Lay analysts placed the onus on medical psychoanalysis, while to those who espoused pluralistic theories, it was the establishment's entrenched and "arbitrary" *theory* that was the target. In each case, the group that suffered exclusion felt the sense of mounting disappointment and cumulative frustration that, as Waelder (1967) has pointed out, is a common base of revolution, which occurs finally after a period of rising expectations.

From a semi-philosophical point of view, this question of "To whom does psychoanalysis belong?" has more theoretical relevance than might be apparent. Thinking about where psychoanalysis fits—whether into the family of science, or among the social disciplines—has always been a provocative intellectual game. Freud discovered, or invented, the science of the mind. But whether psychoanalysis is a science, an art, or a craft (Gray 2000) became a debatable subject. And if it is a science, is it a natural science or not? I (1999) agree with Brenner (1999), who answers that question in the affirmative. Nature makes no exceptions. The mind is derivative of the brain, and ceases to exist when the brain dies. Yet the mind is more than the brain, although it cannot exist without it. After separating psychoanalysis from existential philosophy and claiming the new discipline for science, Hartmann concluded that it belonged not to the physical but the social sciences, which have their own methodologies, criteria, and means of validation. Freud envisioned the field he discovered as an overall science of man. The mind nurtures, and is nurtured by, humanity; it grows into and is fed by its social surround. This does not exclude mental science from the natural science. Natural science must include human science. Nature includes human nature.

All of these apparent polarities—between natural and behavioral science, for example, and between science and art (or craft)— as most of the dualities we have confronted, are better seen as varying degrees of combination. The intellectual issue posed by the broad new array of social and behavioral scientists entering the field—"To whom does psychoanalysis belong?"—does not devolve into lay or medical. Psychoanalysis partakes of both, as it encompasses brain and behavior, body and mind, person and society, and the realms of the physician and of the psychologist/ mentalist both. Neuroscience, the latest area of insight (and of potential false exclusivity), provides one of the partial explanations of the human behavior that is the subject matter of psychoanalysis; psychology and the gamut of social sciences provide the other. Psychoanalysis does not belong to neurology, nor is it totally of sociology or history; it belongs to both and is superordinate to all. It would be unfortunate if the former exclusion of the social scientist were followed by a denigration or exclusion of the physical or medical one. The complete psychoanalyst is a humanistic scientist, a scientific humanist.

The two branches of the psychoanalytic profession, the medical and the lay, share responsibility for both the integrity, and the defects, of its theory. I agree neither with Wallerstein (1998a,b), who attributes the "hegemony" of American ego psychology to its policy of having excluded lay analysts, nor with the opposing view of Richards (1999), who attributes the multiple array of theories to the same exclusionary policy. Both arms of the discipline, medical and nonmedical, have contributed to and distracted from the forward course of theory. Classical contributions were made by Hartmann, a physician; Anna Freud, an educator;

Waelder, a physicist. Divergent or alternative theories have been proposed by Kohut, a physician; Rank, an artist; Stolorow, a psychologist. It is as true now as it was in the beginning that it is not the division between medical and lay analysts that makes for dividing lines within theory, but the division between those who support the essence of Freudian theory and those who obstruct it.

LAWSUITS

As I have said, these ideational and social divisions were not yet institutionalized or legal ones. Lines of cleavage had been established, both theoretical and organizational, and they were getting firmer and broader, but no binding solutions had yet been drawn up. But there were harbingers of change. In the seventies and eighties, as theoretical pluralism and the question of lay analysis gained momentum, a new development made its appearance: the threat of legal action.

The theoretical issue came close to legal confrontation first. The (British) Kleinian analysts now residing on the West Coast were getting ready to apply for Society membership in this country, which raised the question of whether Society members in Los Angeles who held to the new theories would be appointed as training analysts. The first application for membership in LAPSI was that of Susanna Isaacs. Isaacs was an M.D., a Kleinian, and a respected child analyst from Great Britain who had been living in Los Angeles for several years. She applied for membership in the Society (in 1975), and was accepted routinely by the Membership Committee; but in the end she was turned down by the Society after a telephone campaign against her (which occurred even after the disturbed atmosphere created by the British invasion had been uneasily calmed). After an investigation by the I.P.A., to which Isaacs had sent a letter (Kirsner 2000), the threat of a lawsuit (Bail 1991, in Kirsner 2000), and some embarrassment on the part of the American, Isaacs was made a member of the Society a few years later, by which time she had returned to England. During that same period, to retain harmony and ease the theoretical tensions, a large group of new training analysts of mixed theoretical views was appointed in LAPSI in one move. This had never been done before. The effects on the scientific atmosphere of that decision, which trickled down to students for many years, have to this day not been properly assessed. While decisions at that time were made under duress and threats, what was at issue on a larger scale, which to my mind was never faced nor resolved, was a much more subtle question: that is, the right of the American to define what it considers psychoanalysis to be, the right to be the arbiter of its own intellectual base.

While the specific local conflict about theoretical dissent was settled, no principle was established on the general scientific issue: what changes would be made in the American's definition of the minimal standards for psychoanalysis. And the seething question of lay analysis was finally coming to a boil. The threat of legal action came to a head with the institution in 1985 of the well-known lawsuit against the American and International, and several smaller Associations, by a group of psychologists, and the protracted and intense arguments and negotiations that followed (Wallerstein 1998c). When this long struggle was legally resolved in 1988 in favor of the lay analysts, the agreement, which ended the exclusion of nonmedical applicants, was signed for the American by Homer Curtis and for the I.P.A. by Robert Wallerstein, who had struggled sympathetically for lay psychoanalysis for a long time, and who had started a nonmedical track toward psychoanalytic training in San Francisco some years before.

WALLERSTEIN

It is not without significance that Robert Wallerstein, who played such a seminal role in achieving equal status for lay analysts, appeared in a leadership role at exactly the time that the coexisting issue of competing theories was reaching its peak. The resolution of the first problem seemed to call for a similar process for the other. No event gave the mushrooming concept of theoretical diversity as much currency, or such an official stamp, as Wallerstein's (1988) presidential address at the Montreal International Congress in 1987, in which he posed the question "One Psychoanalysis or Many?" and supplied his own definitive answer: Many. All theories, Wallerstein said in his sharply worded address, have equal valence and validity. No one theory has the right by logic or performance to claim superordinacy over any other. I was present when this view was propounded, and could sense the pulse of the audience and the feeling that this was a defining moment in psychoanalytic theory and debate. Wallerstein's view was embraced with excitement, and his receptive audience, which grasped this democratic principle, proceeded to condense into one seemingly homogeneous view a variety of existing divergent theories.

In a view not unlike that of the group around George Klein (who in the sixties had first postulated two theories), Wallerstein now maintained that clinical theory is the common ground uniting all psychoanalytic viewpoints, making them equal and interchangeable, while abstract theories, which are speculative and unconfirmable, serve to separate them. In support of this view, Wallerstein cited a formulation of the Sandlers (1984) about what unites and separates divergent theories. In this paper, the Sandlers, like Wallerstein, moved from a previous unified Freudian, and Anna Freudian, position toward the current pluralistic view. They asserted that the main Freudian system points to the past unconscious, which is more abstract and speculative, while modern, diverse theories aim toward the more accessible, verifiable, and variable present unconscious. This division of the unconscious on the basis of temporal considerations, the Sandlers feel, explains the differences in theory and practice between main and alternative theories.

Although Wallerstein's statement could be seen (and was regarded by many) as a political rather than a scientific one, his strong new formula pervaded the general atmosphere. Psychoanalysts throughout the country supported this principle of multiple equal theories and the American gradually followed suit, eventually coming to stand officially and administratively for the equivalence of divergent theories. Its previous adherence to traditional Freudian metapsychological theory was replaced by a more "liberal " point of view, more in line with that of the International, and when it finally took a stand on the "one theory or many" question, it took it in favor of the latter—a recognition of alternative and equal theories.

Officialdom, therefore, had now institutionalized the fissures appearing and widening in the theoretical tree. This in turn led to major changes in its standards, membership requirements, and scientific programs. A total conceptual change—from one theory of psychoanalysis to an array of psychoanalytic theories—had come about not by discovery but by the public announcement of a new point of view; and this had come about, in its turn, not as a result of scientific advance but in response to social and political developments. Thus a group of new acceptable "paradigms" was created, with no regard to the adequacy of these individual systems to qualify for such consideration on scientific grounds.

COMMON GROUND

That the analytic population rallied to this view was not unpredictable, given the theoretical developments over the previous two decades in this country, and several decades more than that in England, Europe, and the rest of the world. I have a number of differences with the reasoning behind these new conclusions, however. Abstract notions of "equality" may correctly apply to opportunity and licensing, but they are not the criteria by which to decide among explanations and theories. Empirical evidence and scientific methods are more appropriate techniques for discrimination between alternatives.

Many agree easily with Wallerstein's view of the common ground that unites us: clinical theory and practice. However, these do not in actuality equate or bind divergent theories together. In fact there is division within clinical theory itself. Defense and resistance, conflict and compromise, transference and counter-transference, which Wallerstein (1991) offers as common clinical ground, are concepts that are understood as unevenly and as disparately as many more abstract aspects of theory. Not all psychoanalytic schools place conflict and compromise in the forefront clinically; defect and deficiency are in many cases thought to supersede these. Nor are defense and resistance universally agreed upon, either as concept or technique. Even the much-vaunted transference and countertransference are not as common a bond among analysts as one might think. Not only are there differences with regard to the central role of transference, but there are important disagreements as to what transference is. The concept of countertransference, as is well known, divides analysts as much as it unites them. To most of us it is a phenomenon that is always present and has to be recognized on all occasions. Beyond this, however, it is guarded against by some and embraced as useful by others.

Moreover, there is no dearth of common ground among the alternative abstract theories that Wallerstein, and the Sandlers, see as dividing and separating analysts. This includes the shared use of much of Freudian theory: both central concepts of neurosogenesis and derivative theories of technique. Most if not all theories make use of the concepts of the unconscious, anxiety, psychic conflict, trauma, and final psychic outcomes out of a variety of compromise formations. All theories that are psychoanalytic use Freudian theory, employing various combinations of its essential components. There are certainly beliefs that separate theories from each other—Klein from Kohut from Lacan, for example, and each of these from Freud. But these lines of separation exist in both abstract *and* clinical theories. Fenichel's (1945) statement quoted above, "There are many ways to treat neuroses but there is only one way to understand them" (p. 554), articulated the point of view that opposes the new principle of many understandings but one treatment. I feel that Fenichel's generalization better fits my own observations and experiences, and possesses a more logical and satisfying ring.

Sandler (1983) has said, in favor of divergent theories, that there is a discrepancy between public and private statements about the practice of analysis—that analysts commonly profess to be Freudian in public, while in private find other theories more useful. While granting that this may be true, I have pointed out (1990) an opposite (and perhaps coexisting) discrepancy. Analysts commonly speak publicly about major divergences, while privately finding longstanding Freudian concepts—objectivity, the use of transference in the original sense (as displacements from the past), the uncovering of unconscious conflicts, interpretation and reconstruction—comfortably compatible with the practice of analysis.

The Sandlers' distinction between a past and a present unconscious, the basis of Wallerstein's two levels of theory, is in my opinion a strained and inaccurate dichotomy, reminiscent of the separation between analysis by reconstruction and analysis by the here-and-now. Just as analysis deals with the here-and-now *and* reconstruction, with the present transference *and* the repressed past, so does it deal with the unconscious in its entirety, including the temporal aspects, past *and* present, that emerge from the depths to the surface. What the Sandlers call the present unconscious is in fact more akin to what analysts usually call the preconscious. To consider that present level the unconscious, thereby deflecting attention from the characteristic human repository of lifelong repressed content, is to eliminate from view what has always been the main source of psychopathology at which psychoanalysis aims. Although the unconscious is timeless, different aspects of it are available in any analytic hour. Analysis proceeds from the surface down. There is no dividing line in the unconscious between old and new repressions, but a fluid path between them. Certainly there are not different levels that define separate theories. Different aspects of repressed contents, whether from present or past, come close to the surface at different dramatic moments, related to the state of the defenses and resistances.

CHASING THE IRRATIONAL

Since the sixties, which, I feel, is when the forward course of psychoanalytic theory first began to be derailed, psychoanalytic theory has been chasing and trying to overtake the irrational. In many respects, primary process reasoning has become part of the analyzing instrument itself, replacing rational analysis of the irrational. The fallacies I described earlier as ubiquitous and repetitive have come to the fore in full force, and are widely and firmly in operation. In the fallacy of pars pro toto, one part is emphasized and treated as the whole: drive psychology only, or only objects, or ego psychology alone, or transference to the exclusion of reconstruction. In a paradoxical opposite fallacy, the focus is upon the whole *without* acknowledgment of the component parts, a scientific regression to a preanalytic understanding: as when the self is not distinguished from the ego aspect of the whole person that is at a given moment the meaningful part. Or the genetic fallacy holds sway: that the first in a sequence must be the cause of what follows. It is well to keep in mind Anna Freud's (1976) statement that earlier is not necessarily deeper. Similarly, it is not necessary to choose one of a dichotomous pair, as intrapsychic vs. interpersonal, or oedipal vs. preoedipal; both poles may be simultaneously operative, and reciprocally related. Overemphasis of one point on a continuum may obscure a continuous developmental line.

I find it both impressive and regrettable how little contested these lacunae in logic remain. Support of the new views has been accompanied by a turning away from Hartmann, Rapaport, and Freud, and, I add centrally, Fenichel—away from science and intellect in favor of subjectivity. Yet there too in most cases the principle of complementarity applies; the objective and subjective coexist. Intellectualization as a defense is used as an argument against intellect. And as a background affect, nurturing this entire climate of opinion, there seethes a savage antagonism—at times of paranoid proportions—to the "old" American, the repository and representative of the hated and resisted total amalgamated views.

Beginning in the sixties and continuing through the eighties and nineties, misperceptions, misunderstandings, misrepresentations, and straw men have abounded. In one institute, to point out resistance is considered a criticism of the patient, and interpretations are regarded as accusations or confrontations. The first analysis of Mr. Z (Kohut 1979)—whoever the patient and analyst really were—was a flawed analysis, not a condemnation of the classical method. Still, this case and other reanalyses have been falsely used against the theories of previous analysts. In one "modern" presentation of a reanalysis, an analyst who places great emphasis on the new infancy research felt that the original classical analyst had not listened to or believed his patient about earliest mother–child material. In my more reserved view, research findings about infancy can find their way properly into clinical analyses only when knowledge from theory meets data from observation. The "creative leaps" (a phrase used by a patient of mine who complained that I did not make enough of them) between data and theory must not be so wide that the rational ego cannot absorb them.

HOW MANY THEORIES?

The assertion of "many" equal theories poses even more complications. *How* many? Two? Four? More? The "two theories," clinical and abstract, of George Klein, which began the serious division of psychoanalytic theory (although there had been many varied interpretations of aspects of that theory before then), did not remain the division between theories for long. At one point in the progression of theories, some analysts, Cooper (1981, 1992) and Gabbard (1990) among them, favoring closer attention to diagnostic categories, saw three theories and their derivative techniques, which they applied selectively to three different types of patients. Classical theory was for benign, hysterical, neurotic patients; self theory for narcissistic patients; and object-relations theory, following Kernberg (1975), for borderline and more disturbed patients. The Fines (1990) conducted a research study of what analysts of different theories actually do in analysis. They too found clinical differences, and they came to the conclusion that there were four theories: Freud, Klein, Kohut, and Kernberg. Pine (1990) speaks of four also, but a different four than the Fines: drive, ego, self, and object theories. I heard one analyst espouse in a class he was teaching the belief that there is a theory for each patient, and another a theory for each analyst; another spoke of "a cafeteria of paradigms."

IT IS WHAT EACH THEORY OMITS
THAT IS THE PROBLEM

In the actuality of practice, the clinical theories that Wallerstein points to as binding and unifying are no less separatist than the abstract theories that divide us, and that he, with George Klein, feels are insufficiently rooted in observable data. Clinical theory across the spectrum of analytic practitioners is as heterogeneous and fraught with difference as the whole array of abstract supraordinate theories intellectualized from the body of clinical experience. The scaffolding upon which each theory purports to stand contains the distinctive features of each respective theory, and these scaffoldings differentiate theories from each other in practice more than clinical theory binds them, making them more different than alike. What *does* bind many in these different groups together, however, is their reliance in common on the basic psychoanalytic methodology of free association. All share an exploratory stance of relative objectivity in the obtaining and observing of data. What separates theories and the analysts who hold them, and what guides analysts toward the variations in their clinical operations, are the divergences in the systems of understanding that they use to interpret the data obtained by common means.

As I have said before, it is not what each separate theory contributes or emphasizes that splits the field into competitive systems, but what each omits. "None of the [alternate theories] are wrong, but all of them are incomplete" (Rangell 1974a, p. 6). The very earliest dissidents began their differences by leaving out essential elements. Adler focused on power and the ego but omitted drives and the id. Rank pointed to birth and infancy but overlooked childhood. A frequent and passionate point of contention historically has been whether a theory without the oedipal complex, or sexual drives, or defense against these, can be a theory of psychoanalysis. Minus 1 plus minus 1 equals minus 2. Adding together all these omissions would result in an impoverished theory indeed, without instinctual drives, oedipal conflicts, castration anxiety, the sexual etiology of neuroses, and the neurotic anxiety behind sexual psychopathology. The total effect of this addition, when each theory omits, is the ultimate disintegration of psychoanalytic theory. Theory is *de*integrated, instead of the reverse. Integration, and the integrity contained within it, are removed, the latter in both of its senses—wholeness and the moral sense of consistency, disciplined vs. undisciplined scientific principles. Theory is gradually denuded of its essentials, resulting in fragmentation and in a discontinuous individual history.

THE POSITIVE CONTRIBUTIONS OF MANY

None of the exceptions I have taken to the alternative theories is intended to diminish or negate specific contributions made by their authors. The contributions of Melanie Klein on early infantile mentation point in important and helpful directions. Kohut's emphasis on preservation of the self and the role of empathy added valid concepts, as did Alexander's attention to the corrective emotional aspects, both affective and cognitive, of the analytic relationship. In a paper on friendship (1963a), I found the contributions of Alfred Adler most helpful. Adler sowed seeds of ego psychology before Freud came to this. His error, as those of most others, was to discard what had been discovered before. Even Jung's veering to the spiritual was not without value, and is echoed in mainstream psychoanalysis today by emphasis on the affective, the creative, and the unknown.

I am opposed both to omission and to excessive elevation of parts of the whole. It is not with any of the valid contributions of these creative authors that I differ, but with their omissions, as well as their elevation of specific partial aspects of a theory into the basis of a new theoretical system. The main catchwords for which the new-school authors are known are in fact incomplete and unsatisfactory—preoedipality in Kleinian theory, or emphasis on the self in Kohutian—compared to their own more lasting contributions, which have often been considerable and significant. Thus, some of Klein's insights into early childhood, and her specific papers on envy or on the psychopathology of very disturbed states, or Kohut's early papers on narcissism and empathy, could have been added to the main body with more lasting profit than the more charismatic influence both exerted toward forming split-off schools, each diminishing rather than enhancing the total theory. Both would have been known in a less dazzling but more solid and enduring way.

While I am making a case for uniformity of theory, I unequivocally support independence and individuality as well. Every individual or individual group, small or large, is a composite of his, her, or its individual composite of characteristics or internal components. Nor are leaders more uniform or identical than their less visible colleagues. Moreover, the relations between leaders and their constituents are also individualistic, and vary from flexible to rigid, from democratic to autocratic, each with their own stamp. The only way to establish what kinds of relations these are or were would have been through firsthand knowledge and observations, which of course are as subjective as all other human observations or perceptions. And not all leaders of groups can be held responsible for the actions or beliefs of their disciples. From my own direct (but subjective) observations on some of these subjects, and close experiences with the individuals involved, I aver, for example, that Erik Erikson was limited in his agreement with the large separatist social school that claimed to develop under his views. He remained more in conflict between his original classical views and those professed by the "Eriksonian" school of psychology, than was the case for instance with Kohut, who was gratified by the growing distance established by his followers between self psychology and Freudian theory. I do not know first-hand the relationships between the early pioneers and their adherents, or whether there was any division between Jung or Adler, say, and their own "schools." Lacan, however, shortly before his death, in a puzzling and peculiar move, disavowed his many followers in the psychoanalytic world, leaving them bereft and confused. Every analyst deserves an individual hearing.

8

THE 1990s TO 2000: BREAKING THE BONDS AND HOLDING THE FORT

THE FINAL THEORETICAL PATH OF THE CENTURY

As psychoanalysis enters the last decade of the century, heading toward the new millennium, the theoretical course we are fashioning today will determine whether our young science will finish its first hundred years looking forward and up, or on its way to atrophy and survival only as an interesting relic. The present course is a compromise among several forces, intermingled and mixed together. One was the general mood of having outlived a jaded theory—conceived in another age, creative and compelling in its historical context, but hardly applicable now in the face of modern knowledge. Another contributing concept, of increasing interest inside psychoanalysis as well as outside of it, is that a qualitatively new level of neuroscientific explanation, more subject to verifiability and the laws of science, is slowly making psychological explanations appear less relevant. Psychoanalysis, which once sought confirmation in neurophysiology, is now being obscured by it instead as dreams, for example, are seen only as the product of reticular tract activity in the brain stem, not as repressed conflicts.

Paradoxically, intellectual and professional interest in the art and science of psychoanalysis are as lively as ever. The academic disciplines are aware of and responsive to psychoanalytic input, and the intellectual public is open to and eager for analytic explanations. There is still active interest in entering the field. New

York's Waldorf in December teemed with analysts, candidates, participants, and onlookers, and so have the recent Congresses in Barcelona and Santiago. Conversation, debate, inquiry are as animated as ever. Yet conflict and contradiction are visible. More than one institute has had years in which it has failed to register a full incoming class. Psychiatric residencies no longer produce more prospective analysts than neuroscientists. The general press is conspicuously negative toward analysis, writing as though its death knell has already sounded. Scorn and dismissal are particularly evident around the name of Freud. And as I have noted, at the last International Congress held in this country, in San Francisco (1995) in mid-decade, pluralism was celebrated, and alternative theories specifically called for from within the field itself.

Yet not all the emphasis and interest is on what has superseded Freud, and this adds still another level of contradiction. A small but solid segment in all professional meetings keeps its attention on the present state and endurance record of what came *with* Freud and his successors. Amid all the popularity of the competing theories, a significant number in our professional groups retain their affective acceptance of the nuclear building blocks of Freudian theory, and I think that this is true on some core level of most individual analysts as well. Object-relations theorists come to accept drives; interpersonalists do not easily eliminate awareness of defenses; analysts reconsider the role of unconscious anxiety. A strong contributor (Rodman 2001, personal communication) on the subject of Winnicott's history and role criticizes the statement of a colleague that Winnicott replaced Freud. The timelessness of basic theoretical contributions keeps the Freudian system of thought alive and active alongside other, newer additive discoveries.

AN ALTERNATIVE TO ALTERNATIVE THEORIES

There is in fact an alternative to alternative theories, and it has maintained its identity throughout this era of undulating changes. There is more than one answer to the question of one theory or many. Theoretical pluralism has been accepted as though unanimously, yet I myself had posed the same question on several occasions prior to Wallerstein's 1987 address, and each time offered the other answer: One. Throughout the changes of the last thirty years I have favored a unitary theory that is hospitable toward all new advances that are generally considered valid, while retaining previous discoveries that are not expendable and have endured. In a summing-up address to the Congress on how analysts work, I critiqued the excessive emphasis on transference in clinical work in a discussion of case material presented by Anne-Marie Sandler (Rangell 1984a, A.-M. Sandler 1983). I took the same stand, along with Stone, in a 1978 panel discussion in which Gill criticized Fenichel's classic 1940 monograph on technique for favoring defense at the expense of transference (Gill 1978, Panel 1978, Rangell 1980b, Stone 1981b). I also showed, in separate papers, how self (1982b) and object (1985) are both contained within total psychoanalytic theory in a more complete and unified way than they are in the separate theories of self and object. And in an all-day dialogue with Betty Joseph at the International Congress in Jerusalem (Panel 1977), I (1978) questioned the automatic interpretations of transference without clinical data pointing in that direction, as well as the interpretations of infantile mechanisms out of reach of the ego, and the attribution of motivations to the patient below the level of his defenses. Only the availability of a total theory provides and enables the balance necessary to take into account all relevant elements; this includes such matters as when to engage the patient and when to demur. In these views, I am joined by a good many close colleagues, and a significant number of others who express their agreement subtly and more privately.

TOTAL COMPOSITE PSYCHOANALYTIC THEORY

In the ongoing debate over "one theory or many," I favor one total, composite psychoanalytic theory, unified and cumulative:

total because it contains all nonexpendable elements, composite because it is a blend of the old and all valid new concepts and discoveries, and psychoanalytic as fulfilling the criteria for what is psychoanalysis. Every viable contribution made by alternative theories finds a home within this total composite theory. Under its embracing umbrella coexist drives and defense; id, ego, and superego; self and object; the intrapsychic and the interpersonal; the internal and external worlds. A theory like this, parsimonious yet complete, comprises a unitary theory of psychoanalysis.

I am not an "ego psychologist," although I am often automatically considered one. This widespread appellation is another of the common straw-men fallacies. I do not feel that there is a "drive" theory, or an "ego" theory. No theory of psychoanalysis, indeed no theory that purports to explain any human being, can rely on drives alone, or ego alone, or superego only, or the equivalents of these functions in other psychological systems of thought. I have said in many papers that I am an id-ego-superego-internal-external-psychoanalyst-psychosynthesist—"synthesist" because the purpose of psychoanalysis is not only to tease apart but also to put together. I have seen patients who had been subjects of analysis without synthesis. They were left in sorry states. I remember one candidate who was analyzed in a training analysis but never synthesized, or put back together again. I saw him regress from an integrated and successful individual with some encapsulated neurotic traits into a decompensated person in a chronic anxiety state that spilled over into social situations and limited his ordinary adaptedness for the remainder of his life.

REASON AND "THE FIELD" OF PSYCHOANALYSIS: THE PSYCHOANALYSIS OF PUBLIC OPINION

A theory can be unitary without being monolithic. Within a total composite theory, there are many principles of multiplicity, such as overdetermination, multiple function (Waelder 1936), and the multiple metapsychological points of view that Freud converged upon any single psychological phenomenon. The psycho-analytic field does not take to this reasoning easily, however. I am not referring to differences of opinion as to what is rational, but to what I consider a more serious disagreement, widely held, about whether or not the rational should prevail in psychoanaly-sis at all, or even be considered a guide. When I speak against the view, often quoted with fervor from Bion (1970), that an analyst should enter every hour without memory, desire, or understand-ing (which I hold to be both questionable technique and impos-sible of attainment) I am often met with an aggressive disdain of dismaying proportions. Yet although I know that while this popu-lar phrase is on a continuum with Freud's (1912) admonition to analysts not to be too taken with therapeutic zeal, still I believe that at some point a line of reasonableness and reality must be drawn.

At the opening session of the London Congress of 1975, in my dialogue with André Green on "Changes in Analytic Practice and Analytic Experience" (Rangell 1975b), Green (1975), in his cre-ative and imaginative way, emphasized the absence rather than the presence of the analyst, psychic and analytic space, the fear of nothingness, which he relates to the death instinct, and the dread and despair when there is no internal object, not even a bad one. Green (1973) had previously explicated Bion's admonition cited above, explaining that "All knowledge is a loss of truth" (p. 117) and quoting, along with these thoughts, Keats's "nega-tive capability . . . [the ability to be] without any irritable reach-ing after fact and reason" (p. 115). Reflecting on this line of thought, I countered with the reciprocal need to balance the focus on emptiness—to keep our sights on the *presence* of the analyst with all that this brings to the patient, positive and nega-tive, and on the occupants of psychic space, such as unconscious conflicts and defenses against drives. The seeking of reason need not be irritable. I felt the irritability of the audience at this ra-tional approach, however, and heard criticism explicitly later, from many to whom negative space had become the catchword of the moment.

It should be no surprise that psychoanalytic groups differ only in degree from other groups in their affective/cognitive ratios. Robert Stoller once spoke to me a bit apologetically when he found out that while a huge audience came to his session (with slides) on sexual deviations, my simultaneous meeting on a theoretical subject in a nearby room had been sparsely attended. Many psychoanalytic meetings and congresses favor the dramatic over the reasonable. Common human experience tells us that this is not surprising, and so do Freud's (1921) observations about group psychology.

Remarkable and important in the formation of a group, Freud pointed out, are the exaltation of emotion, the feeling of unlimited power, the contagiousness of both affects and thought, and the resulting tendency to uniformity among group members. Dissimilarities among individuals are deemphasized, and the unconscious foundations present in all are exposed and come to the fore. "What is heterogeneous is submerged in what is homogeneous" (1921, p. 74). Affectivity is heightened, judgment and rational processes impaired. A group is impulsive, suggestible, changeable, irritable. It is open to influence, subject to the magical power of words, lacks critical faculty, and feels that nothing is improbable. "Groups have never thirsted after truth" (1921, p. 80). These descriptions are of course extreme, to make their points; a complementary series is undoubtedly operative here, too, and there are groups (usually the smaller ones) that can operate with unimpaired, sometimes even enhanced, rationality.

Watergate and other galvanizing political events in modern American life have led me to an interest in the psychology of public opinion (2003), which I consider a major force in determining and guiding the history of groups. I feel that this has been an underattended area for applied dynamic understanding. Since all life is group life, the psychology of the group is a major determiner of the direction of the history of the planet. This is especially so with the increasing complexity of human living, the burgeoning world population, and the explosions of modern technology. The psychology of groups, therefore, from small and informal ones to nations, is a most important area for applied psychoanalytic insights.

Another source of data fueling my sustained interest in the psychology of public opinion has been my ongoing participant observations of the psychoanalytic body. I regard this special group, although it may rightly be considered a more insight-directed assemblage of individuals than most, as still a litmus test of "groupthink." To maintain clarity on the recurring issues involved requires a careful distinction between the affective, which is characterized by moods and emotions, and the irrational, which is a cognitive phenomenon. While the subject matter of analysis includes both the affective and the irrational, as Fenichel (1945, p. 4) pointed out, the *method* of psychoanalysis employs the affective (and cognitive) but not the irrational. From Robert Fliess (1942) in his discussion of the metapsychology of the analyst, to Isakower (1957) on the analytic instrument, to the modern writers who include the subjective participation of the analyst in analysis of the affective life of the patient—all of whom include the analyst's affects, unconscious and conscious, in the conduct of an analysis—analysts who embrace the affective reverberations of the analyst in the analytic process stop short of crossing the line into the irrational. The goal of exposing primary process in the patient does not replace the enduring role of secondary process thinking and feeling in both the patient and the analyst. The focus of analysis on the unconscious does not eliminate the conscious, nor does the uncommon sense of the unconscious replace the common sense of everyday life. As Fenichel (1941) also states, treatment is through the rational ego; therefore technique "must be arranged according to rational criteria" (p. 13).

It is not rare in analysis for a metaphor to be taken as literal. Had Bion spoken against bringing bias to an hour, rather than recommending against "memory and understanding," his divisive influence would have been less. He would have been remembered, more solidly if more modestly, for his contributions to the psychoanalytic understanding of group behavior, and for his clinical emphasis on observation over imposition of theory, even without the Greek symbols explaining the associative process or his more dubious and mythical admonishments to analysts to abandon their cognitive functions.

A reverse injustice to ideas may occur where the literal becomes metaphoric, probably because of doubts about convictions regarding early mentation. Gill began what turned out to be an extended and valuable correspondence with me (Gill and Rangell 1990–1992, personal communication) when he wrote to object that in my paper on castration (1991) I should have said that the castration complex is a metaphor. Castration anxiety is, of course, widely used as a metaphor, often stretching the point beyond justification. But in the context of my paper, I was referring to the psychoanalytic discovery—the major flash of insight—that castration anxiety is an entity, and a vital one, in unconscious fantasy, and hence in psychic reality. Children, at a certain age, do have a literal fear of castration as punishment for specific forbidden wishes; this is a childhood concept, however irrational, that often survives into adult unconscious life. To miss or avoid this is to overlook an important discovery, and to leave some analyses incomplete.

The border between thing and metaphor cannot be taken lightly, and the analyst has a responsibility to try, at least, to make a distinction between the two. This may be the most "psychoanalytic" contribution of an analysis. How much does the analyst "really mean" what he tells the patient? What is the patient to take away with him? One can err, or be incomplete, or deficient, in either direction, overstressing or underappreciating either the literal or metaphoric. Hostile impulses do not mean wishing to murder. But a fear of being alone can literally mean, in the unconscious, a fantasy and fear of being abandoned by one's mother.

CHANGES IN THE ROLE OF THE ANALYST: A PROCESS UNDER STRAIN

The 1990s strained the rational spine of the analytic process further than ever—to the breaking point, it seemed at times. Along with the fallacious and less-than-rational reasoning I have been describing came a steady, although quiet, change in the very aim and methodology of psychoanalysis. At the end of the first century of their science, a predominant majority of psychoanalysts joined in a reconsideration of the role of the analyst in conducting an analysis, casting doubt both on his possession of a special body of knowledge and on the validity of his accustomed technical stance toward a patient in the service of analytic goals.

This development happened both gradually and in spurts. A thoughtful new proposition would be grasped and lurched forward to an extremist position, and then often tugged the other way in a rescuing pullback. The too-brightly-lit transference is balanced a bit by a beginning look into the interior of the analyst, and countertransference is born. Paula Heimann (1956) establishes this germ of an idea among the Kleinians of Great Britain, and Racker (1968) advances and develops this insight in South America. Both introduce valuable guiding ideas, which they incorporate into general theory. Gill (1979a, 1982a,b), after his excessive emphasis on the transference at the expense of other elements in an analysis, then does the same thing with countertransference: the initial reasonable contributions on countertransference are extended to the point of hypertrophy, and are increasingly brought to the same level of exclusivity as he originally prescribed for the transference.

Gill (1994a) continues the path away from the original view of the psychoanalytic situation toward his two-person psychology, and his final social-constructivist view. The input of the analyst is gradually equated with that of the patient. While in his original work on countertransference Gill encourages the analyst to acknowledge his mistakes—an admonition with which no analyst can disagree—the analyst now has to be aware of his equal role in coconstructing the material of each hour and of the analysis. Gabbard (1995), in a review of the subject, describes countertransference (converging with an increased development of projective identification and enactment) as an emerging area of the common ground that supposedly binds clinical theories together.

Because of such views the scientific life of the psychoanalyst has undergone a metamorphosis; his professional role, tools, and stance have changed into something quite different from the ones introduced a century ago. Some of these changes are gains, some losses. They all must be evaluated according to a comment of Waelder's (1967) that I am perhaps too fond of repeating—"Scientific and technological progress has had victims as well as beneficiaries" (p. 2).

KNOWLEDGE AND AUTHORITY

On the strength of this questioning attitude in the psychoanalytic air, an entire issue of *Psychoanalytic Quarterly* in 1996 was devoted to the subject of "knowledge and authority in the psychoanalytic relationship." Eliciting opinions from across the theoretical spectrum, the editor, Owen Renik (1996), succeeded in sampling the views of a dozen leading analysts on this basic underpinning of analytic thought. Consonant with Wallerstein's conclusion about the equal status of all extant theories, a majority attitude emerges from this chosen group, that the idea of any special psychoanalytic knowledge on the part of the analyst is elusive and questionable. The same holds true for the idea that there is any justified or conclusive position of authority from which the analyst can legitimately impart understanding to the patient.

The contributors reflect, taking off from Renik's suggestive question: "What kinds of expertise can legitimately be claimed by analyst and analysand?" I will capsulize these representative thoughts and views. They are a reliable cross-section of current opinion.

Bollas (1996) is impressed by the oedipal nature of the analytic process itself, and how subjectively each analyst plays either a maternal or paternal role: Kohut the former, Kernberg the latter. Freud himself, in various examples, yields to the knowledge of the patient, with whom he collaborates. Many of his interventions and insights come from his own unconscious. Each participant makes his own truth.

Brenner (1996), one of a minority, predictably holds up the traditional view. The analyst possesses a specific body of knowledge—of the causes of psychopathology—and this is his specific contribution over and above what the patient knows. He uses the authority that stems from this for the benefit of the patient, in keeping with the patient's reason for coming to him. The analyst can never be certain of the validity of what he imparts, but he uses his tools to the best of his ability, by the psychoanalytic method, which is also part of his knowledge. Authority does not mean authoritarianism.

To Chodorow (1996), structural thinking is on the wane. The analytic encounter is mutually constructed rather than intrapsychic. Emphasis on the past reflects a "pretheoretical, taken-for-granted belief" (p. 34) that is intrinsic to Western culture. The Hindu and Buddhist conceptions of life include previous and future lives. The past is a narrative, Chodorow says, quoting Schafer, and the unconscious is of both past and present, quoting the Sandlers. Transference comes equally from present and past. We should be wary when imagining objectivized universal childhood stages or drives that determine later experience. The human capacity to create interpersonal meanings virtually from birth promises more consistency in our understanding of the analytic encounter than present developmental and structural concepts.

Elliott and Spezzano (1996) describe current psychoanalytic debates against a background of modern and postmodern revisionism and deconstructionism, and as part of it. Defining modernism as Kant's "reason"—"that precious child of the Enlightenment"—and the postmodern as the reaction against this toward the relative and uncertain, these authors provide a useful philosophical and epistemological lesson on the place of psychoanalysis in this intellectual sequence. Stressing the ambiguity in every aspect of analysis, they argue that it is better to allow confusion to reign than to aim for universal truths or uniformity. But within their survey and arguments is also the view that "Acknowledging . . .

the plausibility of multiple perspectives does not consign one to accepting that any interpretation is as good as any other" (p. 61). I would say the same about theories.

Hanly (1996) approaches the challenge of the subject by asking whether there is a difference between masculine and feminine authority, and whether this might play a part, for example, in influencing affiliation to Freud as compared to Klein. He then offers a detailed reformulation of the course of the Oedipus complex. Equalizing the formation of the superego in the two sexes, he shows how boy and girl both need to temper their rivalry with the same-sex parent by love and identification and by sublimation of their heterosexual incestuous wishes toward the parent of the opposite sex. Through these reflections, Hanly counters some of Freud's concepts on the feminine superego and on differences between maternal and paternal authority. Rather than a fallacious "argument with respect to authority," he argues, analysis depends upon "the authority of fact and knowledge." When we exploit our transferential parental authority as a substitute for the authority of fact, we "betray the patient's trust." Hanly and Bollas, both discussing aspects of the Oedipus complex, end up in different places with respect to facts and objectivity, Hanly joining more with Brenner in basic concepts.

Hoffman (1996), who with Gill worked out the "social constructivist" position in its most articulated form, emphasizes that a two-sided relationship shapes the analytic encounter. Hoffman points out the inevitable presence of suggestion, the "myth of analytic neutrality," the benign aspect of our interpersonal involvement, the universal "context of ignorance of contexts," the analyst's position "in the middle of the action" as the patient tries to decide what to make of his life. Freud struggled with the educative functions of the analyst. Analysis is a moral enterprise, but analysts need to examine how much they impose the moral value of conformity to social expectations. Hoffman's comprehensive summary, describing the history of the psychoanalytic method, traces the evolution of the psychoanalytic method from a presumed solitary reflection to a subtle, intimate, interrelational activity between the two participants.

Kernberg (1996), who as much as anyone has flexibly used parameters as appropriate extensions of analytic treatment in his work with so-called borderline patients, holds firmly to core principles in assessing present trends in overall psychoanalysis. While recognizing the dangers of authoritarianism and loss of empathy, he emphasizes the value of technical neutrality as the best way to protect the autonomy and freedom of the patient, and eventually to help the analyst integrate the dominant, albeit selected, "facts" of the analytic interchange. From clinical experience with very disturbed patients, Kernberg points to the dangers of exclusive reliance on the here-and-now, of avoiding negative transferences and the analysis of aggression, and of imposing a "conventional" frame on the patient's experience. Enduring theoretical and technical values, with openness to the uncertainties and unknowables of each analytic hour, are the hallmarks of analytic treatment.

Mayer (1996) joins Chodorow in her distrust of traditional ideas about psychoanalytic knowledge and authority. Citing a long list of analysts who feel that familiar theories have derailed us, Mayer echoes Bollas's view that "official psychoanalytic decoding is over," and Stolorow's that "analytic neutrality is a defensively grandiose illusion." She describes the current travails of psychoanalysis as parallel to the revolution in physics; indeed, she points out, a sea change in our scientific world view has put all scientific knowledge "up for grabs" (p. 162), including contemporary theories of psychoanalytic technique. Citing a clinical experience with an analyst in which the crossing of a sexual boundary with a patient helped the analyst understand the patient better and made the patient feel better understood, Mayer goes on to suggest that just as analysis enlarged our understanding of the irrational, changes in our concepts of rationality itself may be in order. Some analysts find certain mystical experiences in Tibetan Buddhism or other Eastern religions provocatively interesting, and that they may help to explain some aspects of psychoanalytic intuition.

McLaughlin (1996), a pioneer investigator of the more subtle aspects of the analytic relationship, examines the power of the analyst vis-à-vis the patient. He carefully dissects issues of influence, distinguishing suggestion, persuasion, authority, and power so as to prevent excesses and to enhance the mutative analytic work. There is no all or none. The useful intermediate band is "the quiet, insensible or gradual exertion of power, often arising from strength of intellect, force of character, eminent position and the like" (p. 202).

Schafer (1996) explores the difficulties of arriving at clinical evidence in the complex interplay of transference and countertransference, emphasizing the ambiguity that is always present. Knowledge, in this context, most often represents new compromise formations based on power relationships between the two participants, one of whom is submissively compliant to the other in the analytic frame. Narrative pluralism is Schafer's belief and perspective. Analysts build upon the metanarratives of their particular theories, undermining their analytic authority. Schafer feels that the so-called school of logical positivism, empiricism, realism, or objectivism, held by those who emphasize rationality, clinical facts, and historical truth, has lost its philosophic following in the present world of critical thought. Psychoanalysis is "an exploratory discipline" (p. 252) rather than a science; the "unsettledness" to which Schafer's views lead him he finds welcome, and intrinsic to the nature of the psychoanalytic enterprise.

In a final overview of the entire Journal issue, Friedman (1996) ties the papers together. In his well-exercised role as a final arbiter, he finds a nucleus of truth in each presentation, but then distinguishes properly between authority based on role and that stemming from knowledge. While the "knowledge type of authority" (p. 264) is the base of our profession, it should be used skillfully and with discretion, and not conveyed to the patient by the authority of relationship.

This is a sampling of the theoretical views of a group of articulate and literate psychoanalysts at the midpoint of the last decade of the psychoanalytic century. They run a gamut: for some analysts, the old endures; for some, everything has changed. For the rest, many original formulations have withstood the test of time, yet a continuous process of modification has produced significant changes in original thoughts and practice. The latter view is most in accord with my own, avoiding as it does the common current fallacy of stressing, usually with a good deal of stridency, the need to be open to new ideas while overlooking the equal necessity to be open to earlier ones that have proven enduring. In a sense, the issue is a modern extension of the question Freud faced at the beginning of the century: whether to give up the seduction theory when he discovered unconscious fantasy, or to add the new to the old.

In keeping again with the theory of complementarity, it is not only possible but necessary to combine the rationality of the modern (and what preceded it) with the freedom and ambiguity of the postmodern within psychoanalytic theory and technical procedure. The positive and empirical have as much of a place in mental life as the subjective and relativistic; clinical facts as much as their varied derivatives. To rigidify at either pole invites stagnation and limitation. For me, it is as impossible to imagine how psychoanalysis can exist without psychoanalytic knowledge and the professional authority that comes with it, as it is to support the rigidification of original discoveries without subjecting them continuously to the process of verification and modification that comes with further experience.

ENACTMENT

These questions of analytic knowledge and authority are part of a rethinking, retesting, and revalidating of ongoing working analytic concepts as they have developed over a century of psychoanalytic practice and theory. Both the theory and its derivative technical procedures are under widespread and necessary scrutiny. Careful monitoring and a continuous need for confirmation and validation are called for and useful, considering the increasingly apparent susceptibility of the analytic position to abuse. The "impossible profession" has become even more impossible since Freud

(1937) named it so, with longer analyses, more ambitious goals of character transformations, and, I add, an increasingly subtle mixture of moral as well as neurotic compromise formations.

In practice, however, the process by which this questioning is implemented requires attention and sometimes modification. Reexaminations of theory and technique tend to follow a common course: a justified inquiry is followed by such exaggerated "correction" that the result is regression rather than progress. An example of this is another phenomenon of the nineties that, along with the cynical doubting of psychoanalytic knowledge, has enjoyed a meteoric rise in popularity and public interest. It arose reasonably out of specific clinical circumstances, but then gained momentum as a general—and thereby questionable—change in methodology. I am referring to the new technical concept of "enactment."

Analysis, which is conducted by verbal interchange, has frequent impasses. There have always been efforts to understand these periods, and to convert them to analytic usefulness. Of course they tax the comfort and patience of analysts (and patients), and they also tend to be accompanied by (among other things) frustration on both sides. Creative solutions are legion; ways to increase spontaneity have always been sought, and are always in order. A call went out from imaginative and intuitive analysts: to overcome impasses otherwise impervious, "do first, think later." Take a chance, trust your (analytic) instincts; you will probably be right. Over time, reported individual instances of such clinical maneuvers became more numerous. When a word was attached to them, and experiences were shared and discussed of this occasional means of acting in a difficult clinical situation, an exception was gradually elevated to a primary tool, and became a more common occurrence. Group contagion, which has resulted in exaggerations of new methods since the inception of psychoanalysis, then took it up, making enactment our latest buzzword, and soon part of the more "liberal" segment of analytic technique.

To enact, etymologically "to act outwardly," from the start was distinguished from the older "acting-out" or "acting-in," which had accrued to themselves pejorative connotations. Actually, I was part of a panel at the International Congress in Copenhagen, in 1967, in which three participants, Anna Freud (1968), Vanggaard (1968), and I (1968c), presented work that sought to remove such stigmatized implications; we described clinical actions, physical or behavioral, inside or outside the analysis, as grist for the analytic mill. In the case of enactments, however, the idea went further. Actions, not words, became the preferred mode of communication, and were considered more spontaneous, real, authentic— somehow more analytically meaningful. Words were felt to be more formal, more controlled, and more easily used in the service of defense. In all such generalizations, there is some truth. Analysts can reverberate to the claims made without much difficulty. Certainly a touch on the arm of the patient as he or she leaves can at times be a more effective communication than a comment. Nevertheless, although this may at times lead to limitations and obstacles, it was a method of *verbal* communication that evolved over time as the hallmark of the psychoanalytic exchange.

For many analysts to whom enactment has become a central technical construct, action has come to rival, if not replace, the centrality of verbal interchange between the two participants in the analytic dyad. The long strain of the silent but thoughtful analyst has been suddenly relieved by a liberating new avenue of expression. Nonverbal communication has always played a role alongside verbal content, but with this new carte blanche an inevitable occasional action, or acting-in, within the analytic exchange by both patient and analyst has hypertrophied into an expectable norm. Analysts admittedly work with their affective instruments. Now they can speak on impulse; they can act first and catch up with their thoughts later. We learn what we think from what we say or do.

As always, clinical experience in this new direction was interesting at first, applied as it was to impasses where many analysts would welcome creative parameters to break a stalemate. Authors such as Chused (1991), Jacobs (1986, 1991), and McLaughlin (1991, 1995) contributed the initial ideas, at first to appropriate material that rightly elicited a positive and appreciative interest. And Busch

(1995a) pointed out, in an inescapable way, how thoughts and action, as the words and the music, always are together in communicating a message, whether in life or in analysis. Words and thoughts are in themselves actions, as Schafer, Busch, and I agree. But, as happens often when innovations are directed to groups for approval, a momentum results, and excesses are quick to follow. As Glover (1949) had warned decades before about the tendency to psychoanalytic fads (he was reacting at that time to the excitement over ego identity), enactment now became a method of the moment, frequently presented and discussed at meetings from local to national. Not as a controlled advance, but driven by the same restlessness and discontent that has repeatedly fueled the cycle of extremism and reversal that I am describing, came the recommendation for enactment as a central feature of psychoanalytic technique.

This cycle runs in an intense but limited sequence. It has no geographical limits. In France, the phenomenon of learning from one's actions is subsumed under a broader concept of *nachträglichkeit* (Faimberg 1997), the retroactive assignment of meaning. During the heyday of the new enactment mode I was on two panels. One (Panel 1995) at the 40th anniversary celebration of the Southern California Institute, had enactment for its chosen theme, and Jacobs (1995), Natterson and Friedman (1995), Spezzano (1995), and I (1997b) presented. In this discussion, widespread use of the technique of enactment seemed to be closely intermingled with the two-person, social constructivist view. More recently, I wrote an invited post-hoc discussion of a previous well-conducted symposium (Panel 1999) on enactment, in which many of the main contributors on the subject presented their views, among them Chused (1999), Renik (1999), Ellman (1999), and Rothstein (1999) (even though this latter author had described himself to me as "a Brennerian"). Limitations of and objections to the concept were raised by Furer (1999), Jacobs (1999), and myself (1999a). By this point in the cycle, retreat was in order, and some were now downplaying the importance of the method. As often happens, its originators had backed up to varying degrees, and were now concurring that limits are necessary. Chused, seeing how far some had come, now declared herself a classical analyst relative to the others. McLaughlin (1996) also promulgated a more balanced and reasonable position.

The theoretical reasoning behind this trend counters the general understanding and the goals of analysis. In normal living, thought is experimental action. In this "postmodern" analytic turn, action becomes experimental thought. Intrapsychic segments of mental activity that are protective in human life, presenting a cautionary preview to the ego before external action is taken, are bypassed. While freedom and spontaneity are desirable goals, the crossing of the line to action, in and out of analysis, is hardly a therapeutic road. Certainly as a model for behavior, this procedure cannot hold. It is better to expose and analyze primary process than to externalize it as a desired mode of behavior.

INTERSUBJECTIVITY

In keeping with these changes, the 1990s also saw the rise of a number of views of psychoanalysis that fell under the general rubric of "intersubjectivity." Since this word captured what all the other movements were aiming to highlight as the defining direction of the new psychoanalysis, it became a popular school under which many of the others were willing to be included. As attention shifted from transference to countertransference in the analytic method, so more and more did the equality and mutuality of the two participants move into the center of the picture. And since it was in the subjectivity of the patient that his conflicts resided, the mutuality of the interchange required, according to some, that the subjectivity of the analyst come equally into focus. While the subjective and affective participation of the analyst had always been included as an integral part of the analytic instrument (although in a limited, patient-centered context), this aspect now acquired a special valence, and joined the other theoretical/technical movements that had accelerated through group contagion.

An extension of this subject that captured much attention was Renik's (1995) introduction of the issue of self-disclosure into the larger field of intersubjectivity. Noting the analyst's "irreducible subjectivity," which I don't question, Renik examined the pitfalls of the concept of analytic anonymity, its impossibility of achievement, and how its limitations should be counteracted. Again, there followed a period of excited use of self-disclosure that many eventually felt to have become excessive; after this more restraint was counseled. The same formula ultimately devolved as had in the case of enactment: that the exchange ideally should be guided by what is in the best interest of the patient.

As psychoanalysis distilled into a diverse group of theories—enactment, intersubjectivity, self-disclosure, and self psychology—the advancing concept of mutuality went so far that at times it seemed that the person no longer existed, only the pair. In the 40th anniversary enactment panel (1995) discussed above, as far as Spezzano or Natterson and Friedman were concerned, all roads led to fusion of self and object. There was never one person or, in the analytic dyad, never a patient alone, but always a fused patient–analyst unit. There was only the two-person, interacting pair, which seemed to approach the Kohutian conception of the selfobject, or the Kleinian one of continuing projective identification. I took issue with this at the time, stating the obvious: that there is a self or person separate from the object. Narcissism, which in general usage I feel has been too widely applied, is in the present instance overlooked. Normal narcissism, the cathexis of the self, is here invisible, as is the self along with it, in these formulations of "only the pair." Mahler's (1972; Mahler and Furer 1968, Mahler et al. 1975) separation-individuation phase seems to have lost its place, not only in psychoanalytic theory but also as her crucial insight and description of that stage in the developmental process reflects and represents life.

This postmodern focus on the pair in psychoanalysis is popular for two reasons. It reflects current sociopolitical concerns about fairness and equality, and since it addresses self and object equally it appeals to both major relational schools. The move from countertransference to coconstruction and a social-constructivist two-person psychology was congruent with the assignment of equal valence to the analyst's and patient's subjectivities. Every movement of theory from intrapsychic to interpersonal, objective to subjective, cognitive to affective, facilitated the inclusive formulation of "intersubjectivity." Yet each of the above pairs of "polarities" might have been more usefully conceived theoretically, and better served in practice, as a complementary series, with the two poles of each pair contributing in varying balances at different times and place. Every analysis is intersubjective, but the roles of each pole on each pair vary with each analysis and at each moment within every analysis.

The fusion of the patient–analyst pair has occurred gradually, but there have been discernible nodal points in that development. The concept that a transference interpretation is the only mutative interpretation, which began with Strachey's (1934) seminal paper, was received with a remarkable universality. This view of the centrality of the patient–analyst pair was taken up energetically by the Kleinians and extended by the object-relationists. It made its way into American ego psychology with Gill's (1982a,b) influential emphasis on the transference and the here-and-now, as opposed to reconstruction and the past. But even more important than the superordinacy that Gill accorded to transference was his quiet change in the definition of transference itself. I first became aware of this at the "Classics Revisited" panel (1978) of the American, at which Fenichel's (1941) monograph on technique was the subject. Gill (1978) disagreed with Fenichel's "defenses first" rule, substituting transference for defenses. Transference, as Gill went on to define it on that occasion, was comprised of *all* feelings directed to the analyst by the patient, not just those from the repressed past.

This change, which I saw as a momentous one, had a strange history. It was virtually never discussed; it was just put into effect. In symmetry with Gill's formulation, countertransference soon came to be seen as its reciprocal: that is, all of the affective reactions of the analyst to the patient, not just the displaced ones from his own past. These changes, with their increasing focus on the current affects of the analytic pair and their relegation to a secondary position of insight into the patient's past, seemed to me to alter completely the method and goal of psychoanalysis.

One polarization that has crystallized out of today's diversity is the one between "interactional" vs. "interpretative" analysis. The former is a composite of the empathic, self- and object-oriented, intersubjective, relational, enactment, and therapeutic immersion methods—all of them centering on relations and interactions. It is considered the "modern, liberal" theory and method, as contrasted with "classical, conservative" analysis, oriented toward objectivity and interpretation. Other political terms are freely used in this context as well, and often pejoratively; Wallerstein (1991), defending the equality of multiple theories, characterized the unified total composite theory as "imperialism by assertion" (p. 288). Yet does not his declaration of equality of theories qualify at least as well for that description, having come about as it did as if by fiat?

The processes of democracy and science are neither interchangeable nor necessarily reciprocal. Popularity has never been the criterion for validation in psychoanalysis. And while the celebration of diversity is appropriate in social affairs, it is parsimonious yet comprehensive explanation that is the goal in scientific understanding, from Einstein in the physical universe to Freud in the psychological one. Science can explain democracy, but democratic processes do not always further science. Discoveries are seldom made by committee; politics can derail science. It would be better to include knowingly a study of political processes within psychoanalysis, than to allow political process to remain invisible and so influence us without our knowledge.

THE ALTERED GROUND

The alternative theories and dichotomies that have occupied the theoretical stage in recent years have one factor in common. They have all questioned long-standing assumptions and theoretical guides, and appear to have superseded them. The ground behind the theory of psychoanalysis has been significantly altered. Historical truth has given way to narrative truth, and reconstruction of the past to the here-and-now. Fantasy has expanded until it excludes reality, and the analyst has been assigned an equal role with the patient in shaping the transference. Countertransference is now as much a subject of the analysis as the transference. The roles of patient and analyst become less and less distinguishable. The conflicts and neuroses on both sides of the couch are thought to require equal attention. In all of these situations the operation of a complementary series has been eschewed in favor of polar positions. It is more realistic to recognize that each of these pairs represents both a set of polar extremes and the intermediate zone that lies between them.

The trend toward equality and democracy in social life can be a distorting force when applied to a scientific field. Political objections to the asymmetry that the goals and methods of analysis impose on the participants has led to questions about whether the analyst has any special knowledge at all, or any "authority" to make an interpretation.

I see this phenomenon as an instance of nihilism sheltering under the larger umbrella of "postmodern" intellectual thought; in psychoanalysis it takes the form of a cluster of fallacies kept in force by the contagious quality of group life. Recent developments have involved a steady progression away from specificity, reality (both psychic and material), delineable repressed contents, circumscribed etiologic agents, definitive psychic traumata, clinical facts, particularized individual development, concrete elements or forces, defined history. The result of this cumulative ambiguity is a skeptical attitude toward *any* search for truth, events, information, or facts, and a compensatory overriding focus on the analytic process itself and certain elements within it. The moral supremacy of democracy is imposed upon the analytic exchange, as it has been applied to science and art in general, as part of a wider postmodern revisionism in intellectual and cultural life. In psychoanalysis, this trend applies more broadly than to the specific question of the analyst's authority. I feel that the logic and veracity of the larger issue, the general postmodern reversal of the values, mores, method, and goals of psychoanalysis, is more important and more needful of examination than any of the various dichotomous debates under its banner. If these were seen in their longitudinal context many of the specific issues would dissolve of their own emptiness, without storm or attention, much as the loud and powerful Soviet Union has faded away.

IN THE MEANTIME, STEADY ADVANCES

In the meantime, even as a diverse and discordant array of theories has appeared over the last few decades, basic psychoanalytic theory and practice have seen a slower but steady stream of expansions, refinements, and modifications. These have deepened the roots and pruned some of the limbs of the psychoanalytic tree of knowledge. They have been more quietly absorbed, but proved more enduring, than many more drastic and stridently proclaimed changes. Many of these contributions lie explicitly within a total theory, as do Gray's work and Busch's on close ego operations, Arlow's on unconscious fantasies or the genesis of interpretations, Brenner's on conflicts and compromise formations, Stone's on the widening scope of analysis, Blum's on preserving the goal and method of reconstruction, and mine on unconscious ego–superego conflicts. Contributions of many other authors either add to existing theory implicitly, or, while ostensibly writing on wider subjects, add concepts that nonetheless relate automatically to a continuing total theory.

In my six decades of activity in the psychoanalytic world, I have acquired the impression that in almost every organized analytic group, inside or outside of the American and the International, there are a number of members who live, either overtly or covertly, in kinship and affinity with what I (1987) consider the core tenets of psychoanalysis: the need to look to intrapsychic conflict for explanations; the need for a sufficiently neutral and objective position to be able to detect such conflict; and the need for a relationship of sufficient mutual trust between the two participants that the analyst can convey such insights usefully to the patient. Many groups pride themselves in being able to point to such a core group, however small, through which they can retain the name "Freudian." I also believe that a significant number of more "liberal" analysts retain enough of these attributes in their professional ego-ideal that essentially they practice as do more traditional analysts, whatever they may call themselves. Operationally, these two segments of the psychoanalytic population augment each other, providing in a large number of practitioners both the necessary objective stance and the warmth needed to go with it. Each individual analyst has his own combination of these attributes.

Although the long era of alternative theories may have distracted us from the main line of psychoanalytic theory development over the last quarter-century, the growth of that main line has never been extinguished. While relatively unheralded by group enthusiasms or even public backing, theoretical thought and clinical research that furthered the deflected theoretical mainstream have continued steadily to this day. The compact nucleus once exemplified by Anna Freud, Hartmann, Rapaport, and Fenichel has been constantly renewed by Stone, Greenacre, Mahler, Arlow, Brenner, Gray, Blum, Richards, Boesky, Busch, and now many younger contributors, all refinding, refining, and advancing the central line of development.

MY OUTLOOKS: SOME SOCIAL EXTENSIONS OF PSYCHOANALYTIC THEORY

Since I am presenting my own odyssey through these scientific waters, I want to describe my own activities, interests, and reflections during these last conflictful decades. I have made one self-imposed choice repeatedly during this era of scientific change:

to remain outside of affectively based group movements, which I feel threaten to swallow up and negate the achievements of a century of scientific goals and methods. Pressures for political correctness, which in our field may hide under psychoanalytic correctness, have accompanied the current alternative theories as much as pressures to conform may have accompanied the "old establishment."

Here are a few casual observations along this line, looking at some of today's key words. One: I often do not agree with the diagnoses of "borderline" or "more disturbed" that are so common these days in presented cases. When I have had the opportunity to see such patients bearing such diagnoses myself, they have mostly seemed to me to be mixed character neuroses. A second popular concept from which I keep a distance is the superordinate role of narcissism; I consider narcissism to be on a par with anxiety in psychopathology. "The culture of narcissism" (Lasch 1979), which for a few years excited a population sensitized by psychoanalytic concepts, has not replaced the "age of anxiety." Anxiety is a property of every age. So are narcissistic conflicts. Another: I cannot grant possession of the mutative function exclusively to transference interpretations, as originally enunciated by Strachey. Although his view quickly garnered almost automatic approval, and has been the politically correct one in clinical discussion since then, I feel that devotion to this idea has reached obsessive and inappropriate proportions. I attend as much to the original neurosis as to the transference neurosis, and direct at least equal analytic and interpretative work to the neurosis with which the patient presented, and which he retains until the multilayered analytic work influences it toward reversal. Finally, as I have indicated throughout this work, I do not agree with the trend toward symmetry of the two participants in the psychoanalytic process. The analyst and the patient have two distinctly different roles.

The subjects that have occupied my own attention over the last three decades reflect these concerns. Such revisions as Holt's (1989) *Freud Reappraised* are commonly reevaluations in the negative sense and concentrate on Freud's limitations. In contrast, I feel that some of my contributions, and those of many others in a similar positive vein, can be thought of as "Freud Furthered." I have worked to advance the theory of anxiety, of the unconscious decision-making process, and of the psychopathology of moral conflicts. I have extended these theoretical interests to an applied psychoanalytic interest in the psychology of political processes and the everyday and every-era workings of the psychology of public opinion (1996, 2003). These latter are manifestations of depth psychology, and as such are as relevant to psychoanalytic science as they are of interest in more superficial studies of social life. Psychoanalytic group political life is not excluded from psychoanalytic attempts to understand.

While concern with moral conflicts (as distinct from neurotic ones) is relevant in analytic work in general, it is indispensable in training analyses, in which the life behavior of future analysts is greatly determined. Moral conflicts, as instinctual ones, must be treated analytically, not moralistically—that is, by analysis of superego conflict and functioning, not by the imposition of one's own values and preferences. A special task exists in this area, for the analyst must separate his own tastes, ambitions, and ideals, and also his theoretical views, from the patient's and from his institution's. Here I underscore Freud's (1940) admonition against the analyst's temptation "to create men in his own image" (p. 175). In view of the long years of training, it is well to be aware of the danger of turning out analytic clones.

I also have an interest in an area of human behavior—more exactly, of humanness—that exists in the gray areas between psychic systems, and over which ego surveillance and control is only partial. The area of sincerity and its lack, and the surrounding affective/cognitive states, are an increasingly important aspect of human feeling and acting, although they remain far outside of psychoanalytic reach or interest. I am referring to the distances between what a person says and what he thinks or feels; between what he thinks and feels and what he does; between what he thinks or feels and what he knows is right. These gulfs, which exist and operate to various degrees and at various levels of consciousness within every individual, color and characterize every interpersonal exchange, and, at both private and public levels, shape the social fabric of our lives. They are intrinsic to our every conversation. These are interests of mine over the long period; they also indicate the reach of which I consider psychoanalysis to be capable.

The "true and false selves" of Winnicott (1958) relate to this subject. In my own journey into this unusual but challenging area of applied analysis, I (2000a,b) have focused psychoanalytic interest on the centrality of these aspects of truth and falsehood in recent political life. I have studied the trait of hypocrisy, both when this came into public prominence in the intimate life of an American president, and in the procedure by Congress to impeach him and the intense contradictory affective reactions that this evoked in the government, in the press, and in the public. There is no lack of interesting incidents along these lines. Even as I write, the historic presidential election of the year 2000 has already superseded the impeachment of the year before, and has filled the news with evidence that at least half of the American population considers hypocrisy to be a dominant operating force at the highest judicial levels of the land. Psychoanalytic understanding can be of aid even in such momentous events.

In a paper delivered for the centennial of the University of Chicago (1992), I dealt with the psychology of public opinion and political process over the last half century, touching upon such phenomena as McCarthy, Watergate, the Hill-Thomas Senate hearings, the Iran-Contra episode, the Rodney King case, the Smith and Tyson rape trials, the L.A. riots, the O.J. Simpson case, and, every four years, the role of the electorate in the election of a president. In all such charged public events, one shining trait and capacity presents itself as worthy of great interest. It too relates to this diffuse segment of character that, I believe, involves all three psychic systems, and we call it *courage*—the will and ability to act against, in the presence of, or after having overcome, anxiety or danger. Psychoanalysis has more to say than it has even begun to know.

NO NEW PARADIGMS

While I wish to avoid the imperialism attributed by Wallerstein (2000) to American ego psychology, I must say that I do not believe that there has been any new paradigm for a total theory of the mind since the advent of psychoanalysis. The simplistic use of Thomas Kuhn's (1970) thinking to claim otherwise supports the view that the recent movement of psychoanalytic theory has been irregular and capricious. Reviewing Kuhn's work shortly after his death, Gladwell (1996) writes that Kuhn "taught that the process of science was fundamentally human, that discoveries were the product not of some plodding, rational process but of human ingenuity intermingled with politics and personality—that science was, in the end, a social process" (p. 32). Kuhn himself, Gladwell states, tried to take back the word "paradigm," suggesting the word "exemplar" instead, but it was too late. "Paradigm" had become the paradigm.

Erikson (1950) said about social crises that times meet the man. Something similar can be said about rapid change in the psychoanalytic culture, which requires both the flash of an idea, and people to receive it and carry it on. This process, however, says nothing about the nature, progressive or regressive, of the new direction. Rational progress need not be plodding, nor does the fact of rapid change validate an idea. One can have as irrational an idea in a flash as a rational one, while social influence can cumulate in destructive as well as constructive directions. There is no simple formula. Progress arises out of the dual influences of social readiness and individual creative thrust. Freud stood upon a social base that both rejected and accepted his offered views; his forward thrust too depended on the extent to which his flashes of insight did meet a receptive soil.

This double aspect of progress may hint at the etiology not only of theoretical advances, but also of the alternation of progress and regress in human history. Historical and cultural environments can stifle as well as stimulate the individual striving into the unknown. The resultant alternation of progression and an equal—or even greater—regression, which Waelder has pointed out in psychological and political life, mimics the alternations in nature, of growth and decline, in plants and animals, and ultimately of life and death.

The qualitative alteration in man's thinking as occurred with the introduction of psychoanalysis a century ago has not been repeated in any of the many changes or advances superimposed since then upon the system Freud devised. On the contrary, this young science, as many other breakthroughs in knowledge, has undergone periods of diminution and retardation in its development, perhaps as many as its periods of progress and growth. These occur when new theories grossly omit hard-won insights, or when uncritical mass movements distort or exaggerate seminal ideas—Freud's as well as any of his successors. This happened, for example, with Strachey's influential paper on transference, and Erikson's (1956) creative work on ego identity. In such cases, the roles of the originators often need to be differentiated from the actions and reactions of their followers. All contributions need to be filtered through the lens of further experience. Freud's (1922) formulation, for example, of the connection of paranoia and repressed fear of homosexual impulses, as brilliant and creative a flash of insight as any, received an addition recently when Blum (1980) wrote that paranoia can also have origins related to trauma experienced at the hands of sadistic persecutors.

With the spread of more variegated and less uniform psychoanalytic thinking has come a sharp decline in the intellectual coherence of the psychoanalytic body of understanding and explanation. Yet within a unified and cumulative total composite psychoanalytic theory, all of the dichotomies that recent diversification has polarized may coexist. Whenever analytic interest is limited to only one of a pair, psychoanalysis is reduced by half. There is no aspect of the human being, from the behavior and structure of the total organism to the functioning of its most microscopic internal components, that can be eliminated from the bank of knowledge without shortchanging the total theory of understanding. Such unification would leave us only the task of establishing the line of demarcation between psychoanalytic and nonpsychoanalytic theories of human behavior. It is the unconscious area of human intrapsychic functioning that is the central domain of psychoanalysis. Many of the psychoanalytic theories that claim independence or separateness give up one or more essential areas of this domain, to that extent ceasing to be psychoanalytic in the comprehensive sense.

BARCELONA, 1997: HONORARY PRESIDENT

In July 1997, at the business meeting of the Barcelona Congress, I was elected honorary president of the International Psychoanalytic Association. I felt, and still feel, awed by this honor. I want to convey my personal thoughts about it, and to reflect on its meaning, in the same spirit in which I look at all developments in the psychoanalytic body: by seeking their theoretical implications and their consequences for psychoanalysis.

This move was not without complex antecedents, conflicts, ironies, and inconsistencies. One result of the alterations in the current psychoanalytic milieu, which I feel was related to the diversity of theoretical convictions and their attendant loyalties, was that the honorary presidency had been vacant for ten years, since the death of Anna Freud. I was the first "modern" person to be awarded this post, my predecessors having been no less than Jones, Hartmann, and Anna Freud. These three had all been virtually automatic choices. One can hardly say that they were elected; only to think their names was to accept them. I was the first analyst who had trained in a complex organized institution to be so honored—and an American, at that. I was also the first whose election had to go through an elected, stratified legislative and executive body comprised of people and theories in less than full harmony and with its own internal pushes and pulls.

Perhaps my election was a bridge from early to modern history, a transition from heroic figures to ordinary ones. The initiator of the process that ultimately bestowed this post on me, and the person who carried it through, was Horacio Etchegoyen, the esteemed first president of the International from South America. Endorsed as it was by the incoming president and secretary, Otto Kernberg and Robert Tyson, my election reflected not provincialism but more likely "one worldism" of theory. In ironic confirmation of Kohut's critical 1969 comment to Anna Freud that the Kleinians liked me, Etchegoyen's initiation of my election did represent one leading Kleinian scholar's view of theoretical leadership in the psychoanalytic world. His decision to act upon it clearly arose not out of regional allegiances or group or personal affinities; it was a decision based on considerations of the science. Equally significant is the fact that the Executive Council, made up of representatives of many different regions and theories, saw fit to second Etchegoyen's suggestion unanimously and to execute it. This confirms my belief that there is a deep, affective identification that links many diverse thinkers together, and that a broad-based uniformity underlies their theoretical diversity.

I wish also to record here, with a frankness that is not the usual rule in social discourse but is required by my goal of conveying even this data in the spirit of a psychoanalyst, my opinion that this event, this breakthrough into the new generation of the office of honorary president, would not have taken place under the administrations of closer "siblings"—that is, if it had been up to "ego psychologists," or North Americans, or psychoanalytic leaders of the Western world, to initiate it. I offer this view not to cast a negative light on any particular group, but in order that a deepening understanding of the specific may shed light on the general. Long participation convinces me that this dynamic, the ambivalence of sibling closeness, is universal in every aspect of human politics, from the nuclear family to the broadest manifestations of group life. Events affecting even the highest office of the international administrative structure of psychoanalysis continue to demonstrate the same unfortunate fusion of science and social forces that has been at the center of my total account of the course of psychoanalytic history.

In the spirit of an oral historian, I will report a bit further on the subject of honorary officers of the I.P.A.. Into the late sixties, and through my two terms as president, it had been customary to elect past presidents as vice presidents after their terms as past president, so as to retain their knowledge and experience on the Executive Council. This happened, for example, with Gillespie and Van de Leeuw before me. Since the number of vice presidents was limited, it can easily be understood that this custom was making opportunities for vice presidential service less and less available to new analytic leaders moving up from the ranks. In 1965 and 1967, therefore, at the Amsterdam and Copenhagen Congresses, a change was made to lessen the congestion in the vice presidential list. Jeanne Lampl-de Groot, Willi Hoffer, and Phyllis Greenacre, three previous vice presidents who were universally respected but who had no interest in higher administrative positions, were elected permanent *honorary* vice presidents. This honored them while keeping the elected office of "regular" vice president open for new and ambitious younger leaders. In keeping with this same goal, when I finished my two terms as president in 1973, I discontinued the tradition of ex-presidents running for vice president after their term as past president, which meant that I would also leave the Executive Council after my serving one year as past president.

New vice presidents now came in regularly, but there were no new honorary vice presidents for the next twenty-two years. In Rome in 1989, during Wallerstein's presidency, Angel Garma was elected honorary vice president as a symbol of affection and respect on the basis of his age, his pioneering career, his many contributions, and his advancing illness, and also to do honor in this way to the newly advanced third-world region (they were to be included for the first time in rotation for the presidency). Two years later, in Buenos Aires in 1991, Sandler as president revived the active use of the honorary vice presidency, nominating for this position (for the first time) a past president, William Gillespie, who had been president in 1959 (his election followed). At his next Congress, in Amsterdam in 1993, Sandler nominated Serge Lebovici, who had succeeded me as president in 1973, for election to the same position. His bypassing me, the only living ex-president between the two that he named, was inexplicable on the basis of seniority, scientific or organizational work, or any other formal criterion. Lebovici told me that he himself wondered about it, and could not explain it. In the years that followed, several analysts, including past officers of the American and the International, noted this discrepancy and wrote spontaneous letters to Sandler recommending that he nominate me to that position; one of these, a former president of the American, suggested an honorary presidency. Some of these letters went unanswered; none were acted upon. Etchegoyen, who knew none of this background, was the president who followed Sandler; he spontaneously nominated me for honorary vice president at his first Congress in San Francisco, and then initiated my nomination for honorary president at his next Congress in Barcelona. Both nominations were unanimously approved by the Executive Council. (Ironically, Sandler told me as the vote for honorary president was coming up at the Council that of course it would be unanimous; he would vote for it.) So I rejoined the Council, more than twenty years after I had left it. At my first meeting back, I remarked that I felt like Rip Van Winkle, viewing a changed world. Except that I had not been asleep during the long gap.

I relate this next memory with some trepidation, fearing that it may be of no general interest, and therefore leave the impression of an entirely self-indulgent account. But I include it as one more corroborative detail of this history, which aims to make visible some record of the interpersonal minutiae upon which decisions can be made, even in a noble and intellectual profession. The relevant background demonstrates a central dynamic of my view of the psychoanalytic century: the fusion of lofty scientific thinking with what might appear petty and personal, and yet that touches people deeply. Sandler's bypassing of me during his presidency rested on a long-festering interpersonal history. He and I had been close theoretical, scientific, personal, and professional comrades from the time we were both young contributors, he in the U.K. and I in the U.S. I met Sandler when I discussed a first paper on fixation by him and Walter Joffe (1967) at a meeting of the American in the fifties. The three of us became close and moved ahead together; my wife and I stayed at the homes of the Sandlers and the Joffes in London and Southern France. Joe Sandler was the one to tell me in 1969 that the British Society had decided to back me for president of the International.

This is what I think then happened. At the Vienna Congress in 1971, Joffe's name came up in consideration for a vice presidential nomination. Sandler was hurt by this; he was Joffe's senior author, his own health was precarious, and he felt that he should have been the one. Neither of them was elected. I recall Sandler telling me that he believed that I had backed Joffe. This was not true, but although I told him so, it seemed to make no difference. This incident terminated the fertile Sandler-Joffe writing team. It also changed my relationship with Sandler permanently. From then on, for three decades and through many congresses and shared events, our relationship remained strained, hardly more than nodding. I record this as a piece of firsthand history, because I feel that such small discordances, if they occur in high places, have disproportionate effects on larger bodies. I believe that such occurrences may illuminate by extrapolation what went on in past generations, all the way back to the pioneers, and what is likely to happen in the future. I also extend these observations of motivations to the course of theory. I believe that such personal, affective stances play a part in shaping opinions and convictions.

I have emphasized, and am now illustrating, that splits in psychoanalysis can influence, and be influenced by, even individual friendships. Where personal bonds remain strong and unwounded, differences in ideas can flourish, and even fructify each other. Where personal links are damaged, ideas can atrophy, or cause further separation. In a review of the Freud/Jung letters, I (1975a) noted this mechanism at work in a not-so-subtle way between those first colleague-pioneers. How the personal relationship dovetails with theoretical outlook, each influencing the other, can be discerned in my relationship with Sandler, in a solitary incident occurring during the period of our long separation. After I (1989b) published a review of a book, a dialogue between Sandler and Anna Freud on *The Ego and the Mechanisms of Defense* (1985), in which I wrote that Sandler's introductory remarks to each chapter in themselves made the book worthwhile, I received a warm and grateful letter from Joe. But this brief connection notwithstanding, I have documented in this narrative the increasing divergences between our theoretical convictions, and the widening personal distance between us, as he moved increasingly toward diversity and the relational, and I to an underlying unified, and still basically Freudian, theory. Toward the end of his life, Joe (Sandler 1995, personal communication) told me, in a brief encounter, that he no longer believed in my type of analysis. Social conflicts affect group relations on the large scale as well as the small, with effects on theory commensurately more global. In a long look back, I would say that Anna Freud's concern, noted by Young-Bruehl, that her staff and students at the Hampstead were always in conflict about their relationships within the British Society, applied to no one as much as to Joseph Sandler. By far the most brilliant of her surrounding group, Sandler was squeezed between the pull of his important Anna Freud association and his natural affinities with the more genial, more social, and larger "independent" group of analysts. Both groups wanted him, and he needed (and could have had) both. This circumstance, given his clarity of mind and his penchant for formulation, led, after Anna Freud's death, to his "contemporary ego-psychological object relations theory."

Arnold Goldberg (1999), in a plenary address calling for the reuniting of classical and self psychology, stated famously that the two Heinzes, Kohut and Hartmann, belonged together. What I missed hearing was that they should never have been separated in the first place. And this applies to other divisions as well. Like "the two Heinzes," ego psychology and object relations always existed together. No person from birth on is ever without the "other" anchored into his mental life. But from some of the early separatists on down to the many relationists and intersubjectivists of modern theory, a phalanx of analysts continues to deflect attention from the center of the individual mind to the space between the individual and his surrounding objects. The two entities are never unconnected. I can only hope that reuniting the two will be seen as a necessary and successful reparation, not the creation of a third new theory combining them.

I recently heard a middle-group British analyst who had just presented a paper in Los Angeles speaking freely in a social situation about the analytic atmosphere in England. The main schism, he volunteered, was with the Kleinians—"They proselytize so damn much." But his group gets along very well indeed with the "contemporary Freudians." I asked him whether there were any analysts in London today who were just Freudians, not "contemporary" Freudians. He could think of one. "He calls himself 'an unreconstructed Freudian'; you know, everything ends with 1915, and stays that way." No one seems to think in terms of any Freudian, including Freud, growing steadily (as Freud in fact did). We analysts have done something horrible to our image inside the field, as well as outside it.

My own theoretical credo stands on a solid integrated platform built originally by Freud and strengthened by the contributions of countless others. This is the reason, I feel, for my election by the I.P.A. as honorary president, in which capacity I may be called upon by the membership at any time. It is a recognition that I represent not one sectional school or regional theory, but all of them—not as many partners equal in explanatory value, but "all" as one. The composite system of thought, the source from which, in my view, clinical life flows and derives its nourishment and direction, is built on the work of many authors, in some cases in toto, in others in pars, all of which fused together make for coherence and an internally consistent body of theoretical knowledge capable of supporting the clinical discipline.

If I may add one deep, personal experience at the business meeting in Barcelona, where the final election occurred, it was that it took place three months after the death of my wife Anita. We had been married just short of sixty years, a period that spanned a shared professional life from the prepsychiatry days of my internship to this latest honor. Anita was loved throughout the psychoanalytic world. I was consoled that she had known about the election, in which she had played so large a part, as it had been voted upon by the Executive Council in London during the year before she died.

9
THE NEW MILLENNIUM

JANUARY 1, 2000

It is here: the new millennium. And psychoanalysis itself is one hundred years old. "The Interpretation of Dreams," a symbol of man's breakthrough into his inner life, has quietly taken its place in the intellectual order of things. The American has just had its annual winter meeting in New York, and the International its summer congress in Santiago. Analysts are off for a two-week hiatus, after which they will return to their chairs behind their patients.

We start the new century with a paradox. As psychoanalytic thinking has become less uniform, there has been a burgeoning quantitative interest in psychoanalytic knowledge and in psychoanalysis as a profession. At the same time, there has been a sharp qualitative decline in the coherence and persuasiveness of psychoanalytic understanding. Buzzing and popular young cities like Berkeley, Boulder, and Austin are rich with therapists, many of them vying for analytic status. The lobby at the Waldorf teemed with analysts and students, all wanting to hear the latest thinking. Yet the authority of analysis is diminished everywhere, its insights alternately accepted, rejected, and repressed. Patients suitable for the training of the eager new candidates are difficult to find, and even senior analysts find analytic patients hard to come by. Yet psychoanalytic terms, and the concepts that go with them—oedipal, defensive, repressed, sublimation—have been absorbed into every language.

This self-contradictory ambience is the result of a combination of forces. One of them is economic: inflation-driven fees make it difficult for many people to finance a five-day-a-week search for their deepest motivations. And even after a century of trial, the profession has not yet demonstrated that there is a sure enough return for the money and the effort that the psychoanalytic process demands. The results of psychoanalysis, in the long run and over time and space, have still to be assessed, and understood.

But all of these issues are part of our science; they can be dealt with. Reality in all its forms and distortions is grist for the psychoanalytic mill, part of what the judging and discriminatory functions of the ego labor to process. Psychoanalysis must live within its own limitations, as it aims to help its patients live within theirs. But with all the restrictions imposed by the external culture—whether in Victorian Vienna where psychoanalysis began or in the postmodern cities where it is practiced today—the treatment of the individual mind must have a place.

Part of the resolution of these difficulties will have to come from the culture. Will modern industrial nations, the hosts of psychoanalysis and the surrounds in which it exists, wish to—and can they—sustain this aspect of individual human striving? These are not easy negotiations to manage. Analysts themselves are not free of the conflicts that managed care, health plans, and insurance companies inflict upon all the healing disciplines, and that make individual treatment programs a war zone. So far we have been able to work out individual ways of navigating in these environments, seeking manageable compromises and adapting ourselves to the limiting conditions. But we analysts have some difficult and vital terrain still to cover, if we are to develop a mature theory and enable our evolving field to meet the harsh requirements of its current reality. To these ends, many changes have taken place already, and others are in progress. Some have been salutary; some have not.

Psychoanalytic theory today, at the portal of the new century, is in a state of flux. The ascendancy of the "many theories" point of view has left the field in an unsettled transition. Trends wax and wane, often in conflict with each other, as analysts seek an intellectual base for their discipline that can both satisfy them as individuals and unite them as colleagues. At this moment in our history psychoanalysis hangs balanced among contradictions, all competing for the path to the future.

COMINGS TOGETHER: MODERN KLEIN AND CONTEMPORARY FREUD

After three decades of disruptive controversy, it is not surprising that we are now seeing attempts at rapprochement and reconciliation. Divisiveness and rancor, if they are intense enough, eventually bring forth calls for cooperation, if only to put a stop to cacophony. After a long period of postmodern revisionism, the pendulum is beginning to swing back again. If we keep in mind Waelder's (1960) observation that progress is an alternation of excesses, we can seize an opportunity for some prudent reassessment. Like the original splits that they purport to heal, the new comings together are made by people as well as by ideas, and so they vary in their rationality, their sincerity, and their staying power. After so many years of diverging theories and techniques, the reasons for the original rifts are not always clearly recalled, so repair is sometimes more approximate than exact. Each new arrangement needs to be assessed on its own, monitored over time, and judged dispassionately for enduring value in the crucible of clinical psychoanalysis.

One important trend that bears watching involves the not-unexpected rapprochement of the theoretical poles that have been pulling the psychoanalytic world apart during much of its existence. Two new groups, originating in England but now thriving everywhere, have chosen labels—"modern Kleinian" and "contemporary Freudian"—that support my contention that psychoanalysts feel both a wish and a need for amalgamation; they represent a realignment that seems to bring our outer reaches closer to an overlapping center. To the many who feel reassured and warmed by this trend, it appears that the common area between the two schools is increasing, and that the extremes at each end are becoming less significant. What could not be achieved in Great Britain by the long and intense Controversial Discussions is now being accomplished naturally, it seems, without conference or debate. It sometimes sounds as if both ends have melted into the middle by sheer good will.

The trend toward unification itself is of course welcome and desirable. Yet a closer look at the process of the changes may still give us pause. Our apparent new harmony seems at times to have a double aspect, not only the rational one that we need to reestablish a sense of security for our field. In fact, on scrutiny some of these new developments demonstrate mechanisms similar to the ones that drove the very disruptions that they now correct—the dominance of the affective over the rational, for instance, or at least the intrusion of the one into the other. In individual compromise formations, surface tranquillity may rest on an underlying substructure of repressed unconscious contents; a similar process may be at work beneath the new appearance of theoretical harmony. We would like to feel new trends toward cooperation as reparative, yet too often there is little evidence of any significant insight into the past. It is ironic that this missing piece should be the one that is the goal of psychoanalysis—insight and the gains in rationality that prevent new iterations of pathological repetition, like our repeated cycles of separation and rapprochement. Some aspects of the new coming together look less like the resolution of an old cycle than the beginning of a new one, where once again theoretical considerations are being determined by social bonds rather than the scientific method. The distorting dominance of affect over ideation can operate in both directions, and it appears to be pushing now toward reunion as it once did toward separatism.

Furthermore, even as indications of rapprochement appear in papers and in panel titles, the behavior of the new groups themselves and of their chosen leaders bears at times a striking resemblance to the divisive behaviors and leaders of the past. In the late 1990s, San Francisco saw a sequence of events that echoed uncannily what had taken place in Los Angeles exactly three decades before. The head of a postgraduate committee initiated an invitation to a leading British Kleinian, who now makes regular teaching visits to an entranced audience. The personnel have changed—the visitor was Hanna Segal then; it is Betty Joseph now—but the message and the results have not. The eloquent visitor is clinically admired and psychoanalytically envied; she "can see right through the material," she "spots the transference at once." An enthusiastic and newly cohesive group rallies around the charismatic teacher whose presence promises ever greater clinical prowess, while the rest of the Institute looks on, observing and wondering. Here are the same technical "innovations" and the same challenging but questionable techniques—analyzing below defenses, premature interpretations, the whole constellation—that disrupted the society to the south in 1969. My own view of the situation and my discussions with San Francisco analysts convince me that the same subliminal acting-out against analysts and Institute, the same displaced transferences to theory, are operating here and now as they did in L.A. thirty years ago.

Even with rapprochement and mutuality in the air, exclusionism, a self-congratulatory stance toward one's own views, and a corresponding devaluation of the views of others are still much in evidence. Articulate leaders of the new "liberalized" groups profess union, but are sent out to developing centers in other cities to promote and teach their own versions of theory. And character defamation continues on both sides. Above all, there is little evidence of change in the central theoretical tenets that maintain division: the structural view among the contemporary Freudians, and decisive early infantile experiences among the modern Kleinians.

FUSION AND SECONDARY REVISION: THE COURSE OF SCHAFER

Roy Schafer's (1999) detailed description of his own theoretical path, "From Heinz Hartmann to the Contemporary British

Kleinians," enables us to look closely at the reasoning behind one analyst's shift over the years from Freud to Klein. Schafer's retrospective highlights a number of crossroads that were crucial to him, and the determinants at each to which he attributes his choice of direction. The final product, however, is at the end subjected to what I feel is the equivalent of the secondary revision by which a dream is given the appearance of coherence and uniformity. The reasoning that he reveals would have led me to very different conclusions.

Schafer and Gill were two important members of the Rapaport group; like George Klein, they went on to carve out new directions. Gill, like Rapaport a most creative architect of American ego psychology, ultimately departed from that system, first with an exclusive focus on transference and then with the adoption of a constructivist position, which made him a major support for the growing relational and intersubjective movements. Schafer also moved away from his early role in ego psychology but eventually became the most prominent ego psychologist to embrace British Kleinianism. As he has traversed this terrain in a dramatic and visible arc, and as he has been an articulate spokesman at every phase of his journey, Schafer's views of his theoretical course lend themselves well to assessment.

His delineation of his journey is complex and instructive. He traces the development of his thinking from his preclinical years with the Rapaport group through a period as chief of testing at Austen Riggs, and then to analytic training in Western New England beginning in 1954. He details his interests and writings, which moved by degrees away from what he came to view as their structural, mechanistic, physicalist moorings to hermeneutics, narration, analytic philosophy, and literary criticism. He eventually became intrigued by, and joined, the modern Kleinian group, attracted, he says, by its focus on the immediate clinical situation, on transference–countertransference dynamics, and on unconscious fantasy. As Schafer describes the pivotal theoretical developments in the journey he narrates, his reasoning at some of these nodes demonstrates the same kinds of assumptions and questionable beliefs that further contribute, in my view, to divisive trends in psychoanalysis. I will examine some of these to illustrate how these assumptions appear in the context of the new "rapprochement."

First, in my view, Schafer conflates the debate about Freudian theory with the problem of lay analysis. The medical model behind ego psychology, he states, made it a conservative, traditional theory that "dominated psychoanalysis as a physicalistically-conceived science" (p. 344), while a nonmedical model would have allowed a more liberal view. This is a widely accepted juxtaposition that is not borne out by the facts, as I believe I have shown. Anna Freud, Robert Waelder, Ernst and Marianne Kris, and David Rapaport were all nonmedical analysts, but all were unconflicted about traditional Freudian structural theory. And there is no need to document how many medical analysts have led, or followed, one divergent anti-Freudian movement after another. The view that Schafer espouses continues to attract adherents, but it is a myth, and its persistence is unfortunate, as it distracts us from the long-term project within psychoanalysis—to master some day the border between psyche and soma; to cross back and forth between the brain and mind. This challenge, far more than turf wars, will ultimately determine our future direction and make for clarity.

Schafer's move away from the traditional view began, he relates, when he was struck by how little permission Freudian theorists gave for appreciation of early development. My own experience of this was very different, as was that of my contemporaries in training. Freud's (1905a) "Three Essays" on sexuality are replete with considerations of the early postnatal and pre-oedipal periods, and these concerns are maintained throughout Freud's opus. They are maintained as well in Hartmann's (1950) detailed expansions of constitutional givens and Rapaport's (1953) discussion of built-in defenses and other very early ego mechanisms. Schafer was not a clinical analyst when he did his close theoretical ego work with Rapaport in the early forties, and I believe that this fact is relevant to his feeling that early life was not included in Freud's developing theories. It was many years later, after his analytic training and clinical work began, that the substrates behind primitive states, and the special importance of their preoedipal origins, came to the fore for him; perhaps that explains the discrepancy between his experience and mine. As I have had occasion to say before, attention to the oedipal in Freudian theory and practice never denied the importance of the preoedipal. However, belief to the contrary remains a prevalent misunderstanding of Freudian theory and teaching.

I also see very differently a number of the historical developments on which Schafer reflects retrospectively. For example, as he comes to experience the reach of psychoanalysis into the more disturbed states, Schafer appreciates the "total-situation viewpoint" (p. 342), "which is not limited to the content of the patient's remarks" (p. 343). For this development he gives credit to "the groundbreaking work" of Betty Joseph on the transference and the nonverbal aspects of the clinical situation, as well as Paula Heimann's contributions on the use of the countertransference in the total situation to understand the patient better. But although these are important considerations, none of them—the widened scope, the nonverbal content, the transference and countertransference contributions—belongs exclusively to the Kleinian, or any other, partial tradition. They are part of general psychoanalysis. Indeed, the orientation toward total psychoanalysis is not itself a Kleinian contribution; Schafer himself cites Zetzel, Jacobson, and Leo Stone, for also approaching a "total-situation viewpoint," although he dismisses their contributions by explicitly limiting the latter to "an ego-psychological framework" (p. 342). "More and more—a tightly knit, monolithic theory that guided all clinical work seemed to me to be untenable" (p. 343), Schafer writes. Yet I have demonstrated that Freudian theory is not monolithic, and to what a large degree it contains, and embraces, multiplicity.

Trying to maintain his original roots while putting down new ones, Schafer sees himself as continuing the work of Hartmann, who was for many, he says, "too rarefied (i.e., complex and difficult to master) but who showed us the way to the highest development of Freud's general theory" (p. 350). "The consistent Kleinian attention to defense and the role of unconscious fantasy," Schafer states, makes them "ego psychologists of another color" (p. 349), and Betty Joseph's "groundbreaking work . . . conveys its own kind of ego-psychological orientation" (p. 342). Further linking Klein to Hartmann (with some difficulty, it seems to me), Schafer states that Hartmann systematically opened up the contemporary object-relational thinking of the Kleinian school. This reminds me of a comment Gill made to me once to the effect that if Rapaport had lived, he would have become a supporter of self psychology. In the same vein, Schafer states that it was the Kleinian emphasis on adaptation that drew him to that school. But historically, it was Hartmann, not Klein, who introduced and emphasized adaptation; in fact Klein at one point was conspicuously dismissive of external reality. By such strained linkages, which portray neither Hartmann nor Klein accurately and which obscure the real gap that Schafer traversed when he moved from one theory to the other, Schafer describes Hartmann's work as the baseline of his developmental path.

Unlike Hartmann (and Freud), Schafer does not see "why one needs to infer . . . an instinct for sexuality or . . . aggression"; he feels it is only necessary to include "reference points of sex and aggression . . . in the psychoanalytic situation." It is not ultimate origins or general psychology that lie at the center of analytic interest, he writes, "[but only] clinical operations and their results" (p. 352). In this emphasis on the immediate and shunning of the abstract, Schafer's thinking resembles George Klein's. Yet the clinical and abstract operate together; this is as true in Kleinian psychoanalysis as in any other kind. In a discussion of the "contemporary British Kleinians," Schafer (1999) says that "the two major Kleinian frames of reference for situating clinical phenomena, the depressive and the paranoid-schizoid positions, have greatly facilitated my clinical understanding and added to the effectiveness of my clinical interventions" (pp. 352–353). This may indeed have been his experience, but I would say that these supposed infantile states have generally not been reachable by the world's non-Kleinian analysts. I concur with Brenner (1999) that such memories as the Kleinians describe are not consonant with the cerebral development of that age. Claims that these states can be reconstructed from the data provided by transference/countertransference interactions seem to me equally implausible. Trying further to link with Hartmann, Schafer writes, "The Kleinians' work is oriented toward facilitating adaptation. . . . They see the primitive forces of narcissism and destructiveness [as] obstacles to . . . creative relations within the self . . . and with the community at large, as emphasized particularly by Hanna Segal" (p. 352). As this thinking is hardly specific to Klein, I do not consider it a compelling argument for a new orientation.

Schafer suggests that the Kleinians stress action. By their emphasis on unconscious fantasy and the immediate clinical situation, their interest is "always cast in terms of someone doing something to someone else" (p. 349). In another theoretical phase of his own, Schafer had written a new "action language" (1976) for psychoanalysis which, like George Klein's (1970) writings on the person as agent, described action outside metapsychology and the structural view. I have described my own writings (1971a, 1989a) on a psychoanalytic "action theory" which ascribe action, agency, and responsibility within the Freudian structural system. Schafer refers to none of these earlier detailed views on action theory. It is, moreover, difficult to see how the (Melanie) Kleinian system to which he *does* ascribe advances in action theory has addressed, let alone added to, this subject.

In presenting such explicit rationales for his conversion from ego psychology to Klein, Schafer, one of our most thoughtful analysts, shows us (also in Schafer 1997) the justifications, as they might appear to Kleinians, for separating their theory from the main Freudian body. What becomes apparent in Schafer's description of his own theoretical odyssey, however, is (a) that much of what drew the author to the Kleinian system was already present within the central body; and (b) if the insights of the new theory that *are* original, such as the infantile paranoid and depressive constellations, are agreed upon as valid phenomena, they can and should be added to the central theory. Any true elaborations achieved by the Kleinian or any other system belong in the main theory, which would be incomplete without them as they are incomplete without the main theory.

Since the rationales adduced by Schafer do not alone appear to account for his conversion, it might be that affective factors have played a part along with them—factors such as whom he likes or dislikes, his friendship with Betty Joseph, or a possibility that Schafer himself suggests: "It may have been simply due to chance influences" (p. 340). All of these commonly affect the course of theory.

UNITY WITH DISAVOWAL: FONAGY

Nevertheless, Schafer in his revisions—such as the explanations he gives of how he retains parts of Hartmann—does seek to fuse past and present insights. Some theorists are moving toward another kind of rapprochement, seeking instead a unity that explicitly discards previously held views that many consider central to the psychoanalytic enterprise. That is the approach taken by Fonagy in a 1999 essay reversing the psychoanalytic view of recovered memories. In a statement as bold as it is shocking, Fonagy writes, "Some still appear to believe that the recovery of memory is part of the therapeutic action of the treatment. There is no evidence for this and in my view to cling to this idea is damaging to the field" (p. 215). He goes on to say, "Therapies focusing on the recovery of memory pursue a false god" (p. 220). More important than this opinion as an individual statement is the fact that it appeared in an invited guest editorial in the *International Journal*, and thus has the appearance of an officially sanctioned view.

Fonagy's reasoning relies for support on modern neuroscience in a way that demonstrates both the opportunity and the need to delineate more accurately the boundary between the neurologic and the psychological—that is, how brain activity and psychological processes are related. Early object relations are laid down in brain mechanisms too early to be remembered, Fonagy points out, referring to the same neurophysiological facts that I, in agreement with Brenner, hold responsible for the inaccessibility in analysis of the infantile mechanisms postulated by Klein.

Fonagy distinguishes between declarative or explicit memory, which is involved in conscious retrieval of information about the past, and procedural or implicit memory, from which information may be retrieved without the experience of remembering. He points out that early experience is formative, but that it is retained in parts of the brain separate from those where autobiographical memories are encoded, stored, and retrieved. Procedural memory (which involves content-free skills like playing the piano and driving, and which does not require intentional or conscious recollection of experiences) and the declarative memory involved in conscious recollection are neurophysiological systems completely independent of each other. The hippocampus and temporal lobes operate in what Fonagy calls "autobiographical" events, and subcortical structures such as the basal ganglia, cerebellum, and amygdala in "implicit memory" or "emotionally charged experiences" (pp. 216–217). In relating these concrete physical descriptions to the clinical level, Fonagy states that Betty Joseph discovered the discrepancy between these two types of memories before cognitive neuroscience did. That is why she feels we should not rely on what is verbalized and remembered. Rather, "the bedrock of [the patient's] personality" (p. 217), the relationship between the uncomprehending mother and the infant who feels unable to be understood, is conveyed only in the total interpersonal situation in the here and now—that is, in the transference–countertransference interaction of the psychoanalytic hour. Here Fonagy (and Joseph, in Fonagy's selection of quotations) both disparage childhood memory and aim beyond it to the internal state of the infant. In support of these assertions, Fonagy cites Sandler's papers on role responsiveness (1976), on the past and present unconscious (Sandler and Sandler 1987), and on the false memory controversy (Sandler and Sandler 1997).

With this line of reasoning, Fonagy gives neurophysiological support to a broad group of modern analysts who have shifted their interest in recent years from reconstruction to the here-and-now, from past to present, from memory and history to corrective experience. While Fonagy credits this development to the Kleinian school, there are many non-Kleinians, both inside and outside analysis, who also take a negative view of insight and reconstruction, and who suspect the veracity of recovered memories. Concentration on transference and the analytic experience has been characteristic of many groups: the early Kleinians applying the influential views of Strachey; the object-relations analysts; the modern revisers of both Klein and Freud; Gill and the ego psychologists who followed him on the centrality of the here-and-now; the analysts of many schools who focus on the countertransference; and the relational and intersubjective analysts, for whom interchange within the analytic pair has superseded the pursuit of the past. All of these can now point to the findings of neuroscience as confirmation of their beliefs.

In fact, however, although the new links between cerebral visualization studies and mental processes are exciting and promising, their scientific value is not yet clear. The relation between the brain and the mind has occupied the interest of a multitude of analysts and neuroscientists over the years. To attribute the "discovery" of the separation between memory systems to Betty Joseph is misleading on that account alone. And to equate her clinical "discovery" with what neuroscientists later demonstrated is questionable as well. There has not yet been any definitive determination of how much the organic "causes" the mental, or the behavioral the somatic. We do not yet know to what extent the two are correlative, or what other qualitative mechanisms might influence their association. Most dubious of all in this series of arguments, however, is Fonagy's assumption that the new demonstration of organic cerebral changes should stop analysts from trying to undo the results of repression, and to relinquish their attempts to influence this dynamic process by means of a therapeutic procedure whose goal is to liberate the contents under the defense.

The interrelationships between the physical and the mental are among the most complex in human science. Advances in elucidating them have indeed been made, as Fonagy notes, but these have not yet achieved a form usable for psychoanalytic or even neurological purposes. A more diffuse interface is in fact at issue than that between mind and brain; this is one that involves the whole body. At a meeting of the German Psychoanalytic Association in 1983 on psychosomatic processes, I said, "It is difficult to achieve a scientific explanatory balance for the organic and psychological together. Chemical, pharmacologic, endocrinologic, neuroanatomical, electrical and radiologic studies have resulted in a massive advance in knowledge of somatic, especially central nervous system functioning. But all of these combined continue to add up to an advance on the physiological side of the border, coming toward the psychological but not into it. Endorphins, which protect against pain, do not answer the riddles of anxiety; nor do anxiolytic agents or antidepressant drugs cast light on the psychological causes, mechanisms or results of anxiety or depression. Even in the field of sleep and dream research, where the border between the psychic and somatic is often the field of investigation, knowledge accrues on each side, not, I am afraid, between the two. Gerard (1959) stated that not every twisted thought leaves a twisted molecule. And Kety (1960) pointed out that there can one day be a chemistry of memory but not of memories. The same applies to dreaming as compared to dreams. Our understanding of the conditions of sleep and the timing of dreams is continuously expanded, but not equally the analytic knowledge of the contents of the dream. The psychological contents of anxiety or depression cannot be gleaned from the chemicals which can exert an influence on the clinical severity of the respective affects" (2000b, pp. 181–182). While that statement was made twenty years ago and has never been updated, I feel that it still holds.

Expressing his preference for narrative over historical truth, Fonagy says, "As psychoanalysts, we know that patients cannot possibly remember why they behave as they do," and "The only way we can know what goes on in our patient's mind [is] in the transference" (p. 217). Not all analysts concur with Fonagy's sure assertions, however. Do we know with certainty that memory cannot seep from the procedural past unconscious to the declarative present unconscious, and from there to the preconscious and maybe further, through a lifetime of recurrent instances of the repetition compulsion? Stone (1973) proposes a middle ground between these two views: As there are archaic defenses and resistances, mostly beyond the reach of analysis, might there not also be unconscious memories, and unconscious insights deriving from them, that exert their effects in life whether or not psychoanalysis can tap them?

Fonagy does not fail to extend his theory of neurosogenesis to the process of treatment and cure. "Therapeutic action," he says, "lies in the conscious elaboration of preconscious relationship representations, principally through . . . the transference" (p. 218). Psychic change is a function of a shift of emphasis between object relationships: a change in implicit memory leads to a change in the procedures a person uses in living with himself and with others. "Memory is tremendously important but as a mediator, . . . for communicating about the nature of internal representations of object relationships, not as an account of history, be it accurate or inaccurate" (p. 218). If we are serious about object relations theory, he implies, and serious that object relations are psychic structures that organize behavior, then it is these structures, not the events that might have contributed to them, that must be the focus of psychoanalytic work. Psychoanalysis works by modifying procedures rather than by creating new ideas.

This new model that Fonagy suggests in essence eliminates historical reconstruction and insight into the past as a means of effecting change in human functioning (see Blum 1979, 1994a,b). It counters, Fonagy says, "the majority of ego-psychologists [who] have continued to place emphasis on the therapeutic efficacy of reconstruction for a variety of clinical and theoretical reasons" (p. 215). Fonagy formulates his views—and those of Betty Joseph and Joseph Sandler, among others—on the irrelevance and inaccessibility of declarative memory, while still relying on the effectiveness of therapy via the transference to affect implicit memory, and so to bring about automatic procedural alterations in patterns of object relations; thus in effect he leap-frogs over a later, more mature and developed phase to an earlier period of childhood and infancy. I have pointed out something similar, although on a larger scale, in the history of the Los Angeles splits. In 1950, the Southern California Society (SCIPIE) split from LAPSI to favor cultural over oedipal etiology; in 1970 and following, after the Kleinian influx into the city, the same group came to favor the preoedipal over the oedipal. The oedipal phase was bypassed from both developmental directions.

In this revised view of the psychoanalytic process, Fonagy has contributed the definitive modern theory of the independent British object-relations group. Clearly his is a new and sophisticated statement of the raison d'être of object-relations theory, and I do not think it has been presented before, at least not with such an authoritative stamp. From the start, the "middle" group has been identified by what it was not—not Kleinian, not Anna Freudian—rather than by an identifying theory of its own; Fairbairn's theory was a partial exception, but it was never specifically adopted as a theoretical guide. Object relations theory, which many came to prefer to classical drive theory, grew out of the contributions of many prolific but independent British authors—Winnicott, Balint, Bowlby, Gillespie, Khan, Klauber, Limentani, and others—who were never particularly tied together as a unit. In the United States, allied American "middle" object-relations analysts such as Kernberg and Modell also pursued individualistic ways. So did the Blancks (1986), who presented their own version of a combined ego psychology and object-relations approach.

But object-relations theory, however well articulated, does not replace Freudian structural metapsychologic theory, any more than Kleinian theory does, or any more than conflicts among relationship representations preclude conflicts between ego and id. These new views, like all views that express only one pole of a complementary dichotomy, need to be expanded and balanced. Each of Fonagy's assertions about etiology and therapy is half of a pair. Issues around repressed memories have played a crucial role throughout psychoanalytic history, in the arguments of believers and skeptics alike. The questionable veracity of recovered memories baffled Freud and Fliess from the beginning. Confronted with this challenge, Freud discovered fantasy; he realized that seduction and fantasy are *both* important, as are *both* reality and imagination. This recognition was one of the first unifications in the new field, and one that I consider a model. Certainly any automatic value of insight alone must be questioned; I questioned it myself in the paper "From Insight to Change" (1981b). But to eliminate altogether any contribution of insight, memory, or a liberated and expanded availability of past history and experience is to turn back the analytic clock. The most constructive way to use Fonagy's admonitions about recovered memories or reconstructions of the past is to consider them metaphors against overuse, in the same category as Bion's recommendation to eliminate memory, knowledge, and desire.

There is of course a place for introjected self and object ego representations in intrapsychic life (and psychoanalytic theory has included them; see Jacobson 1963) but not at the expense of other, so far useful mechanisms of understanding. Again, it is what is conspicuously left out, and in this instance forcefully interdicted—the development of psychopathology out of the defense against repressed contents—that produces regression rather than advance in psychoanalytic knowledge.

The juxtaposition of these two powerful summaries of modern psychoanalysis illustrates an interesting and paradoxical development. Both Schafer and Fonagy are reporting on current British positions. Schafer attests that Kleinian tenets on infantile dynamics have had a helpful influence on his clinical reach and understanding; Fonagy, from his object-relations standpoint, considers that those very dynamics that Schafer so values must exist in a time zone outside the reach of accessible memory or clinical reconstruction. Schafer is willing to extend the concept of repression further back than he did previously; Fonagy thinks that the concept of repression is to be eliminated, along with its associated techniques and goals. Yet both cite Betty Joseph in support of their opposing views.

It is worth noting, as we debate the desirability of pluralism versus a unified theory, that there is no more "proof" of the equal value of all theories than there is for the validity of recovered memories. Both of these concepts depend ultimately on the convictions developed over the professional life spans of practicing analysts. In my view, abstract conceptualization *is* part of our common ground, in contradistinction to Wallerstein's (and Sandler's) belief that it is only the clinical ground that we hold in common. The concepts that divide the field are not the abstract but the partial ones, the single sides of the coins, the false dichotomies, the denials of complementarity. Fonagy's innovations are but another case in point: the true debate is not over repressed memories or none, over forgetting or remembering, but over the proportions of each and the relations between the two. Chefetz (1999), countering Fonagy and Target (1997), says that the central problem in his patients is that they are remembering, *not* forgetting. They don't *want* to remember. They want to forget. But they are reminded in their sleep by nightmares, and in their days by intrusive flashbacks. Trauma can be remembered too much as well as too little; this has been analytic wisdom from the start, and has been confirmed in the clinical experience of many analysts. It is the states of tension between two opposing forces that define any particular instance of psychopathology. Unwelcome memories, disturbing remembrances, may break through repression into ego-dystonic thought. But breaches can also occur through an outburst into action, physical or verbal. Or through an emotional storm into yet another external channel of drive discharge, the realm of affects. Analysis may bring about insights into any of these three possible outcomes of repression.

The analyst does not have an easy task. Rejection of memories can produce as much unpleasure as can the memories themselves. The damage that Fonagy fears from the analytic search for memories may result equally from the opposite goal of preventing remembering. Discrimination is necessary, as it has been since

Freud came to his conclusion about seduction and fantasy, about outer and inner: it is always both that apply, not one. As for concerns about the veracity of recovered memories, understanding need only be "good enough," a concept found useful in other contexts by Erikson and Winnicott. Fonagy and Target hold analysts to an impractical standard when they assert that memories cannot be remembered, or that, in cases of reports of sexual abuse, "such recovered memories are very likely to be mistaken" (Target 1998, p. 1025). There can be general agreement, I believe, that the pursuit of memories, as of knowledge, is a valid process, even though the results may never be absolute or complete.

RAPPROCHEMENTS: CONTINUING CONFLICTS

I have presented in some depth the approaches of two prominent individuals to the resolution of theoretical conflicts. There are many other possible approaches, and they are becoming apparent on both the individual and the institutional scale. Attempts at resolution can be as complex, at times as contradictory, as were the original separations. The desire for harmony does not automatically dissolve ambiguity.

Attempts at fusion between separated systems are prominent now. I have already cited several striking examples: Goldberg's (1999) comment about "the two Heinzes," and Greenberg's (1998) restoration of drives to object-relations theory are just two of these. A recent issue of *JAPA* (2001) devoted to "Controversial Discussions" refers back to the struggles in Great Britain six decades ago in the context of the present search for reconciliation. In the target paper of that issue, Greenberg (2001) presents an even more interesting reversal of positions; in a statement reminiscent of Waelder, he notes that psychoanalysis "has grown as a discipline under the impact of one inspired theoretical excess after another" (p. 359). Distinguishing himself still further from Mitchell, and concurring with critics of his own partial theories, Greenberg speaks of adding, not replacing; theory, he says, should accommodate both relational theory in particular and "the accumulated wisdom of traditional psychoanalytic thought" (Gabbard in his "Introduction to Greenberg" [Gabbard 2001, p. 356]).

These new views permit questions, and explorations, that relationists have traditionally opposed. Greenberg now asks whether his colleagues have focused too much on analyzing transactions—whether their emphasis on the dyad and two-person analysis does not risk "losing touch with other dimensions, uniquely private and personal, of the patient's experience" (p. 372). Perhaps the analyst, rather than struggling with the nature of his own participation and trying to be a new or good object, might do more for the patient by "immersing himself more receptively in an ancient experience of his patient's that was engulfing the two of them" (p. 375). These are powerful intrapsychic one-person themes from an inspiring leader of the two-person, relationist school. Two of Greenberg's colleagues in theory, Crastnopol (2001) and Pizer (2001), in fact take issue with him on his revisionist views, feeling that he overstates the relationist position and does not do it justice.

Greenberg's close associate Mitchell, who sadly died in 2001 at the age of 54, was eulogized in a 2002 issue of *Gender and Sexuality* that featured as lead articles two papers (2002a,b) written by Mitchell early in his career. In these he depathologized homosexuality at a time when this was a very unusual public position to take. A number of other contributors to the volume note how much Mitchell in these papers was committed to the principles of ego psychology and to Hartmann's and Rapaport's views on autonomy and the genetic fallacy (Chodorow 2002, Drescher 2002).

Other significant authors are also tending back toward a more traditional orientation. Michels (2001), an articulate spokesman for pluralism, has commented that although abstinence and neutrality may be myths, they are powerful and vital myths, not empty concepts, and that we ignore them at our peril. Wallerstein himself now anticipates a convergence of his and my differing views. "I think there may now be a converging of our positions," he wrote me in April of 2001, in a personal exchange on the sub-

ject of pluralism versus a unitary theory. Elsewhere, he states that
there are recent "tell-tale signs of significant convergences, at least
on the clinical and technical level . . . that may indeed be the harbingers of a not too far off coming together at ever higher levels
of theoretic conceptualization, perhaps ultimately at the level of
an encompassing and transcending unified general theory or metapsychology. . . . I would submit that they express our next coming development as a field" (2000, pp. 23–24).

Radical departures are being openly reversed as their proponents move back toward more central positions. Enactment is
viewed with a new skepticism, and self-disclosure is now judged
by how useful it proves to be to the patient. Some analysts who
took the lead in asserting equal roles for patient and analyst also
note the intrinsic asymmetry between the analytic pair (as Gill
1994b; Hoffman 1998).

But it seems to me a necessary caution to examine these reparative trends with the same analytic eye as we bring to bear
on the divisive ones. Even theoretical positions that go by such
names as "contemporary Freudian," or "modern Kleinian," or
even "Freudian-self-object-relations theory" may come about
more for social or affective reasons than for scientific or intellectual ones, and like other theoretical developments they need to
be examined for their specific contents. It has not always been
clear in the discussions of "common ground," for example, what
constitutes a common theory of understanding; clinical theories
may differ in as many ways as abstract theories. And even apparent agreement does not always bridge differences, let alone
heal them. While Greenberg has come to include drives in his
relational theory, the drive motivations he acknowledges, *safety*
and *effectance,* are quite distinct and distant from the sexual and
aggressive instincts of traditional theory. The inclusion of drives
goes a certain distance toward harmony, but the drives that
Greenberg identifies have little in common with those of the analytic system from which the relationists separated themselves.

In making a point of this I do not imply that there is no room
for differences. However, differences where they exist should be

recognized, and not be obscured under a veil of apparent similarity. The new drives that Greenberg suggests are easily subsumed, in a more comprehensive formulation, under ego functioning— along with the signal process for anxiety or safety and the ego's myriad contributions to integration and mastery. The signals of anxiety or safety in a unified theory address a layer of dangers scarcely acknowledged in intersubjective theory, and Greenberg's choices of drives in fact seem to point less toward that than to Freud's original instinct theory, in which he first postulated the self-preservative instincts. In another reflection, which limits somewhat his previous statement about partial theories being carried to theoretical excess, Greenberg (2001) comments, "Each new theory . . . is wonderful and surprising, the more so for being narrowly focused on a partial truth" (p. 360).

Wallerstein, who has played a major role in the present culture of pluralism, is giving mixed messages too in his own move toward rapprochement. His (2000) prediction of an encompassing unified theory is a welcome and promising start, but some of the opinions that accompany it point, in my opinion, to possible continuing conflicts. In his view that a new transcendent theory is arising, Wallerstein (2000, 2002a) looks to the integrative writings of Kernberg and Sandler. Kernberg, he says, has made a strong contribution to commonality in clinical practice and theory from which we may ultimately "painstakingly fashion a more truly scientific and unified broader theoretical structure that could then take its proper place as a full partner within the whole array of human sciences" (2000, pp. 24–25). But the kinds of integration that Wallerstein reasons might derive from Kernberg's views have been known and appreciated for forty or fifty years, in a steady and evolutionary way within general theory: as, for example, in Eissler's (1953) classical writing on parameters, and in Leo Stone's "widening scope" paper (1954).

Wallerstein's attribution to Sandler of this new integration and unity is even more puzzling. It was precisely to Sandler's recent writings that Wallerstein originally turned in support of his influential plea for pluralism in 1987. To turn now to this same author as the platform for unification seems to me both ironic and implausible. Speaking for pluralism in the past, Wallerstein high-lighted Sandler's papers on the past and present unconscious. Today, he cites these same papers in support of the opposite view. He points to some of Sandler's earlier work as well, such as his 1976 paper on role responsiveness, and his leadership of the Index Project of the Hampstead Clinic, which researches the whole gamut of analytic terms and concepts. But it is widely known that Sandler, the leading spokesman for Freudian theory during Anna Freud's lifetime, became in the post-Anna Freud period the theo-retician who reached out most actively to the other two branches of the British psychoanalytic community, sometimes alienating his former colleagues in the process.

Members of both the Freudian and the middle groups in Great Britain have taken strong issue with the proposed alterations in-troduced by the Sandlers in their series of papers on the past and present unconscious. Yorke (2001) states that in general these would be found congenial to the great majority of analysts today who emphasize the here-and-now over the past, a position he himself finds incompatible with the main tenets of Freudian psychoanalytic theory. Rodman (2001, personal communication), citing a telephone conversation with Pearl King, writes me that King said about the same papers "that they [the Sandlers] had thrown out lots of good Freud, that they had cut up the unconscious and made analysis into relationship therapy. She [King] would like to give a paper called 'What Has Happened to Psychoanalysis in the British Society?'" The jury is still out as to whether Sandler, who led what Fonagy (2001) in an obituary called "the quiet revolution that psychoanalysis underwent after the war" (p. 815), succeeded in amalgamating his Freudian theory with his new allegiances toward the end of his life. In Wallerstein's (2000) own words on Sandler's theoretical course, "[The] guiding intellectual thread [that] clearly emerged [was] the incremental transformation of the traditional Freudian . . . paradigm . . . into a more object-relational model" (p. 25).

I agree that the complete theoretical system of the future may indeed contain some of the elements that Wallerstein has in mind, including those he singles out from Kernberg and Sandler. But I think that no theory can claim unification that omits enduring elements of any other theory that developed over the course of the psychoanalytic century. Sandler's "transformation of the traditional Freudian drive/structural psychoanalytic paradigm [into] fluctuating feeling states embedded in internalized object relationships" (Wallerstein 2000, p. 25) does not replace the structural psychic systems and the conflicts and interplay among them.

In a series of articles that refer at times to total composite theory but more often to American ego psychology in general, Wallerstein (1998b, 2002a,b,c,d) repeatedly refers to the concept of ego psychology as a variant of "the monolithic hegemony of the ego psychology metapsychologic paradigm, with imperialistic intent" that dominated American psychoanalysis in the prepluralistic era. This is a surprising position when seen from the long view, because for most of that period Wallerstein himself was very much a part of American theory, and one of the important members of the group under Rapaport in Topeka who did not join George Klein's original secession under the banner of "Two theories or one?" Wallerstein's negative view of ego psychology appears to have begun after his rise to leadership in the I.P.A., and more especially during his strong advocacy for lay analysis. Before that, he had kept himself quite separate from George Klein and the extreme views of Gill in their early phases, and he had been closely related to me in common views about psychoanalysis, psychotherapy, and Freudian theory. I remember him telling me as he was reading Kohut's first book on an airplane trip from New York to San Francisco in the mid-seventies, "Heinz Kohut has left psychoanalysis."

I believe that Wallerstein's metamorphosis developed out of the same mistaken conflation of theory with the problem of lay analysis that I described in the context of Schafer's theoretical shift. Both of these creative leaders seem to me to have displaced ideas and affects about the frustrating and disappointing attitude of the American toward lay analysts onto another central aspect of the psychoanalytic discipline: that is, the theory that was prominent at the time in that same American. Even after the question of lay eligibility had been (properly) opposed and successfully resolved, Wallerstein went on to attribute other controversial developments to the American's opposition to lay analysis. But the issues he raises about matters of administration, education, and standards are independent of theory and require resolution whatever theory is ascendant. While Wallerstein's leadership on the lay analysis question was vital and valid, he fails to recognize the importance of the role of the American in preserving the Freudian theoretical opus, in support of which leading American analysts, both medical *and* lay, have served as the main protectors and the clearest protagonists.

Opposite trends co-exist. On one hand, competing theories strive to distinguish themselves from each other. Kohut, for example, bristled at being linked to Alexander by the concept of a corrective emotional experience. And when some of Kohut's disciples (Shane 1993) suggested an affinity with Mahler, Kohut dismissed this summarily as well. Similarly, object-relations theorists have been firm in differentiating themselves from earlier interpersonalists. Schafer (1999), who favors narrative over historical truth, has made clear his differences with Spence (1982a,b). Still, even while analysts preoccupy themselves with such strained distinctions, real but subtle trends of reunion are also at work. Underneath the new "convergences" and the unresolved disagreements that may underlie them, basic aspects of technique have been moving away from the new excesses and back toward the classical, reflecting accompanying modifications in the guiding theory of therapy. Through these modifications, the composite theory has been expanding even while divergent schools vociferously define and refine themselves. Loose but significant theoretical amalgamations occur without fanfare. Agreements quietly form on the large issues: self, object, drives, neutrality. All need to be included in any adequate whole. The quasiofficial pluralism of the eighties and nineties has encouraged diverse theories, and discouraged, perhaps, the recognition that too many lines of division may make for incoherence. But actual clinical practice continues to draw from all sources of theory, while retaining the basic core concepts of traditional psychoanalysis to a degree that is not always acknowledged.

For a while self psychology considered separating from the main body of psychoanalysis, and a newborn International Society for Self Psychology held international congresses parallel to the I.P.A.'s. But eventually there was more pressure to amalgamate with the American and the International than there was in the other direction, especially after Kohut's death. Kleinians and leaders of the self and intersubjective schools began to appear on programs of the American, often with great honor. These are positive developments in their potential for goodwill and for dialogue, and in the hope that they embody for eventual unity. We are beginning to see agreement on necessary inclusions, as well as on exclusions. The concept of the oedipal has held, as have newer notions about preoedipal development and psychological life in infancy. The fact of constitutional givens is accepted, as well as the importance of the life-determining experiences that begin to accumulate immediately after birth. The self is included, but so are the drives and the notion of developmental deficits. In the technique of this modern total psychoanalysis, the use and role of empathy is accepted as routine—along with an objective analytic attitude.

Administrative movements parallel these scientific ones as societies struggle with forces of separatism and the wishes for union. In Philadelphia, whose society split in two around 1950, reunification has already taken place. Yet new splits are still occurring in Italy, Buenos Aires, Brazil, Colombia, and elsewhere, and new societies are still being formed in cities where older groups already exist, such as San Francisco, Los Angeles, Seattle, and Chicago. Here too the wish to reunite overlaps with an enduring inability to live together. Both the wish and the inability are the result of the old confluence of ideas and people, of theories and attitudes about the common work of psychoanalysis. In the comings together as much as in the splittings apart, theoretical conflict continues. The two older Societies in the city where I live are energetically exploring union, but the reasons appear to be not so much intellectual as practical and logistical. Agreement about the science of psychoanalysis is not very visible, and personal distrust is still manifest. But the economic advantage of pooling resources is unquestionable, and is the main incentive for reuniting. This is not how it was when analysts valued most their common theory of understanding.

The true amalgamation of ideas comes in steps, and in those steps the manifest and the latent are not always identical. Every instance of change needs to be evaluated separately as to how much apparent agreement is authentic, how much is accommodation, and how much is deceptive, to others or even to one's self. There is no doubt, however, that new experiences, and new interpretations of old observations and experiences, have altered the convictions of many analysts, leading to a common ground that is theoretical as well as clinical. I believe that our patients—including the ones who are analytic candidates—will over time encourage further consensus, as they call attention to the inadequacies of our theories, expand the Kleinian vision to the oedipal and later stages, and soften the rigid aspects of too-literal Freudian analysts. Our patients have, or they develop in analysis, a preconscious recognition of unconscious life; they become aware of their dreams, their drives, their sexuality and aggression, their anxieties, their defenses, and the connection between development and the etiology of their symptoms. I have been asked lately by a number of institutes to lecture on aspects of ego, drive, and structural theory. These are groups that see themselves as Kleinian, self-psychological, intersubjective, or eclectic in orientation, but are beginning to desire a more complete representation of certain aspects of psychoanalytic theory in their training and curricula.

It is a total psychoanalytic theory that is being confirmed and strengthened by these modern reparative developments, not the coexistence and equivalence of the separate systems that preceded them. This unification is the hope, and in my opinion the inevitable direction, of the future, if reason is to triumph and if confidence and intellectual conviction are to return.

REGROUPING

History, in this case the history of a theory, is complex, the product of a crisscrossing of ideas, methods, and motivations. People group and people regroup. In a paper on friendship, I (1963a) described one pattern of group development—there is a working up to a peak of intimacy, and then a decline into increasing ill will, distrust, recrimination, and finally a painful breakup. The history of psychoanalytic groups is a fertile source for the study of such interpersonal cycles, in which social groups hold power for a time, then decline, taking their "in" theories with them. I experienced this phenomenon personally and dramatically in Los Angeles, but it occurs just as definitively if less acutely throughout the psychoanalytic world. The compromise formation of eclecticism is the immediate external outcome. The view that theory does not matter is a cynical (or exhausted) next step in the sequence, but it conveniently dismisses the real advances that have been made over the psychoanalytic century, and avoids dealing with the problems that inevitably come with them. There are clusters of analysts everywhere, tired or confused by the raging passions of the last thirty years, who have come either privately or publicly to this dour conclusion.

A group may pull toward it a leader who embodies its chosen criteria, or a charismatic leader may attract a group. Contrarily, a group may change its loyalty, abandoning an old leader to follow a new one. Both individual and group psychology influence such movements, and analysts themselves are aware of these fluctuations. George Klein's change of direction demonstrated how a group can re-form; Schafer and Gill show how individuals can steer their own changes. Gill's individualism, over the course of his successive positions, has been striking, and with every change he brings an audience with him. In fact Michels (1994), bestowing the Sigourney award upon Gill, said that the best argument against what Gill said at any time is what he said before—which (ironically, to me) he meant by way of praise.

Individual and group movements are influenced by external events as well. This is another way of looking at the important development I have described before—how Sandler and Wallerstein, who had been the most spirited leaders of the Hampstead symposia during Anna Freud's lifetime, came after her death to stand for analytic views quite opposite to hers. Object relations had actually always been part of, and fitted coherently into, Freudian theory and did not need a separate theoretical system. Similarly, Sandler's views on the representational world (Sandler and Rosenblatt 1962) and on role-responsiveness (1976), widely (and rightly) appreciated, were always syntonic with object-relations views, and under Anna Freud's strong influence he continued to maintain them within the Freudian system. But Sandler's extension of these ideas to the present and past unconscious, and his (1990) more definitive movement, continued later by Fonagy, to conflicts between self and object representations in the ego, a view of conflict that would have been unacceptable to Anna Freud, gained momentum after her death. Groups then developed around these new ideas, strengthening them.

Ironically, there are two dominant clusters of opinion in the current analytic culture that appear to cohabit as though they were compatible, although in actuality they are mutually exclusive. One group of theorists (who have come together from self, object, and coconstructionist ego schools) centers on subjectivities: the analyst's as well as patient's; the here-and-now; the participatory, contributing, coconstructing role of the analyst; the dominant role of the transference, the ubiquitous transference–countertransference interplay. A second active and enthusiastic culture, built mostly around the Kleinian nucleus, looks for pathogenesis in very early development—not only in the paranoid and depressive positions of early Klein, but also in genetic and immediately postnatal inputs. These two clusters are equally pressing and equally confident, but their foci are mutually exclusive. One looks to the very dimmest past, while the other eschews looking to the past at all.

LOOSE UNITY, THE LATEST REVERSAL, AND BRENNER'S CHANGE

So a mélange of combinations exists during these transitional days. In Britain, always a fountainhead, Schafer (1997) discerns modern Kleinians, contemporary Freudians, and standard Freudians. Ellman and colleagues (1998) divide "modern Freudians" in the United States into self-Freudians, Freudian object-relationists, self-object Freudian analysts, Kleinian Freudians, Freudian Kleinians, and other combinations. Richards (2000) has divided contemporary Freudians further into "ego psychologists, conflict theorists, defense analysts, and separation-individuation analysts." There are contemporary ego psychologists, modern conflict theorists, and contemporary structuralists (Richards and Lynch 1998). If all these new categories increase the challenge of matching a patient with an analyst, the saving grace is that these distinctions can often be ignored in favor of criteria more applicable and enduring than labels.

I cannot say that I consider myself a member of any of these categories. Especially (and I think this will surprise many friends) I do not consider myself to be a "contemporary Freudian." I think I am a "developed Freudian"—that is, one who has retained the enduring insights and formulations of an evolving general psychoanalytic theory and added such new ones as he thinks have earned inclusion. I have differences with several widely accepted contemporary Freudian views; although these do not separate me from that group on the basic issues, nevertheless they differentiate my developmental path from that of some of my colleagues. Thus, with Anna Freud and a minority of other analysts, I continue to find the topographic and even the economic points of view useful. In contrast, the contrary positions of Arlow and Brenner (1964) and Gill (1963) are taken for granted by most contemporary Freudians. And as I listen to clinical presentations, it seems to me that many of the "contemporary" group quite automatically add "and depressive affect" whenever they describe the role of "anxiety," and refer routinely to compromise formation as the explanation of all psychic outcomes. Both of these latter views represent agreement with modern formulations of Brenner.

Brenner and I have agreed on most points of basic theory, and in a discussion of one of his recent papers, I (2002) agreed with his (2002b) view of psychoanalysis as a natural science. However, we have had some differences in the past, and I do take issue with a number of Brenner's recent conspicuous modifications of traditional concepts. Our differing views of Freud's two theories of anxiety are longstanding. As far as more recent differences are concerned, I continue to find defense mechanisms useful clinically. I (1978) also believe that anxiety stands behind all other affects, including the depressive, and supersedes them all as the motive for defense; and I (1995) disagree with Brenner's (1974) definition that affects include an ideational component. In my view, two separate elements, affects and ideation, intertwine.

But we have a much larger area of difference now, one that I feel has implications and consequences as yet hardly tapped. I feel that the concept of compromise formation, introduced by Freud but in its present use automatically associated with Brenner, has been accorded too exclusive a role in the determination of psychic outcome. In his view that compromise is the sole mechanism of psychic outcome, Brenner has overlooked the place of choice, especially unconscious choice. I have referred already to a series of papers in which I argue that unconscious choice of one component of conflict over another may also occur, and that compromise is not always the automatic, and not always the elected, choice. When compromises do occur, they too are "chosen," unconsciously as consciously.

This major area of abstract (but crucial) theorizing opened for me in the sixties, and in its development has gradually separated me from Brenner on the central subject of agency. In his 1982 overview of analytic theory, Brenner takes issue with Waelder

(1936), who considers the ego the central problem-solving agency. "The most serious weakness of this formulation," writes Brenner, "is Waelder's assumption that the ego is a steering agency—that it is like a little man, a homunculus, in a sort of driver's seat of the psychic apparatus" (1982, p. 117). Brenner has never said so, but his objection to Waelder's formulation applies equally to my views on the unconscious decision-making function of the ego, which I described in 1963(b,c) in papers on intrapsychic conflict, and made explicit in 1971(a). This "homunculus" objection leaves open the question of how in mental life decisions are made, and negates the contributory explanations of the structural point of view, upon which to that point Brenner had been a supreme authority. In my (1986) elaboration of the executive functions of the ego I said that "A diminutive whole person [homunculus] would still be in need of an explanation as to the specific agency within this new miniature whole which performs this active function" (p. 13).

Perhaps I should not have been surprised when this disagreement was followed much later by Brenner's more radical questioning of the structural point of view itself. As I bring this book to a close, Brenner (1994, 1998, 2002a) has gradually been defining a more drastic divergence from traditional theory than any he has taken before. On the basis of (what he feels to be) observable evidence, available psychoanalytic data, and further theorizing about optimum explanations, Brenner first suggests (1994), and then affirms (2002a) that the tripartite division is invalid and should be discarded.

It is not possible to overstate how this pronouncement shook followers of psychoanalytic theory. In an overall formulation that implicitly had to include the subject of agency, Brenner substitutes the whole person for the system ego. "Instead of positing 'an ego,' the new theory speaks simply of an individual, of a person, and of that person's mind. Not of 'the self' . . . but simply of a person or individual in the ordinary, colloquial meaning of the words" (Brenner 1994, p. 482). In this view Brenner joins ranks with George Klein and his supporters, who regarded the total person as agent. The role of the ego in relation to the person, the question of the specific "doer" within a complex psychic apparatus, is no longer an issue; it ceases to exist. Yet without these same psychic components that Brenner would now discard, psychoanalysis in my opinion loses the very area of knowledge that affords its unique understanding—the unconscious intrapsychic sequence of testing for anxiety, and the external outcomes that result. Without this, the issue of relative responsibility for actions and behavior becomes less distinct.

Brenner (2002a) does not specifically deal with these areas in his new and startling suggestion. He does, however, in his careful and succinct manner, delineate the evidence and thought that led him to his new conclusion, and in examining these, I find some of his reasoning open to question. One piece of "evidence," for example, is that Freud's original description of the "distinguishing characteristics [of] the systems or structures into which he proposed to divide the mind"—that is, that the id functions by primary process, is solely concerned with pleasure-seeking, and takes no account of external reality, and that the ego operates by secondary process, obeys the rules of logic, and takes reality into account—has turned out with further experience not to be accurate. In practice, Brenner says, there is considerable overlap: the id does not entirely ignore reality; instinctual wishes can be formulated in words; the ego is not entirely mature or logical, and so on (pp. 400–402). From these observable facts, however, I would not conclude that "there is no part of the mind that functions as the ego is supposed to do," or dismiss the other two structures similarly. These subsequent observations do not invalidate structural theory, but refine and modify it. Freud himself described such an amended view specifically and positively. As he struggled with these complexities, he assayed several diagrams (1923, p. 24, 1933, p. 78) in his attempts to deal with the ambiguities; he wrote with regard to the psychic systems that "[there are no] sharp frontiers like the artificial ones drawn in political geography. . . . After making the separations we must allow what we have separated to merge together once more" (Freud, 1933, p. 79).

Another of Brenner's lines of reasoning is also in my opinion a non sequitur. Brenner points out that psychic systems started out as explanations of symptoms and pathological conflicts, but that we know now that conflict is ubiquitous and part of normal life. I do not feel, however, that these two facts speak against the concept of structural systems; rather they extend its usefulness and demonstrate its reach. Hartmann's comment that normal, adult mental life is conflict-free was not made, as Brenner states, to point out a previous misconception, but to make the point that conflict-free aspects coexist regularly with the conflictual aspects of life. My own analysis of the intrapsychic process underscores both sides of this situation: that conflicts are involved in both the normal and pathological, and that choices are made that *are* conflict-free. Freud himself (1901) from the beginning pointed to conflicts and compromise formations in normalcy as well as in pathology, and in the mundane events of "everyday life."

I feel that the structural theory is still the apex of psychoanalytic theory, much of whose power would be lost without it. No description of intrapsychic process, with its ongoing scanning for safety or anxiety and its myriad possible psychic outcomes, normal or pathological, can exist without the structural view. My own conclusion from sixty years of psychoanalytic observation is that there is no aspect of human mental life that the structural view does not illuminate. *Ego, id,* and *superego* have rightly become part of our language. This is one instance in which a popular development has coincided with a more controlled and enduring professional experience.

The idea of psychic structures has always encountered opposition: for being mechanistic (G. Klein 1973), for fear of reification (Beres 1965), for the reasons Brenner gives in his (1982) "homunculus" criticism. But along with his own warning, Beres (1965) points out that these objections can be obviated by imagining the psychic agencies as what they are—metaphors, not concrete things. "The metaphorical use of the terms 'id,' 'ego' and 'superego' has become a part of psycho-analytic language and need not be given up. Metaphor is a basic element in language and serves as illustration and as emphasis in scientific discourse as well as in ordinary discourse. It is when metaphor is treated concretely . . . that it leads to a false sense of understanding" (p. 56). The antidote to reification is not to reify.

WHEN THE DUST SETTLES

The current division within psychoanalysis of "interpretation versus interaction" may be an interim split, aiming toward a new unification. If present rapprochements continue, the ultimate remaining dichotomy will be between analytic and nonanalytic psychotherapies. The mid-century question about what is psychoanalysis and what is not still exists, although in a new form and with new overtones. The new wave of eager analytic aspirants still faces, although in a vastly more flexible professional environment, the daunting and necessary task of defining what this discipline is and will be, and what its borders are. The widened field of the analytic therapies will still derive its theory of understanding and the spine of its technique from the parent theory of psychoanalysis.

Once, any move toward reassurance on an analyst's part was considered a movement away from analysis and toward psychotherapy. But as the analytic attitude has evolved over the years toward empathy, a more overt subjectivity, and a more prominent attention to countertransference, psychoanalysis has absorbed a wide swath of the middle band between the two disciplines, incorporating comfortably into the psychoanalytic interchange a larger segment of the analyst's affects and previously private cognition than had been considered desirable or even permissible in earlier days. Yet to be complete and fair, Edward Bibring's paper on the span of therapeutic principles had defined and left room for a flexible continuum as far back as 1954. And even as unification progresses, radical changes are still being introduced that bring with them the need to distinguish between those that constitute advance and those that introduce fresh divisions. Fonagy, speaking at the meeting of the American in Philadelphia in 2002 (Panel 2002) on whether free association is still fundamental as part of the psychoanalytic method, prefers "free conversation" instead. Does such a recommendation that an established aspect of the psychoanalytic method be dismissed enlarge the pool of analytic data, or remove the very method that gave access to the unconscious? A coming conference (Symposium 2003) will critically review some of the basic concepts that have guided the clinical work in our field for over a century: neutrality, free association, evenly hovering attention, psychoanalysis vs. psychotherapy, and termination.

In the meantime, a more enduring and internally coherent practice is coming into existence, albeit modified over the years. There are many analysts sufficiently guided by the basic aspects of psychoanalytic theory to be considered psychoanalysts in the context of total psychoanalytic theory. Even those who profess allegiance to different schools may aspire, and learn, to understand their patients at the level of the unconscious and to treat them by the analytic method—of obtaining material, understanding this data analytically, and imparting this to the patient in an affective ambience favorable for the task. More of the bottom line exists than is given credit.

This is the common ground that binds analysts together. It is a unity that has long existed, and it needs to be more openly articulated. Analysts approve a unified theory even as they argue for separate preferred points of view. That a single unified theory is a quite universal aim was why, in my opinion and in spite of the many creative divisions it has initiated, the British Society has remained a model for *not* splitting, even though so many other groups have taken that road as the way out of their disagreements. As separate and exclusionary as the three British courses became, they remained under one administrative roof. This was prophetic. While the effort at the time to establish a common understanding (by means of the "Controversial Discussions") did not succeed, hope was never lost. Today various combinations in the British Society are still working at finding common theoretical ground.

There is no doubt that the average classical analyst of today is not the same person as the analyst of earlier days. There was some truth in the early caricatures of the silent, nonresponsive analyst—the one who thought, when his patient said hello, "I wonder what he meant by that?" I remember plenty of clinical incidents of my own that would be embarrassing today. It is also true that analysts in earlier times were for the most part also kind and thoughtful, even while they kept their third ears alertly open. The evolution of the psychoanalytic process (Rangell 1968a) toward a desirable (one can never say ideal) mixture of science and humanity began within the main psychoanalytic fold, and has continued to develop gradually through the contributions to it of analysts of many stripes. Change has been steady and continuous, away from the early caricatures and toward a relaxed and human analyst with a broad and flexible technique. The concept of the analyst as a mirror was a distortion, but for legitimate technical goals. Beginning with Freud, psychoanalysts have reflected back to their patients what they project. That was the intent of the mirror metaphor, and it was a constructive one. This is the same stance that makes possible the therapeutic use of transference. And while I oppose any vision of analysis that limits itself to transference alone, neither can I espouse any view of psychoanalysis without it. The analyst is also a human being and always was—or should have been. The much-repeated story of Freud feeding his hungry patient exaggerates the point, but nonetheless it may be taken as a challenge about limits: how far we can ignore them, and how far we sometimes step over them ourselves.

I am a much freer analyst today than I was in the forties and fifties. I enjoyed Leo Stone's reply in an interview at the American late in his life: "What's wrong with telling the patient you will be in Vermont on your vacation?" But this latitude does not obviate an analytic attitude and the objective stance on which it depends. That is a sine qua non if the procedure is to remain analysis. The way the analyst greets the patient when he enters the room, how he says hello, marks him and his method. The analyst is human, is there for the patient—but he means business, analytic business.

He will protect the patient—but he will also analyze him. The patient knows this, and appreciates it, and feels valued—but what he expects is analysis. Mistakes may be made. Slippages may occur. That is part of being human. But the analysis, and the analytic method, will be there too.

A psychoanalyst today still has something specific that makes him a psychoanalyst—a special knowledge of the structure and dynamics of intrapsychic conflicts and their pathological derivatives. With this knowledge and the theory that derives from it, the analyst positions himself among the patient's conflicting forces, and from that viewpoint can conduct and oversee a resulting reparative process. This constitutes a new experience for the patient, a psychoanalytic one.

At this moment in scientific history, analysts and nonanalysts alike are looking intently to the neurosciences. We have come full circle back to where the field was when I entered it, I and my whole generation of young physicians who were trained in neurology and attracted to the study of brain and mind. Such complementarity with the neurosciences is welcome and exciting; so is the expanding field of psychopharmacology. But even as study and experience in these areas increase, and even as ever deeper depths are plumbed, the same theoretical pitfall as I have been tracking throughout this book remains: the danger of throwing out the lusty baby we have been trying to bathe.

Suppose, for instance, that scans of the brain record activity in the amygdala when the loss of a loved one is followed by depression. The scientist needs to draw his conclusions carefully. What is cause, what is effect, what are the sequences, what are the connections? What relationship do these phenomena have with each other? Are they accompaniments, supplements, substitutions? Are we any closer to the ultimate mystery than Freud was in 1893, when he gave up his effort to fathom the synapse between neuron and thought, the gap between nerve cell and affect? Are these spaces knowable? Psychologists, psychoanalysts, and social scientists, as well as neuroscientists and philosophers, are all thinking about this, but as yet there is no common view.

We can now visualize activity in the basal ganglia during affective reactions, but not its cognitive contents or its psychological meaning. What a person feels anxious or depressed *about* cannot be learned by discharge maps. But the studies continue, and psychoanalysts should continue to be a part of them.

As we enter our 21st century, and psychoanalysis enters its second, I venture that our science will extend its scrutiny beyond a broad attention to neuroses, psychoses, and borderline states to a more microscopic focus on the interstices of general life. We will look for a better understanding of agency, of the choices and decisions people make at the threshold of action. We will learn to assess responsibility more complexly, exploring degrees of activity/passivity as well as consciousness/unconsciousness. None of these are all-or-none issues, but relative; the complementary series will retain its place. To see only the whole person, as in preanalytic days, and not these component parts, is to lose our own special vision. Yet the opposite also obtains. As each human being, the most intricate machine on the planet, is one person, that person's mind, with its infinite parts, is also a whole. And the theory to encompass it is the unified theory of psychoanalysis.

The map of the superego will also be enlarged in the period ahead, and the maze of its interrelationships with the ego clarified. This too will allow concepts of integrity, responsibility, accountability, and moral conflict to take their places within psychoanalytic theory, alongside the neuroses and the instinctual conflicts that have dominated it up to now. There are other more subtle psychic states, too, always present within and between individuals—sincerity, hypocrisy, and courage have yet to find their place under the analytic lens.

Psychic determinism was exposed in the first century of psychoanalytic discovery, but equivalent attention has not yet been paid to psychic autonomy—to human freedom. Hartmann began to study it in 1939, but there is still a long journey ahead. Only determinism and freedom together can encompass the conflicts, obstacles, and potentials that characterize human life, and expand our understanding of human choices, possibilities, and limitations.

In its liberating potential, psychoanalysis, matured in a century of growth, has much to contribute to democracy. That is why totalitarian states have always felt the need to oppose or prohibit it. It is time for autonomy and freedom to move to center stage. In line with my central message, however, they will not claim the whole stage, but will share it with determinism. Life is a combination of what has to be, and what we make of that.

APPENDIX I
Anita Rangell's
"A Day with the Wolf Man"

The accompanying pages are notes written by my wife, Anita, about the better part of a day she spent driving Freud's Wolf Man around Vienna in our rented Beetle in the summer of 1963. We had come to Vienna from the Soviet Union, having visited Russia with a small group of analysts after the Stockholm Congress. The meeting had been arranged by our friend Muriel Gardiner. We four had coffee in the Mozart Café, then drove around a bit together. After dropping Muriel off, I had to leave, and Anita spent the rest of the day with Dr. Pankejeff as he showed her "his Vienna." Her direct memoirs of this occasion appear on the adjacent pages. Kurt Eissler later asked Anita to write up a more formal version of her impressions for the Freud Archives. In addition, an expanded account of her experience and some following contacts have been published in the *American Psychoanalyst* as "A Brush with History" (1990, Vol. 24, No. 3, pp. 7 and 11).

Also pictured is a letter we received from the Wolf Man subsequent to this visit, in return for having sent him some photographs I had taken at that time. This letter, in the Wolf Man's handwriting, may enable those who can learn from handwriting as well as from being fluent in German writing and expressions, to fathom further insights into this famous and enigmatic man.

Anita saw Dr. Pankejeff again in 1971, during the Vienna Congress, while I was busy with Congress affairs. She describes in her published article a still warm but more sober individual. The Wolf Man died in 1979 at the age of 92. A final note took place

317

at the International Congress in Helsinki in 1981, where Anita attended a Special Evening Discussion Group on the Wolf Man's final years and the value of his experiences with psychoanalysis. In his last years, based on new material, he had become critical of Freud, and felt that he had been exploited by all the analysts who had taken care of him, from "the Professor" on. As she spoke on this occasion, Muriel Gardiner, whose generosity had gone a long way toward supporting the Wolf Man in his later years, could not restrain her tears of sadness and disappointment at the irony, and perhaps the complex reality, of the human condition learned from this patient almost to the end.

Anita Rangell died in April, 1997.

⑦

My Most Unforgettable Character

Our meeting had been carefully arranged by a beneficent psychoanalyst, a maternal, wealthy woman, who had supported this old patient of Freud's. We met in Vienna, summer, 1963. Stepping from the clear sunlight of the Ring into the red plush and rococo gilt of the Mozart Café, I found a slightly decadent and tarnished atmosphere, a perfect setting for this strange encounter. I was beset by the tragic, intimate, kind

details of this man's life, his
dreams of wolves, his obsessions,
which were common knowledge to
any reader of Freud. I felt ill
at ease, embarrassed; I knew too
much. As far as I knew, he
was told that he was meeting
the wife of a Californian psychoanalyst.

Suddenly, out of the dimness,
my hand was being kissed with
Viennese effusiveness. A slight,
meticulously dressed man of a faded
uncertain elderliness introduced
himself to me. He was Dr. P.,

2.

Sigmund Freud's Wolf-Man.
He had a dapper, somewhat anxious
air as he looked at me with
his friendly grey eyes. His
aristocratic Russian lineage
now out despite the worn look
of his fine old-fashioned suit.
With his lofty brow and elegant
mustache, I could see him
ruminating in Chekov's Cherry
Orchard.

I sank down on the red
velvet banquette beside him.
It was to be fun after all.

7:30 PM - May 14 - Julia

We were immediately served the
Viennese Coffee mit Schlag.

~~We were immediately served the
Viennese Coffee mit Schlag.~~

But a momentous decision was to be
made about the pastries on the
proffered tray. I chose an
elaborate chocolate creation.
He selected the same. It
was an unspoken confirmation of
approval. My thoughts of
his painful case history and
years of torment were quickly
dispelled with the sweet goodness

3.

of the whipped cream. Even now,
rich chocolate which clings to the
palate revives this scene at
the Mozart Café. Viennese
pastry is just as effective as
Proust's Madeleines in recollecting
the past.

As the coffee mit schlag
disappeared, so did the scrim
of silence lift. In half-English
and German, Dr. P. reminisced
about the "Professor." After all,
he was the favored patient
of the founder of psycho-analysis.

Did I know there was a difficult
time when the Professor helped
him financially? Any discomfort,
the sensitivity about discretion,
was all mine.* He myself-man
behaved much more like artin,
and I hung on to every word.

* To the contrary, he was aglow
with pride as he recalled the
chosen past. It gave meaning
to his latter years.

APPENDIX II
Wolf Man's Letter
(with translation)

Wien
10/I 1964

Lieber Doktor Rangell:

Bitte entschuldigen Sie mich, dass ich Ihnen deutsch schreibe
und nicht englisch. Ich kann wohl einen englischen Brief
lesen und verstehen, aber meine Kenntnisse der englischen Sprache reichen nicht aus, um in dieser Sprache
einen Brief schreiben zu können. Ich hätte hiezu die Hilfe
meines englischen Professors gebraucht, der aber leider
derzeit krank ist.

Vor allem danke ich Ihnen herzlichst für die mir
geschickten Fotos und Ihre Glückwünsche zu den Weih-
nachtsfeiertagen und zum Neuen Jahr. Ich finde die
Fotos für sehr gut gelungen und freue mich sehr,
dass Sie die Liebenswürdigkeit hatten, mir diese
schönen Bilder zu schicken.

Auch ich habe sehr angenehme Erinnerungen von
unserem Beisammensein im Herbst vorigen Jahres
behalten und würde mich sehr freuen Sie und
Ihre Frau Gemahlin auch in diesem Jahre in Wien
begrüssen zu können.

Ich nehme nun diese Zeilen zum Anlasse, Ihnen
und Ihrer Gattin alles Gute und Schöne für das
Jahr 1964 zu wünschen und verbleibe mit
besten Empfehlungen und herzlichsten Grüssen

Ihr sehr ergebener
Sergej Pankejeff

Vienna
1/10/1964

Dear Doctor Rangell:

Kindly excuse me [please accept my apologies] for writing in German and not in English. Though I am able to read and understand a letter in English my knowledge of the English language is not sufficient to be capable of writing a letter in that language. To do that [in order to do that] I would have needed the help of my English teacher who unfortunately is presently ill.

First of all I sincerely thank you for the photos and your best wishes for Christmas and for the New Year. I find the photos very felicitous and I am very glad that you were so kind as to send these lovely photos to me. I, too, have very pleasant memories of our meeting in the fall of last year and I would be very happy to welcome you and your wife again this year in Vienna. I take this letter as an opportunity to wish you and your wife all the best for the year 1964 and I remain with best wishes and warmest regards

Very respectfully yours . . .

References

Abraham, H. C., and Freud, E. L., eds. (1965). *A Psychoanalytic Dialogue: The Letters of Sigmund Freud and Karl Abraham, 1907–1926*, trans. B. Marsh and H. C. Abraham. London: Hogarth Press.

Adler, A. (1973). Alfred Adler's individual psychology. In *Major Contributors to Modern Psychotherapy*. New Jersey: Hoffmann-La Roche.

Alexander, F. (1950). *Psychosomatic Medicine. Its Principles and Applications*. New York: Norton.

——— (1954). Some quantitative aspects of psychoanalytic technique. *Journal of the American Psychoanalytic Assocation* 2:685–701.

Alexander, F., Eisenstein, S., and Grotjahn, M., eds. (1966). *Psychoanalytic Pioneers*. New York: Basic Books.

Arlow, J. A. (1952). Psychodynamics and treatment of perversions. *Bulletin of the American Psychoanalytic Association* 8:315–327.

——— (1969). Unconscious fantasy and disturbances of conscious experience. *Psychoanalytic Quarterly* 38:1–27.

——— (1979). The genesis of interpretation. *Journal of the American Psychoanalytic Association* 27:193–206.

Arlow, J. A., and Brenner, C. (1964). *Psychoanalytic Concepts and the Structural Theory*. New York: International Universities Press.

Baudry, F. (1994). Revisiting the Freud–Klein controversies fifty years later. *International Journal of Psycho-Analysis* 75:367–374.

Baum, O. E. (1981). The quadripartite training structure. *Newsletter, American Psychoanalytic Association* 15:3.

Beres, D. (1965). Psychoanalytic notes on the history of morality. *Journal of the American Psychoanalytic Association* 13:3–37.

Bergmann, M. S. (1999a). The dynamics of the history of psycho-analysis. Anna Freud, Leo Rangell and Andre Green. In *The Dead Mother, The Work of Andre Green*, ed. Gregorio Kohon, pp. 193–204. London and New York: Routledge.

——— ed. (1999b). *The Hartmann Era*. New York: Other Press.

Bibring, E. (1954). Psychoanalysis and the dynamic psychothera-pies. *Journal of the American Psychoanalytic Association* 2:745–770.

Bion, W. R. (1962). *Learning from Experience*. London: Heinemann.

——— (1970). *Attention and Interpretation*. New York: Basic Books.

Blanck, R., and Blanck, G. (1986). *Beyond Ego Psychology*. New York: Columbia University Press.

Blum, H. P. (1979). The curative and creative aspects of insight. *Journal of the American Psychoanalytic Association* 27 (Suppl.): 41–69.

——— (1980). Paranoia and beating fantasy: an inquiry into the psychoanalytic theory of paranoia. *Journal of the American Psychoanalytic Association* 28:331–361.

——— (1994a). The value of reconstruction in adult psychoanaly-sis. *International Journal of Psycho-Analysis* 61:39–64.

——— (1994b). *Reconstruction in Psychoanalysis. Childhood Revis-ited and Recreated*. Madison, CT: International Universities Press.

Bollas, C. (1996). Figures and their functions: on the oedipal struc-ture of a psychoanalysis. *Psychoanalytic Quarterly* 65:1–20.

Bowlby, J. (1969–1980). *Attachment and Loss*, 3 vols. New York: Basic Books.

Brabant, E., Giampieri-Deutsch, P., Haynal, A., and Falzeder, E., eds. (1993–1996). *The Correspondence of Sigmund Freud and Sandor Ferenczi*, trans. P. T. Hoffer. Vol. 1: 1908–1914, Vol. 2: 1914–1919. Cambridge, MA: Harvard University Press.

Brenner, C. (1974). On the nature and development of affects: a unified theory. *Psychoanalytic Quarterly* 43:532–556.

——— (1982). *The Mind in Conflict*. New York: International Universities Press.

——— (1994). The mind as conflict and compromise formation. *Journal of Clinical Psychoanalysis* 3:473–488.

———— (1996). The nature of knowledge and the limits of authority in psychoanalysis. *Psychoanalytic Quarterly* 65:21–31.

———— (1998). Beyond the ego and the id revisited. *Journal of Clinical Psychoanalysis* 7:165–180.

———— (1999). *Reflections on psychoanalysis.* Paper presented to the New York Psychoanalytic Society, June 13.

———— (2002a). Conflict, compromise formation, and structural theory. *Psychoanalytic Quarterly* 71:397–417.

————(2002b). Reflections on psychoanalysis. *Journal of Clinical Psychoanalysis* 11:7–37.

Breuer, J., and Freud, S. (1893–1895). Studies on hysteria. *Standard Edition* 2.

Busch, F. (1992). Recurring thoughts on unconscious ego resistances. *Journal of the American Psychoanalytic Association* 40:1089–1115.

———— (1995a). Do actions speak louder than words? *Journal of the American Psychoanalytic Association* 43:61–82.

———— (1995b). *The Ego at the Center of Clinical Technique.* Northvale, NJ: Jason Aronson.

Chefetz, R. A. (1999). The recovered memories controversy. Letter to the editor. *International Journal of Psychiatry* 80:375–378.

Chodorow, N. J. (1996). Reflections on the authority of the past in psychoanalytic thinking. *Psychoanalytic Quarterly* 65:32–51.

———— (2002). Prejudice exposed: on Stephen Mitchell's pioneering investigations of the psychoanalytic treatment and mistreatment of homosexuality. *Studies in Gender and Sexuality* 3:61–72.

Chused, J. F. (1991). The evocative power of enactments. *Journal of the American Psychoanalytic Association* 39:615–640.

———— (1999). Four aspects of the enactment concept: definitions; therapeutic effects; dangers; history. *Journal of Clinical Psychoanalysis* 8:9–62.

Clinton, W. J. (1999). Address, Millennium Celebration, Jefferson Memorial, Washington, December 31.

Cocks, G., ed. (1994). *The Curve of Life: Correspondence of Heinz Kohut, 1923–1981.* Chicago: University of Chicago Press.

Cooper, A. (1981). Some current issues in psychoanalytic technique. In Richards, A. D., Self theory, conflict theory, and the problem of hypochondriasis. *Psychoanalytic Study of the Child* 36:319–337. New York: International Universities Press.

────── (1992). *Psychoanalysis today: One method or more?* Unpublished manuscript.

Crastnopol, M. (2001). Commentary to Greenberg, J. (2001), pp. 386–398.

Curtis, H. (1985). Clinical perspectives on self psychology. *Psychoanalytic Quarterly* 54:339–378.

Dean, J. (1976). *Blind Ambition.* New York: Simon & Schuster.

Drescher, J. (2002). In memory of Stephen Mitchell, Ph.D. *Studies in Gender and Sexuality* 3:95–109.

Dunbar, H. F. (1954). *Emotions and Bodilily Changes,* 4th ed., New York: Columbia University Press.

Eissler, K. R. (1953). The effect of the structure of the ego on psychoanalytic technique. *Journal of the American Psychoanalytic Association* 1:104–143.

Elliott, A., and Spezzano, C. (1996). Psychoanalysis at its limits: navigating the postmodern turn. *Psychoanalytic Quarterly* 65:52–83.

Ellman, C. S., Grand, S., Silvan M., and Ellman, S. J., eds. (1998). *The Modern Freudians: Contemporary Psychoanalytic Technique.* Northvale, NJ: Jason Aronson.

Ellman, S. J. (1999). Four aspects of the enactment concept: definitions; therapeutic effects; dangers; history. *Journal of Clinical Psychoanalysis* 8:9–62.

Erikson, E. H. (1950). *Childhood and Society.* New York: Norton.

────── (1956). The problem of ego identity. *Journal of the American Psychoanalytic Association* 4:56–121.

Faimberg, H. (1997). Misunderstanding and psychic truths. *International Journal of Psycho-Analysis* 78:439–451.

Farber, S., and Green, M. (1993). *Hollywood on the Couch.* New York: William Morrow.

Feldman, M. (1990). Common ground: the centrality of the Oedipus complex. *International Journal of Psycho-Analysis* 71:37–48.

Fenichel, O. (1933). An outline of clinical psychoanalysis. *Psychoanalytic Quarterly* 2:260–308.

────── (1941). *Problems of Psychoanalytic Technique.* New York: Psychoanalytic Quarterly.

────── (1945). *The Psychoanalytic Theory of Neurosis.* New York: Norton.

Ferenczi, S. (1926). *Further Contributions to the Theory and Technique of Psycho-Analysis.* London: Hogarth.

Ferenczi, S., and Rank, O. (1923). *The Development of Psychoanalysis.* New York: Dover, 1956.

Fine, S., and Fine, E. (1990). Four psychoanalytic perspectives: a study of differences in interpretive interventions. *Journal of the American Psychoanalytic Association* 38:1017–1047.

Fisher, C. (1956). Dreams, images and perception. *Journal of the American Psychoanalytic Association* 4:5–48.

Fliess, R. (1942). The metapsychology of the analyst. *Psychoanalytic Quarterly* 11:211–227.

Fonagy, P. (1999). Guest editorial: memory and therapeutic action. *International Journal of Psycho-Analysis* 80:215–225.

———— (2001). Obituary. Joseph Sandler (1927–1998). *International Journal of Psycho-Analysis* 82:815–817.

Fonagy, P., and Target, M. (1997). Perspectives on the recovered memories debate. In *Memories of Abuse. True or False?*, ed. J. Sandler and P. Fonagy, pp. 183–216. London: Karnac Books.

Freud, A. (1936). *The Ego and the Mechanisms of Defense.* New York: International Universities Press, 1946.

———— (1967). Comments on trauma. In *Psychic Trauma*, ed. S. Furst, pp. 235–245. New York: Basic Books.

———— (1968). Acting out. *International Journal of Psycho-Analysis* 49:165–170.

———— (1976). Changes in psychoanalytic practice and experience. *International Journal of Psycho-Analysis* 57:257–260.

———— (1980). Scientific forum on the significance of insight in psychoanalytic theory and practice. *Bulletin of the Hampsted Clinic* 3:139.

Freud, S. (1887–1902). *The Origins of Psycho-Analysis. Letters to Wilhelm Fliess, Drafts and Notes: 1887–1902*, ed. M. Bonaparte, A. Freud, and E. Kris. New York: Basic Books, 1954.

———— (1893). Project for a scientific psychology. In *The Origins of Psycho-Analysis*, pp. 347–351. New York: Basic Books.

———— (1895). On the grounds for detaching a particular syndrome from neurasthenia under the description "anxiety neurosis." *Standard Edition* 3.

———— (1900). The interpretation of dreams. *Standard Edition* 4 & 5.

———— (1901). The psychopathology of everyday life. *Standard Edition* 6.

—— (1905a). Three essays on the theory of sexuality. *Standard Edition* 7.

—— (1905b). Jokes and their relation to the unconscious. *Standard Edition* 8.

—— (1912). Recommendations to physicians practicing psychoanalysis. *Standard Edition* 12.

—— (1915). Instincts and their vicissitudes. *Standard Edition* 14.

—— (1915–1917). Introductory lectures on psychoanalysis. *Standard Edition* 16.

—— (1917). General theory of the neuroses. *Standard Edition* 16.

—— (1920). Beyond the pleasure principle. *Standard Edition* 18.

—— (1921). Group psychology and the analysis of the ego. *Standard Edition* 18.

—— (1922). Some neurotic mechanisms in jealousy, paranoia and homosexuality. *Standard Edition* 18.

—— (1923). The ego and the id. *Standard Edition* 19.

—— (1925). Some additional notes on dream-interpretation as a whole. *Standard Edition* 19.

—— (1926). Inhibitions, symptoms and anxiety. *Standard Edition* 20.

—— (1930). American Medical Journal. Quoted in *American Psychoanalyst* 24:3, 1990.

—— (1933). New introductory lectures on psychoanalysis. *Standard Edition* 22.

—— (1937). Analysis terminable and interminable. *Standard Edition* 23.

—— (1940). An outline of psychoanalysis. *Standard Edition* 23.

Freud, S., and Jones, E. (1908–1939). *The Complete Correspondence of Sigmund Freud and Ernest Jones, 1908–1939*, ed. R. A. Paskauskas. Cambridge, MA, and London: Belknap Press of Harvard University Press, 1993.

Friedman, L. (1996). Overview: knowledge and authority in the psychoanalytic relationship. *Psychoanalytic Quarterly* 65: 254–265.

Fromm, E. (1941). *Escape From Freedom*. New York: Farrar & Rinehart.

Fromm-Reichmann, F. (1954). Psychoanalytic and general dynamic conceptions of theory and therapy: differences and similarities. *Journal of the American Psychoanalytic Association* 2:711–721.

Furer, M. (1999). Comments on the enactment panel. *Journal of Clinical Psychology* 8:62–71.

Gabbard, G. O. (1990). *Psychodynamic Psychiatry in Clinical Practice.* Washington, DC: American Psychiatric Press.

——— (1995). Countertransference: the emerging common ground. *International Journal of Psycho-Analysis* 76:475–485.

——— (2001). See Greenberg, J. (2001).

Gabbard, G. O., and Gabbard, K. (1999). *Psychiatry and the Cinema.* Washington, DC: American Psychiatric Association Press.

Gales, M. (1998). Lovelines. *Southern California Psychiatrist* 46:1–2, 16.

Gedo, J. E. (1979). *Beyond Interpretation: Toward a Revised Theory for Psychoanalysis.* New York: International Universities Press.

Gerard, R. W. (1959). Neurophysiology. In *American Handbook of Psychiatry,* Vol. 7, ed. S. Arieti, pp. 1620–1638. New York: Basic Books.

Gill, M. M. (1954). Psychoanalysis and exploratory psychotherapy. *Journal of the American Psychoanalytic Association* 2:771–797.

——— (1963). *Topography and Systems in Psychoanalytic Theory (Psychological Issues, Monogr. 10).* New York: International Universities Press.

———, ed. (1967a). *The Collected Papers of David Rapaport.* New York: Basic Books.

——— (1967b). In memoriam. David Rapaport, 1911–1960. In *The Collected Papers of David Rapaport,* ed. M. M. Gill, pp. 3–7. New York: Basic Books.

——— (1967c). Introduction to Rapaport, D. (1953). Some metapsychological considerations concerning activity and passivity. In *The Collected Papers of David Rapaport,* ed. M. M. Gill, pp. 530–568. New York: Basic Books.

——— (1973). Introduction to George Klein's "Two Theories or One?" *Bulletin of the Menninger Clinic* 37:99–101.

——— (1978). The transference in Fenichel's *Problems of Psychoanalytic Technique.* Panel on Psychoanalytic Classics Revisited. American Psychoanalysis Association, New York, December.

——— (1979a). The analysis of the transference. *Journal of the American Psychoanalytic Association* 27:263–288.

——— (1979b). Psychoanalysis and psychotherapy: 1954–1979. Atlanta, October 20: Psychoanalysis and psychotherapy: a revision. *International Review of Psychoanalysis* 11:161–180, 1984.

——— (1982a). *Analysis of Transference, Vol. 1. Theory and Technique.* Madison, CT.: International Universities Press.

——— (1982b). *Analysis of Transference, Vol. 2. Analysis of Transference: Studies of Nine Audio-Recorded Pychoanalytical Sessions.* New York: International Universities Press.

——— (1994a). *Psychoanalysis in Transition. A Personal View.* Hillsdale, NJ: Analytic Press.

——— (1994b). Comments on "neutrality, interpretation, and therapeutic intent." *Journal of the American Psychoanalytic Association* 42:681–684.

Gill, M. M., and Klein, G. S. (1964). The structuring of drive and reality. David Rapaport's contributions to psychoanalysis and psychology. In *The Collected Papers of David Rapaport*, ed. M. M. Gill. New York: Basic Books, 1967.

Gillespie, W. (1980). Book review of Segal (1979). *International Journal of Psycho-Analysis* 61:85–88.

——— (1992). Book review of King and Steiner (1991). *International Journal of Psycho-Analysis* 73:161–164.

Gladwell, M. (1996). "My jaw dropped." *The New Yorker*, July 8.

Glover, E. (1949). *Psychoanalysis*, 2nd ed. London: Staples.

Godley, W. (2001). Saving Masud Khan. *London Review of Books* 23:4, 22 Feb. 1–4.

Goldberg, A. (1999). Between empathy and judgment. *Journal of the American Psychoanalytic Association* 47:351–365.

——— (2001). Cited in Ilahi, M. N. (2002). New perspectives from an overview of the Congress. *International Journal of Psycho-Analysis* 83:257–261.

Gray, P. (1973). Psychoanalytic technique and the ego's capacity for viewing intrapsychic activity. *Journal of the American Psychoanalytic Association* 21:474–494.

——— (1982). "Developmental lag" in the evolution of technique for psychoanalysis of neurotic conflict. *Journal of the American Psychoanalytic Association* 30:621–655.

——— (1994). *The Ego and Analysis of Defense.* Northvale, NJ: Jason Aronson.

——— (2000). On the receiving end. *Journal of the American Psychoanalytic Association* 48:219–236.

Green, A. (1973). On negative capability—a critiical review of W. R. Bion's attention and interpretation. *International Journal of Psycho-Analysis* 54:115–119.

——— (1975). The analyst, symbolization and absence in the analytic setting (on changes in analytic practice and analytic experience)—in memory of D. W. Winnicott. *International Journal of Psycho-Analysis* 56:1–22.

Greenberg, J. (2001). The analyst's participation: a new look. *Journal of the American Psychoanalytic Association* 49:359–381.

Greenberg, J. R. (1998). Quoted in Richards, A.D. Essay on relational psychoanalysis. (Personal communication.)

Greenson, R. R. (1965). The working alliance and the transference neurosis. *Psychoanalytic Quarterly* 34:155–181.

——— (1969). The origin and fate of new ideas in psychoanalysis. *International Journal of Psycho-Analysis* 50:503–515.

Greenson, R., and Wexler, M. (1969). The non-transference relationship in the psychoanalytic situation. *International Journal of Psycho-Analysis* 50:27–39.

Grinberg, L. (1995). Psychic reality: the impact on the analyst and on the patient today—an introduction to the Congress topic. *International Journal of Psycho-Analysis* 76:1–2.

Grosskurth, P. (1991). *The Secret Ring. Freud's Inner Circle and the Politics of Psychoanalysis*. Reading. MA, Menlo Park, CA, and New York: Addison-Wesley.

Hanly, C. (1996). Reflections on feminine and masculine authority: a developmental perspective. *Psychoanalytic Quarterly* 65:84–101.

Harris, B., and Brock, A. (1992). Freudian psychopolitics: the Rivalry of Wilhelm Reich and Otto Fenichel, 1930–1935. *Bulletin of the History of Medicine* 66(4):578–612.

Harris, J. R. (1998). *The Nurture Assumption*. New York: Free Press.

Hartmann, H. (1939). *Ego Psychology and the Problem of Adaptation*. New York: International Universities Press, 1958.

——— (1947). On rational and irrational action. In *Essays on Ego Psychology*, pp. 37–68. New York: International Universities Press, 1964.

——— (1950). Comments on the psychoanalytic theory of the ego. In *Essays on Ego Psychology: Selected Problems in Psychoanalysis Theory*, pp. 113–141. New York: International Universities Press, 1964.

—— (1960). *Psychoanalysis and Moral Values.* New York: International Universities Press.

Heimann, P. (1956). Dynamics of transferences. *International Journal of Psycho-Analysis* 37:303–310.

Hendrick, I. (1942). Instinct and the ego during infancy. *Psychoanalytic Quarterly* 11:33–58.

Hoffman, I. Z. (1996). The intimate and ironic authority of the psychoanalyst's presence. *Psychoanalytic Quarterly* 65:102–136.

—— (1998). *Ritual and Spontaneity in the Psychoanalytic Process. A Dialectical Constructivist Point of View.* Hillsdale, NJ: Analytic Press.

Holt, R. R. (1972). Freud's mechanistic and humanistic images of man. In *Psychoanalysis and Contemporary Science*, Vol. 1, ed. R. R. Holt and E. Peterfreund, pp. 3–24. New York: Macmillan.

—— (1973). *The crisis of metapsychology.* Paper read at the American Academy of Psychoanalysis.

—— (1976). Drive or wish? In *Psychology vs. Metapsychology. Psychological Issues*, Monogr. 36, pp. 158–195. New York: International Universities Press.

—— (1989). *Freud Reappraised: A Fresh Look at Psychoanalytic Theory.* New York: Guilford.

Horney, K. (1937). *The Neurotic Personality of Our Time.* New York: Norton.

Hunter, V. (1994). *Psychoanalysts Talk.* New York and London: Guilford.

Ilahi, M. N. (2002). New perspectives from an overview of the Congress. Report of Panel. *International Journal of Psycho-Analysis* 83:257–261.

Isakower, O. (1938). *Problems of supervision.* Report to the New York Psychoanalytic Institute.

—— (1957). The analyzing instrument of Otto Isakower, M.D.: evolution of a psychoanalytic concept. *Journal of Clinical Psychoanalysis* 1, 1992.

Jacobs, T. J. (1986). On countertransference enactments. *Journal of the American Psychoanalytic Association* 34:289–308.

—— (1991). *The Use of the Self: Countertransference and Communication in the Analytic Situation.* New York: International Universities Press.

——— (1995). *Delphiniums blue and geraniums red. On enactments and collusions in the analytic process.* Paper presented at Panel, November 18.

——— (1999). Comments on the enactment panel. *Journal of Clinical Psychoanalysis* 8:71–77.

Jacobson, E. (1952). *The speed-pace in psychic discharge processes and its influence on the pleasure–unpleasure qualities of affects.* Paper read at the Panel on the Theory of Affects, rep. L. Rangell. *Bulletin of the American Psychoanalytic Association* 8(3/4):300–315.

——— (1953). The affects and their pleasure–unpleasure qualities in relation to the psychic discharge process. In *Drives, Affects, and Behavior,* ed. R. M. Loewenstein, pp. 38–66. New York: International Universities Press.

——— (1963). The self and the object world. *Journal of the American Psychoanalytic Association* Monograph II. New York: International Universities Press.

Jacoby, R. (1986). *The Repression of Psychoanalysis: Otto Fenichel and the Political Freudians.* Chicago: University of Chicago Press.

Jones, E. (1920). Editorial. *International Journal of Psycho-Analysis* 1:4.

——— (1953–1957). *The Life and Work of Sigmund Freud,* 3 vols. New York: Basic Books.

Jung, C. G. (1915). The theory of psychoanalysis. *Psychoanalytic Review* 2:29–51.

Kernberg, O. F. (1975). *Borderline Conditions and Pathological Narcissism.* New York: Jason Aronson.

——— (1996). The analyst's authority in the psychoanalytic situation. *Psychoanalytic Quarterly* 65:137–157.

Kety, S. S. (1960). A biologist examines the mind and behavior. *Science* 132:1861.

King, P., and Steiner, R. (1991). *The Freud–Klein Controversies 1941–45.* London and New York: Routledge.

Kirsner, D. (2000). *Unfree Associations Inside Psychoanalytic Institutes.* London: Process Press.

Klein, G. S. (1970). *Perception, Motives, and Personality.* New York: Knopf.

——— (1973). Two theories or one? *Bulletin of the Menninger Clinic* 37:102–132.

Klein, M. (1957). *Envy and Gratitude. A Study of Unconscious Sources.* New York: Basic Books.

Kohut, H. (1966). Forms and transformations of narcissism. *Journal of the American Psychoanalytic Association* 14:243–272.

—— (1968). The psychoanalytic treatment of narcissistic personality disorders—outline of a systematic approach. *Psychoanalytic Study of the Child* 23:86–113.

—— (1971). *The Analysis of the Self.* New York: International Universities Press.

—— (1977). *The Restoration of the Self.* New York: International Universities Press.

—— (1979). The two analyses of Mr. Z. *International Journal of Psycho-Analysis* 60:3–27.

Kris, A. O. (1977). Either–or dilemmas. *Psychoanalytic Study of the Child* 32:91–117.

—— (1984). The conflicts of ambivalence. *Psychoanalytic Study of the Child* 39:213–234.

—— (1985). Resistance in convergent and in divergent conflicts. *Psychoanalytic Quarterly.*

Kuhn, T. S. (1970). *The Structure of Scientific Revolution*, 2nd ed. Chicago: University of Chicago Press.

Lasch, C. (1979). *The Culture of Narcissism. American Life in an Age of Diminishing Expectations.* New York: Norton.

Levenson, E. (2001). Presentation to Panel, Feb. 23.

Loewald, H. (1960). On the therapeutic action of psycho-analysis. *International Journal of Psycho-Analysis* 41:16–33.

—— (1978). *Psychoanalysis and the History of the Individual.* New Haven, CT: Yale University Press.

Loewenberg, P. (1990). A conversation with Peter Loewenberg. *American Psychoanalyst* 24:8–11.

Mahler, M. S. (1972). Rapprochement subphase of the separation-individuation process. *Psychoanalytic Quarterly* 41:487–506.

Mahler, M., and Furer, M. (1968). *On Human Symbiosis and the Vicissitudes of Individuation: Vol. 1. Infantile Psychosis.* New York: International Universities Press.

Mahler, M. S., Pine F., and Bergman, A. (1975). *The Psychological Birth of the Human Infant: Symbiosis and Individuation.* New York: Basic Books.

Mahler, M. S., and Rangell, L. (1943). A psychosomatic study of maladie des tics (Gilles de la Tourette's Disease). *Psychiatric Quarterly* 17:579–603.

Masson, J. (1984). *The Assault on Truth: Freud's Suppression of the Seduction Theory.* New York: Farrar, Straus & Giroux.

———— (1990). *Final Analysis.* Reading, MA: Addison-Wesley.

May, R. (1969). *Love and Will.* New York: Norton.

Mayer, E. L. (1996). Changes in science and changing ideas about knowledge and authority in psychoanalysis. *Psychoanalytic Quarterly* 65:158–200.

Maza, C. (1999). Affective display in the Southern Hemisphere. *PANY Bulletin* 37:7–11.

McGuire, W., ed. (1974). *The Freud/Jung Letters: The Correspondence between Sigmund Freud and C. G. Jung,* Bollingen Series 94, trans. R. Manheim and R. F. C. Hull. Princeton, NJ: Princeton University Press.

McLaughlin, J. T. (1991). Clinical and theoretical aspects of enactment. *Journal of the American Psychoanalytic Association* 39:595–614.

———— (1995). Touching limits in the analytic dyad. *Psychoanalytic Quarterly* 64:433–465.

———— (1996). Power, authority, and influence in the psychoanalytic dyad. *Psychoanalytic Quarterly* 65:201–235.

Meissner, W. W. (1987). Discussion remarks, in Sandler 1987b, pp. 195–196.

Menninger, K. (1938). *Man Against Himself.* New York: Harcourt Brace.

Michels, R. (1994). Introduction for Mary Sigourney Prize to Merton Gill, New York, December 16.

———— (2000). The case history. *Journal of the American Psychoanalytic Association* 48:355–375.

———— (2001). Commentary to Greenberg, J., pp. 406–410.

Mitchell, S.J. (2002a). Psychodynamics, homosexuality and the question of pathology. *Studies in Gender and Sexuality* 3:3–21.

———— (2002b).The psychoanalytic treatment of homosexuality. Some technical considerations. *Studies in Gender and Sexuality* 3:23–59.

Nagler, S. H., and Rangell, L. (1947). Peroneal palsy caused by crossing the legs. *Journal of the American Medical Association* 133:755–761.

Natterson, J. M. (1991). *Beyond Countertransference: The Therapist's Subjectivity in the Therapeutic Process.* Northvale, NJ: Jason Aronson.

Natterson, J. M., and Friedman, R. J. (1995). *Enactments as an intersubjective event.* Paper presented to Panel, November 18.

Needles, W. (1978). Notes on the differentiating function of the ego. *Journal of the American Psychoanalytic Association* 26:49–68.

Novick, K. K., and Novick, J. (1998). An application of the concept of the therapeutic alliance to sadomasochistic pathology. *Journal of the American Psychoanalytic Association* 46:813–846.

Nunberg, H., (1931). The synthetic function of the ego. In *Practice and Theory of Psychoanalysis*, pp. 120–136. New York: International Universities Press.

Nunberg, H., and Federn, E., eds. (1967). *Minutes of the Vienna Psychoanalytic Society.* New York: International Universities Press.

Panel (1962). *The significance of intrapsychic conflict.* Chairman: H. H. Tartakoff. Reporter: J. C. Nemiah. American Psychoanalytic Association, New York, December 8.

——— (1967). *On acting-out and its role in the psychoanalytic process.* International Psychoanalytic Association, Copenhagen, July 28.

——— (1977). *Different types of anxiety and their handling in the psychoanalytic situation.* Dialogue, B. Joseph and L. Rangell. Chairman: E. Gumbel. International Psychoanalytic Congress, Jerusalem, Israel, August 3.

——— (1978). *Psychoanalytic classics revisited*: Problems of Psychoanalytic Technique, *by Otto Fenichel.* Moderator: A. M. Cooper. American Psychoanalytic Association, New York, December 15.

——— (1979). *Psychoanalysis and psychotherapy: twenty-five years later.* Southern Regional Psychoanalytic Societies and Atlanta Psychoanalytic Society, Atlanta, October.

——— (1984). *Projection, identification, projective identification.* First conference of the Sigmund Freud Center of the Hebrew University of Jerusalem. Chair: J. Sandler. May 27–29.

——— (1989). *Common ground in psychoanalysis: clinical aims and process.* International Psychoanalytic Congress, Rome, July 31–Aug. 4.

—— (1995). *Therapist–patient enactments: recognizing, understanding and working with them.* 45th Anniversary of the Southern California Psychoanalytic Society and Institute, Los Angeles, November 18.

—— (1999). Enactment: an open panel discussion. IPTAR, October 18. *Journal of Clinical Psychoanalysis* 8:7–92.

—— (2001). *What analysts do. Interpretation and beyond.* Combined psychoanalytic sponsorship, New York, February 23–25.

—— (2002). Is free association still fundamental? American Psychoanalytic Association, Philadelphia, May 18.

Paskausas, R. A. (1993). *The Complete Correspondence of Sigmund Freud and Ernest Jones, 1908–1939.* Cambridge, MA and London: The Belknap Press of Harvard University Press.

Pine, F. (1990). *Drive, Ego, Object, and Self: A Synthesis for Clinical Work.* New York: Basic Books.

Pizer, B. (2001). See Greenberg, J. 2001, pp. 411–417.

Racker, H. (1968). *Transference and Countertransference.* New York: International Universities Press.

Rado, S. (1969). The action self. In *Adaptational Psychodynamics. Motivation and Control,* ed. J. Jameson and H. Klein. New York: Science House.

Rangell, L. (1942). Cerebral air embolism. *Journal of Nervous and Mental Disorders* 96:542–555.

—— (1945). Acute spinal epidural abscess as a complication of lumbar puncture (with Glassman, F.). *Journal of Nervous and Mental Disorders* 102:8–18.

—— (1947). Peroneal palsy caused by crossing the legs (with Nagler, S. H.). *Journal of the American Medical Association* 133:755–761.

—— (1951). The role of emotions in cardiovascular disorders. *Annals of Western Medical Surgery* 5:610–618.

—— (1952a). Report of panel: the theory of affects. *Bulletin of American Psychoanalysis* 8:300–315.

—— (1952b). The analysis of a doll phobia. *International Journal of Psycho-Analysis* 33:43–53.

—— (1953). Psychiatric aspects of pain. *Psychosomatic Medicine* 15:22–37.

—— (1954a). Similarities and differences between psychoanalysis and dynamic psychotherapy. *Journal of the American Psycho-analytic Association* 2:734–744.

——— (1954b). Report of panel: Psychoanalysis and dynamic psychotherapy—similarities and differences. *Journal of American Psychoanalysis* 2:152–166.

——— (1954c). The psychology of poise, with a special elaboration on the psychic significance of the snout or perioral region. *International Journal of Psycho-Analysis* 35:313–332.

——— (1955a). *The quest for ground in human motivation.* Presented at meeting of the West Coast Psychoanalytic Societies, San Francisco, October 29.

——— (1955b). On the psychoanalytic theory of anxiety: a statement of a unitary theory. *Journal of the American Psychoanalytic Association* 3:389–414.

——— (1963a). On friendship. *Journal of the American Psychoanalytic Association* 11:3–54.

——— (1963b). The scope of intrapsychic conflict. Microscopic and macroscopic considerations. *Psychoanalytic Study of the Child* 18:75–102.

——— (1963c). Structural problems in intrapsychic conflict. *Psychoanalytic Study of the Child* 18:103–138.

——— (1965a). Some comments on psychoanalytic nosology—with recommendation for improvement. In: *Drives, Affects, Behavior*, vol. 2, ed. M. Schur, pp. 128–157. New York: International Universities Press.

——— (1965b). The scope of Heinz Hartmann. *International Journal of Psycho-Analysis* 46:5–30.

——— (1965c). Chairman's Address: the relationship between child analysis and the theory and practice of adult psychoanalysis. Abstracted in Casuso, G., Report of Panel. *Journal of the American Psychoanalytic Association* 13:159–171.

——— (1967). Psychoanalysis, affects, and the "human core": on the relationship of psychoanalysis to the behavioral sciences. *Psychoanalytic Quarterly* 36:172–202.

——— (1968a). The psychoanalytic process. *International Journal of Psycho-Analysis* 49:19–26.

——— (1968b). A further attempt to resolve "the problem of anxiety." *Journal of the American Psychoanalytic Association* 16: 371–404.

—— (1968c). A point of view on acting out. *International Journal of Psycho-Analysis* 49:195–201.

—— (1969a). The intrapsychic process and its analysis: a recent line of thought and its current implications. *International Journal of Psycho-Analysis* 50:65–77.

—— (1969b). Choice-conflict and the decision-making function of the ego. A psychoanalytic contribution to decision theory. *International Journal of Psycho-Analysis* 50:599–602.

—— (1971a). The decision-making process. A contribution from psychoanalysis. *Psychoanalytic Study of the Child* 26:425–452.

—— (1971b). Obituary, Dr. Heinz Hartmann. 134th Bulletin of the International Psychoanalytic Association. *International Psychoanalytic Association* 51:567.

—— (1972). Aggression, Oedipus, and historical perspective. *International Journal of Psycho-Analysis* 53:3–11.

—— (1974a). A psychoanalytic perspective leading currently to the syndrome of the compromise of integrity. *International Journal of Psycho-Analysis* 55:3–12.

—— (1974b). Affects and the signal process. Abstracted in *Journal of the American Psychoanalytic Association* 22:612–625.

—— (1975a). Book review of the Freud/Jung letters, ed. W. McGuire. Bollingen Series 94, trans. R. Manheim and R. F. C. Hull. *American Journal of Psychiatry* 132:980, September.

—— (1975b). Psychoanalysis and the process of change. *International Journal of Psycho-Analysis* 56:87–98.

—— (1976). Lessons from Watergate: A derivative for psychoanalysis. *Psychoanalytic Quarterly* 45:37–61.

—— (1978). On understanding and treating anxiety and its derivatives. *International Journal of Psycho-Analysis* 59:229–236.

—— (1980a). *The Mind of Watergate*. New York: Norton.

—— (1980b). A neglected classic X: Otto Fenichel's "Problems of Psychoanalytic Technique." *Journal of the Philadelphia Association of Psychoanalysis* 7:93–103.

—— (1981a). A view on John Gedo's revision of psychoanalytic theory. *Psychoanalytic Inquiry* 1:249–265.

—— (1981b). From insight to change. *Journal of the American Psychoanalytic Association* 29:119–141.

—— (1981c). Psychoanalysis and dynamic psychotherapy. Similarities and differences twenty-five years later. *Psychoanalytic Quarterly* 50:665–693.

——— (1981d). *Leaders and led: from official politics to psychoanalytic group life.* Congress summary: Statements by leaders of special discussion groups. 32nd International Psychoanalytic Congress, Helsinki, July 30, p. 51.

——— (1982a). Transference to theory: the relationship of psychoanalytic education to the analyst's relationship to psychoanalysis. *Annals of Psychoanalysis* 10:29–56.

——— (1982b). The self in psychoanalytic theory. *Journal of the American Psychoanalytic Association* 30:863–891.

——— (1983). *The enduring armature of psychoanalytic theory and method.* Address to The Psychoanalytic Forum, American Psychoanalytic Association, Philadelphia, PA, April 28. In *Psychoanalysis—The Science of Mental Conflict: Essays in Honor of Charles Brenner,* ed. A. D. Richards and M. Willick, pp. 89–106. Hillsdale, NJ: Analytic Press, 1986.

——— (1984a). The analyst at work. Madrid Congress. Synthesis and critique. *International Journal of Psycho-Analysis* 65:125–140.

——— (1984b). The Anna Freud experience. *Psychoanalytic Study of the Child* 39:29–43.

——— (1985). The object in psychoanalytic theory. *Journal of the American Psychoanalytic Association* 33:301–334.

——— (1986). The executive functions of the ego. *Psychoanalytic Study of the Child* 41:1–37.

——— (1987). A core process in psychoanalytic treatment. *Psychoanalytic Quarterly* 56:222–249.

——— (1988). The future of psychoanalysis: scientific crossroads. *Psychoanalytic Quarterly* 57:313–340.

——— (1989a). Action theory within the structural view. *International Journal of Psycho-Analysis* 70:189–203.

——— (1989b). Book review of *The Analysis of Defense: The Ego and the Mechanisms of Defense Revisited,* by J. Sandler with A. Freud (New York: International Universities Press, 1985). *Journal of the American Psychoanalytic Association* 37:245–251.

——— (1990). *The Human Core. The Intrapsychic Base of Behavior,* Vol. 1: *Action Within the Structural View,* Vol. 2: *From Anxiety to Integrity.* Madison, CT: International Universities Press.

—— (1991). Castration. *Journal of the American Psychoanalytic Association* 39:3–23.

—— (1992). *Psychoanalysis, moral conflicts, and the political process.* Inaugural Aaron Hilkevitch Lecture. The University of Chicago Centennial, Chicago, IL, June 11. Reported in *Medicine on the Midway*, by P. Routman, Fall 1992, pp. 16–17.

—— (1993). From anxiety to integrity: the paradigmatic journey of psychoanalysis. The 1993 Simmel-Fenichel Lecture of the Los Angeles Psychoanalytic Society and Institute, Los Angeles, CA, March 5.

—— (1995). Affects. In *Psychoanalysis: The Major Concepts*, ed. B. E. Moore and B. D. Fine, pp. 381–391. New Haven, CT: Yale University Press.

—— (1996). Moral conflicts, public opinion, and the political process. In *Psychoanalysis at the Political Border. Essays in Honor of Rafael Moses*, ed. L. Rangell and R. Moses-Hrushovski, Chap. 14. Madison, CT: International Universities Press.

—— (1997a). Into the second psychoanalytic century. One psychoanalysis or many? The unitary theory of Leo Rangell, M.D. *Journal of Clinical Psychoanalysis* 6(4): 451–612.

—— (1997b). Communication within the analytic dyad. A view of enactment. *Journal of Clinical Psychoanalysis* 64:35–45.

—— (1998). Psychoanalysis at the millennium. A unitary theory. *Samiksa, Journal of the Indian Psychoanalytical Society* 2:1–12. Also in *Psychoanalytic Psychology* 17:451–466, Summer, 2000.

—— (1999a). My view on enactment and related revisions. *Journal of Clinical Psychoanalysis* 8:77–93.

—— (2000a). A psychoanalytic view of the impeachment process: the psychoanalysis of hypocrisy. *Psychoanalytic Dialogues* 10:309–313.

—— (2000b). Psyche and soma: leaps and continuities. *Journal of Clinical Psychoanalysis* 9:173–200.

—— (2002). Discussion of Brenner. "Reflections on psychoanalysis" and parallel reflections. *Journal of Clinical Psychoanalysis* 11:96–114.

—— (2003). The psychoanalysis of public opinion. (In preparation.)

Rangell, L., and Glassman, F. (1945). Acute spinal epidural abscess as a complication of lumbar puncture. *Journal of Nervous and Mental Disorders* 102:8–18.

Rank, O. (1947). *Will Therapy and Truth and Reality.* New York: Alfred A. Knopf.

———— (1952). *The Trauma of Birth.* New York: Robert Brunner.

Rapaport, D. (1950a). *Emotions and Memory.* New York: International Universities Press.

———— (1950b). On the psychoanalytic theory of thinking. In *The Collected Papers of David Rapaport,* ed. M. M. Gill. New York: Basic Books, 1967.

———— (1951a). The autonomy of the ego. *Bulletin of the Menninger Clinic* 15:113–123.

———— (1951b). *Organization and Pathology of Thought.* New York: Columbia University Press.

———— (1952a). Quoted in Gill and Klein, 1964, p. 356.

———— (1952b). An attempt to systematize the fragments of the psychoanalytic theory of affects. Paper read at the Panel on the Theory of Affects, rep. L. Rangell. *Bulletin of the American Psychoanalysis Association* 8(3/4):300–315.

———— (1953). On the psychoanalytic theory of affects. *International Journal of Psycho-Analysis* 34:177–198.

———— (1958). The theory of ego autonomy: a generalization. *Bulletin of the Menninger Clinic* 22:13–35.

———— (1960a). On the psychoanalytic theory of motivation. In *Nebraska Symposium on Motivation,* M. R. Jones, pp. 173–247. Lincoln, NE: University of Nebraska Press.

———— (1960b). The Structure of Psychoanalytic Theory: A Systematizing Attempt. *Psychological Issues,* Monograph no. 6. New York: International Universities Press.

———— (1967). Some metapsychological considerations concerning activity and passivity. In *The Collected Papers of David Rapaport,* ed. M. M. Gill, pp. 530–568. New York: Basic Books.

Rapaport, D., and Gill, M. M. (1959). The points of view and assumptions of metapsychology. *International Journal of Psycho-Analysis* 40:153–162.

Reed, G. S., and Baudry, F. (1997). Susan Isaacs and Anna Freud on fantasy. *Journal of the American Psychoanalytic Association* 45:465–490.

Reich, W. (1933–1934). *Character Analysis.* New York: Touchstone, 1974.

Reichmayr, J., and Muhlleitner, E., eds. (1998). *Otto Fenichel: 119 Rundbriefe (1934–1945)*. 2 Vols. Frankfurt and Basel: Stroemfeld Verlag.

Reider, N. (1953). A type of transference to institutions. *Bulletin of the Menninger Clinic* 17:58–63.

Renik, O. (1993). Countertransference enactment and the psychoanalytic process. In *Psychic Structure and Psychic Change. Essays in Honor of Robert S. Wallerstein*, ed. M. J. Horowitz, O. F. Kernberg, and E. M. Weinshel, pp. 137–160. Madison, CT: International Universities Press.

——— (1995). The ideal of the anonymous analyst and the problem of self-disclosure. *Psychoanalytic Quarterly* 64:466–495.

——— (1996). Editor's introduction. Knowledge and authority in the psychoanalytic relationship. *Psychoanalytic Quarterly* 65.

——— (1998). The analyst's subjectivity and the analyst's objectivity. *International Journal of Psycho-Analysis* 79:487–497.

——— (1999). Four aspects of the enactment concept: definitions; therapeutic effects; dangers; history. *Journal of Clinical Psychoanalysis* 8:9–62.

Richards, A. D. (1999). A. A. Brill and the politics of exclusion. *Journal of the American Psychoanalytic Association* 47:9–28.

——— (2000). *A plea for a measure of humility: psychoanalytic discourse at the turn of our century*. Unpublished manuscript.

Richards, A. D., and Lynch, A. A. (1998). From ego psychology to contemporary conflict theory: an historical overview. In *The Modern Freudians: Contemporary Psychoanalytic Technique*, ed. C. S. Ellman, S. Grand, M. Silvan, and S. J. Ellman. Northvale, NJ: Jason Aronson.

Rosenblitt, D. L. (1999). Who speaks for child analysis? *American Psychoanalyst* 33:8–18.

Rothstein, A. (1999). Four aspects of the enactment concept: definitions; therapeutic effects; dangers; history. *Journal of Clinical Psychoanalysis* 8:9–62.

Sandler, A.-M. (1983). *The psychoanalyst at work: a European perspective*. Clinical presentation to the International Psychoanalytic Congress, Madrid, July 25.

Sandler, J. (1960). The background of safety. *International Journal of Psycho-Analysis* 41:352–356.

——— (1976). Countertransference and role-responsiveness. *International Review of Psychoanalysis* 3:43–47.

——— (1983). Reflections on some relations between psychoanalytic concepts and psychoanalytic practice. *International Journal of Psycho-Analysis* 64:35–45.

——— (1987a). The concept of projective identification. In *Projection, Identification, Projective Identification*, ed. J. Sandler, pp. 13–26. Madison, CT: International Universities Press.

——— (1987b) *Projection, Identification, Projective Identification*, ed. J. Sandler. Madison, CT: International Universities Press.

——— (1990). On internal object relations. *Journal of the American Psychoanalytic Association* 38:859–879.

——— (1993). On communication from patient to analyst: not everything is projective identification. *International Journal of Psycho-Analysis* 74:1097–1107.

Sandler, J., and Freud, A. (1983). Discussions with Anna Freud on *The Ego and the Mechanisms of Defence: the Ego and the Id at Puberty. International Journal of Psycho-Analysis* 64:401–406.

Sandler, J., with Freud, A. (1985). *The Analysis of Defense: The Ego and the Mechanisms of Defense Revisited.* New York: International Universities Press.

Sandler, J., and Joffe, W. G. (1967). The tendency to persistence in psychological function and development, with special reference to fixation and regression. *Bulletin of the Menninger Clinic* 31:257–271.

——— (1969). Towards a Basic Psychoanalytic Model. *International Journal of Psycho-Analysis* 50:79–90.

Sandler, J., and Rosenblatt, B. (1962). The concept of the representational world. *Psychoanalytic Study of the Child* 17:128–145.

Sandler, J., and Sandler, A.-M. (1984). The past unconscious, the present unconscious, and interpretation of the transference. *Psychoanalytic Inquiry* 4:367–399.

——— (1987). The past unconscious, the present unconscious, and the vicissitudes of guilt. *International Journal of Psycho-Analysis* 68:331–341.

——— (1997). A psychoanalytic theory of repression and the unconscious. In *Recovered Memories of Abuse: True or False?*, ed. J. Sandler and P. Fonagy, pp. 163–181. London: Karnac Books.

Savitsky, N., and Rangell, L. (1950a).The ocular findings in multiple sclerosis. *Multiple Sclerosis and the Demyelinating Diseases* 28:403–413. Published for the Association for Research in Nervous and Mental Disorders.

——— (1950b). On homonymous hemianopsia in multiple sclerosis. *Journal of Nervous and Mental Disorders* 111:225–231.

Schafer, R. (1976). *A New Language for Psychoanalysis.* New Haven, CT: Yale University Press.

——— (1996). Authority, evidence, and knowledge in the psychoanalytic relationship. *Psychoanalytic Quarterly* 65:236–253.

——— (1997). *The Contemporary Kleinians of London.* Madison, CT: International Universities Press.

——— (1999). Recentering psychoanalysis: from Heinz Hartmann to the contemporary British Kleinians. *Psychoanalytic Psychology* 16:339–354.

Seeley, J. (1967). *The Americanization of the Unconscious.* Philadelphia and New York: International Science Press.

Segal, H. (1979). *Klein.* London: Fontana Modern Masters.

Segel, N. P. (1981). Narcissism and adaptation to indignity. *International Journal of Psycho-Analysis* 62:465–476.

Shane, M. (1993). Personal communication. March 5.

Shevrin, H. (1976). Rapaport's contribution to research. *Bulletin of the Menninger Clinic* 40:211–228.

Simmel, E. (1944). War neuroses. In *Psychoanalysis Today*, ed. S. Lorand, pp. 227–248. New York: International Universities Press. Reprinted from: *Kriegesneurosen und "Psychisches Trauma"* (*War Neuroses and "Mental Trauma"*). Munich: Otto Nemnich, 1918.

Spence, D. P. (1982a). Narrative truth and theoretical truth. *Psychoanalytic Quarterly* 51:43–69.

——— (1982b). *Narrative Truth and Historical Truth.* New York: Norton.

Spezzano, C. (1995). *From transference as distortion to enactment as being: What have we gained and what have we lost?* Paper presented to Panel, November 18.

Spitz, R. (1959). *A Genetic Field Theory of Ego Formation.* New York: International Universities Press.

——— (1965). *The First Year of Life.* New York: International Universities Press.

Stanford Studies in International Conflict and Integration: Crisis and Crises (1963). *Stanford Today*, Series 1, no. 4.

Stein, M. (1979). The restoration of the self. *Journal of the American Psychoanalytic Association* 27:665–680.

Sterba, R. F. (1934). The fate of the ego in analytic therapy. *International Journal of Psycho-Analysis* 15:117–126.

Stern, D. N. (1985). *The Interpersonal World of the Infant*. New York: Basic Books.

Stolorow, R. D., Brandchaft, B., and Atwood, G. E. (1983). Intersubjectivity in psychoanalytic treatment. *Bulletin of the Menninger Clinic* 47:117–128.

———— (1987). *Psychoanalytic Treatment: An Intersubjective Approach*. Hillsdale, NJ: Analytic Press.

Stone, L. (1954). The widening scope of indications for psychoanalysis. *Journal of the American Psychoanalytic Association* 2:567–594.

———— (1973). On resistance to the psychoanalytic process. Some thoughts on its nature and motivations. *Psychoanalytic Contemporary Science* 2:42–73.

———— (1979). *Psychoanalysis and psychotherapy 1954–79*. Read at Symposium on Psychoanalysis and Psychotherapy: Twenty-five Years Later, Atlanta, October 20.

———— (1981a). Some thoughts on the "here and now" in psychoanalytic technique and process. *Psychoanalytic Quarterly* 50:709–733.

———— (1981b). Notes on the noninterpretive elements in the psychoanalytic situation and process. *Journal of the American Psychoanalytic Association* 29:89–118.

Strachey, J. (1934). The nature of the therapeutic action of psychoanalysis. *International Journal of Psycho-Analysis* 15:127–159.

Strozier, C. B. (2001). *Heinz Kohut, the Making of a Psychoanalyst*. New York: Farrar, Straus & Giroux.

Sullivan, H. S. (1953). *The Interpersonal Theory of Psychiatry*. New York: Norton.

Tarachow, S. (1963). *An Introduction to Psychotherapy*. New York: International Universities Press.

Target, M. (1998). Book review essay. The recovered memories controversy. *International Journal of Psycho-Analysis* 79:1015–1028.

—— (1999). Response to Chefetz. *International Journal of Psycho-Analysis* 80:378–381.

Thompson, C. (1950). *Psychoanalysis: Evolution and Development.* New York: Hermitage House.

Van Dam, H. (1988). Leo Rangell, the crypto-child psychoanalyst. *Los Angeles Psychoanalytic Bulletin* Winter: 30–38.

Vanggaard, T. (1968). Contribution to symposium on acting out. *International Journal of Psycho-Analysis* 49:206–210.

Waelder, R. (1934). The problem of freedom in psychoanalysis and the problem of reality testing. In *Psychoanalysis*, ed. S. A. Guttman, pp. 101–120. New York: International Universities Press.

—— (1936). The principle of multiple function: observations on overdetermination. *Psychoanalytic Quarterly* 5:45–62.

—— (1960). *Basic Theory of Neurosis.* New York: International Universities Press.

—— (1962). Psychoanalysis, scientific method, and philosophy. *Journal of the American Psychoanalytic Association* 10:617–637.

—— (1963). Psychic determinism and the possibility of predictions. *Psychoanalytic Quarterly* 32:15–42.

—— (1967). *Progress and Revolution.* New York: International Universities Press.

Wallerstein, R. S. (1988). One psychoanalysis or many? *International Journal of Psycho-Analysis* 69:5–21.

—— (1991). *The Common Ground of Psychoanalysis.* Northvale, NJ: Jason Aronson.

—— (1998a). The new American psychoanalysis. *Journal of the American Psychoanalytic Association* 46:1021–1043.

—— (1998b). The I.P.A. and the American Psychoanalytic Association: a perspective on the Regional Association agreement. *International Journal of Psycho-Analysis* 79:553–564.

—— (1998c). *Lay Analysis: Life inside the Controversy.* Hillsdale, NJ: Analytic Press.

—— (2000). The trajectory of psychoanalysis: past and future. *Samiksa* 54:17–28.

—— (2002a). The growth and transformation of American ego psychology. *Journal of the American Psychoanalytic Association* 50:135–169.

—— (2002b). APsaA-I.P.A. history: determinants of the certification and training analysts issues. *American Psychoanalyst* 36:14.

———— (2002c). The common ground. *Affiliate Council Newsletter* 4:1,6,7.

———— (2002d). The organizational maturation of the I.P.A. *International Psychoanalysis* 11:24–26.

Weiss, J., and Sampson, H. (1982). Miniseries. San Francisco Psychoanalytic Institute.

———— (1986). *The Psychoanalytic Process.* New York: Guilford.

Winnicott, D. H. (1953). Transitional objects and transitional phenomena. *International Journal of Psycho-Analysis* 34:89–97.

———— (1958). *Collected Papers. Through Paediatrics to Psychoanalysis.* New York: Basic Books.

———— (1965). *The Maturational Processes and the Facilitating Environment.* New York: International Universities Press.

Wolf, E. (1994). Interview. In *Psychoanalysts Talk*, by V. Hunter, pp. 141–191. New York: Guilford.

Yorke, C. (2001). The unconscious: past, present and future. In *Within Time and Beyond Time. A Festschrift for Pearl King*, ed. R. Steiner and J. Johns, pp. 230–251. London and New York: Karnac.

Young-Bruehl, E. (1988). *Anna Freud: A Biography.* New York: Summit.

Zilboorg, G. (1941). *A History of Medical Psychology.* New York: Norton.

Index

Abraham, K., 9, 19, 20, 38
Academy of Psychoanalysis, 109, 114
Action, psychoanalytic theory of, 193–196
Adler, A., 8, 21, 23, 30, 31, 47, 99, 229, 231
Affect, theory development, 39–40
Aggression, World War I, psychoanalytic theory, 26–27
Alexander, F., 21, 30, 39, 63, 92–93, 96–97, 100, 101, 103, 108, 109, 111, 186, 214, 299
Alternative theories, 236–237
American Psychoanalytic Association (APA), 4, 32, 44, 93, 97, 109–110, 114, 115, 127, 128, 136, 208–214, 221
Analyst role, 242–244
Anna O. case (Freud), 19
Anti-Semitism, 136n2
Anxiety, 28, 188–189, 260

Arlow, J., 64, 66, 68, 77, 78, 79, 84, 93, 106, 145, 148, 150, 151, 152, 184, 258, 304
Army Air Force, 84–86
Atkin, S., 64
Authority, knowledge and, psychoanalytic theory, 244–249

Bail, 220
Bailey, P., 61, 62
Balint, 210
Barcelona Congress (IPA, 1997), 265–272
Bartelmez, G., 61
Baudry, F., 59, 177
Beres, D., 308
Bergmann, M., 170–171, 175
Berman, S., 85
Bernfeld, S., 92
Bibring, E., 77, 108, 309
Bibring, G., 77, 108, 161, 164
Bion, W., 17–18, 130, 133, 170, 181, 210, 217, 239, 241

Bird, B., 148
Blanck, G., 290
Blanck, R., 290
Bloom, W., 61
Blum, H. P., 77, 264, 289
Boesky, D., 77
Bollas, C., 244, 246, 247
Borderline diagnosis, 260
Bornstein, B., 161
Bowlby, J., 155
Brabant, E., 20
Brain, 61–62, 285–287, 312–313
Brandschaft, B., 130, 131, 132, 133, 134
Brenner, C., 77, 78, 84, 93, 184, 213, 218, 245, 258, 284, 304–309
Brenner, I., 184
Breuer, J., 3, 19, 21, 38
Brill, A. A., 32, 66, 98, 105
British Psychoanalytic Society, 176–181
Brock, A., 74
Brunswick, D., 91, 103, 104
Buchanan, D., 63
Bucy, P., 62
Busch, F., 77, 194, 251–252, 258

Carlson, A. J., 61
Castration anxiety, 89
Center for Advanced Study in the Behavioral Sciences, Stanford University, 118–120
Charcot, J.-M., 38
Chefetz, R. A., 292

Child analysis, 157–162, 165, 177–179
Chodorow, N. J., 245, 247, 294
Chused, J. F., 251, 252, 253
Cocks, G., 147, 154
Compromise of integrity syndrome, 196–202
Cooper, A., 227
Copenhagen Conference (IPA, 1967), 251
Crastnopol, M., 294
Curtis, H., 155
Cushing, H., 61

Davidoff, L., 63
Davison, C., 64
Dean, J., 200–201
Decision-making function, of ego, 193–196
Defenses, intellectualization as, 18
Deri, F., 91, 103, 104
Dora case (Freud), 19
Drescher, J., 294
Drives
  aggression, World War I, 26–27
  relational theory and, 7
Dunbar, F., 96

Education. See Psychoanalytic education
Ego, decision-making function of, 193–196
Ego psychology, 94–95, 97, 112, 263, 266, 280
Eisenstein, 39

Eissler, K. R., 148, 151, 296
Eissler, R., 152
Eitingon, M., 163
Ekstein, 161
Elliott, A., 245
Ellman, S. J., 252, 304
Enactment, 133, 249–253
English, 100
Erikson, E. H., 98, 118, 186, 230, 263, 264
Etchegoyen, H., 266, 268
Ethical issues, 128–129, 136

Faimberg, H., 252
Fairbairn, W. R. D., 10, 133, 217
Fantasy, 291, 293
Farber, S., 138–139
Fascism, 57–58
Federn, E., 20
Fenichel, H., 91
Fenichel, O., 17, 27, 52, 58, 73–77, 89, 91, 92, 94–95, 96, 100, 101, 103, 104, 106, 183, 224, 226, 237, 241, 255
Ferenczi, S., 8, 17, 19, 21, 23–24, 31, 38, 39, 96, 100, 109, 170
Film industry, 123
Fine, E., 228
Fine, S., 228
Fleming, J., 214
Flexner, 98
Fliess, R., 3, 20, 21, 38, 46, 241, 291
Fonagy, P., 182, 285–293, 297, 303, 309–310

Ford Foundation (Center for Advanced Study in the Behavioral Sciences, Stanford University), 118–120
Freud, A., 9, 12, 28, 77, 78, 94, 98, 111, 112, 124, 125, 129n1, 131, 132, 137, 147, 148–152, 154, 155–175, 177–184, 219, 222, 226, 251, 265, 266, 270, 281, 297, 303
Freud, E., 129n1
Freud, S., 3, 4, 5, 7, 10, 12, 18–28, 32, 38, 39, 40, 44, 46, 47–48, 50, 58, 60, 62, 65, 68, 69, 73, 74, 77, 86, 91–92, 94, 96, 97, 98, 99, 111, 112, 124, 125, 131, 135, 142, 164, 168, 170, 176, 182, 183, 188, 193–194, 197, 200, 201, 217, 218, 219, 228, 238–239, 240, 244, 246, 249–250, 260–261, 264, 271, 277–279, 281–283, 291, 305, 307, 308
Friedman, L., 248, 254
Friedman, R. J., 252
Fromm, E., 29, 30, 31
Fromm-Reichmann, F., 31, 108
Furer, M., 252, 254
Futterman, S., 67

Gabbard, G. O., 123, 227, 243, 294
Gabbard, K., 123
Gales, M., 207

Garma, A., 267
Gerard, R. W., 288
Gershwin, G., 64
Gill, M., 31, 77, 78, 107–109, 112, 125, 142, 144, 195, 237, 242, 243, 246, 255, 280, 283, 295, 298, 302–303, 304
Gillespie, W., 132, 165, 166, 168, 267
Gitelson, F., 162, 166
Gitelson, M., 110–111, 166
Gladwell, M., 263
Glover, E., 252
Godley, W., 136n2
Goldberg, A., 270, 293
Goldwater, B., 114
Gray, P., 77, 194–195, 258
Green, A., 169, 170, 171, 175, 239
Green, M., 138–139
Greenacre, J., 77, 267
Greenberg, J., 293–296
Greenson, R., 85, 86–88, 91, 92, 93, 103, 104, 106, 117, 128, 131–132, 136–141, 166, 173, 174, 184, 202, 207
Grinberg, L., 50
Grinker, R., 62
Grosskurth, P., 20
Grotjahn, M., 92, 103
Group effects, 87–90, 240–242, 302–303
Guttman, S., 136

Hampstead Clinic, 157–161, 162, 165–166, 171, 172, 176, 177–178, 180–181

Hanly, C., 246
Harris, B., 74
Harris, J. R., 46
Hartmann, H., 12, 28–29, 41, 77, 93, 94, 105, 112, 124, 136, 163, 164, 171, 183, 189, 195, 200, 201, 218–219, 265, 270, 279, 282, 283, 308, 313
Hassin, G., 62–63
Heimann, P., 243, 282
Helsinki Congress (IPA, 1981), 183
Hendrick, I., 194
Historical truth, narrative truth and, 257
Hitler, A., 74, 99
Hoffer, W., 267
Hoffman, I. Z., 246, 295
Holt, R. R., 142, 260
Horney, K., 5, 29, 30, 31, 57, 109, 124, 126
Humanism, 58, 179

Ideation, theory development, 39–40
Institute of Contemporary Psychoanalysis, 206
Integrity, compromise of, syndrome, 196–202
Intellectualization, as defense, 18
International Psychoanalytic Association (I.P.A.), 4, 129, 130, 137, 144–155, 156–157, 158, 164, 166, 172, 211, 214, 220
Barcelona Congress (1997), 265–272

Copenhagen Conference
    (1967), 251
Helsinki Congress (1981), 183
Jerusalem Congress (1977),
    237
London Congress (1975), 239
Montreal Conference
    (1987), 222
Paris Congress (1973), 168–
    169, 196, 198
Rome Congress (1969),
    144–155
San Francisco Congress
    (1995), 236
Vienna Congress (1971),
    156–157, 159, 161,
    162–165, 168, 171,
    175–176, 183, 269
Intersubjectivity, 133, 204,
    253–256, 270–271
Intrapsychic realm, 112
Irrationality, 39–40, 226–227
Isaacs, S., 220
Isakower, O., 11, 241

Jacobs, T. J., 251, 252
Jacobson, E., 74, 77, 93, 107,
    282, 291
Jacoby, R., 74
Jerusalem Congress (IPA,
    1977), 237
Joffe, W., 269
Johnson, L. B., 114, 211
Jones, E., 9, 19, 20, 21, 23,
    38, 47, 49, 163, 164,
    176, 183, 265
Joseph, B., 130, 133, 181,
    237, 282, 283, 285, 286,
    287, 289, 292

Jung, C. G., 8, 17, 20, 21, 23,
    30, 31, 38, 47, 99, 229–
    230, 231

Kant, I., 245
Kardiner, A., 32
Keats, J., 239
Kernberg, O., 181, 217, 227,
    228, 244, 247, 266, 296,
    298
Keschner, M., 70
Kety, S. S., 288
Khan, M., 136, 137
King, P., 9, 59, 137, 177, 297
Kirsner, D., 116, 134, 135–
    136, 139, 220
Klein, G., 5, 125, 142, 143,
    196, 227, 228, 280,
    283, 284, 298, 302,
    306, 308
Klein, M., 9, 10, 21, 23, 47,
    111, 124–125, 131, 133,
    134, 170, 175, 176, 177,
    178, 179, 181, 182, 185,
    217, 228, 229, 246, 277–
    279, 303
Knight, R., 137
Knowledge, authority and,
    psychoanalytic theory,
    244–249
Kohut, H., 5, 10, 21, 23, 30,
    31, 124, 129n1, 133,
    145, 146–155, 156, 159,
    172, 174, 185, 186, 198–
    199, 217, 220, 227, 228,
    230, 231, 244, 266, 270,
    299, 300
Kris, A., 194
Kris, E., 93, 98, 106, 281

Kris, M., 147, 149, 151, 161, 162, 281
Kubie, L., 139–140
Kuhn, T., 263

Lacan, J., 23, 170, 217, 231
Laible, E., 163
Lampl de Groot, J., 147, 158, 162, 267
Lasch, C., 260
Lawsuits, 220–221
Lay analysis, 97–99, 216–220, 221, 281, 298, 299
Lebovici, S., 267–268
Levy, N., 92, 103, 104
Lewin, B., 77
Lewy, E., 91, 103
Linn, L., 67
Little Hans case (Freud), 19
Loewenberg, P., 104
Loewenstein, R., 93
London Congress (IPA, 1975), 239
Los Angeles, California, 90–94, 116–117
Los Angeles Psychoanalytic Society (LAPSI), 100, 103–105, 126–141, 202–208, 216, 220–221, 290
Luckhardt, A., 61
Lustman, 151
Lynch, A. A., 304

Maguire, I., 129, 133
Mahler, M., 71, 77, 93, 161, 254, 299
Marmor, J., 92, 103, 104
Marx, K., 58, 74
Masserman, J., 63

Masson, J., 46, 134, 169
May, R., 202
Mayer, E. L., 247
McGuire, W., 20
McLaughlin, J. T., 247–248, 251, 253
Medical psychoanalysis, 95–99
Medical school, 61–63
Meltzer, 130
Memory, 285–291
Menninger, K., 86, 95
Menninger, W., 84
Menninger Clinic (Topeka, Kansas), 5, 141–144, 203
Metaphor, 308–309
Meyer, A., 31, 66, 93
Michels, R., 24, 294–295, 303
Mitchell, S. J., 293, 294
Monroe, M., 117
Montreal Conference (IPA, 1987), 222
Muhlleitner, E., 58, 74
Munk, M., 91
Murray, J., 84, 85

Nafziger, H., 64
Narcissism, 199, 260
Narrative truth, historical truth and, 257
Natterson, J. M., 252, 254
Neo-Freudians, 103, 111
Neurology, 63–66, 89
Neuroscience, 235, 285–289, 312–313
Newman, L., 149, 156
Newman, R., 156
Nixon, R. M., 134, 198, 200–201, 211
Novick, J., 208

Novick, K. K., 208
Nunberg, H., 20

Object-relations theory, 290–
    291, 299
Omissions, in psychoanalytic
    theory, 7–8, 30, 228–229

Paradigms, 263–265
Paris Congress (IPA, 1973),
    168–169, 196, 198
Peck, G., 86
Piers, G., 213
Pizer, B., 294
Postmodernism, 144, 257
Projective identification, 181–
    182
Psychoanalysis
    current status of, 275–314
    public confidence in, 3, 236,
        275
    scientific status of, 12–13
Psychoanalytic education, 127–
    128, 161, 209–210
Psychoanalytic theory
    of action, 193–196
    advances in, 258–259
    alternative, 236–237
    analyst role, 242–244
    appeal of, 17–18
    downward turn in
        development of, 123–
        124
    enactment, 249–253
    flaws and fallacies in, 45–49
    fragmentation of, 3, 5–7, 18,
        29–34, 99–105, 124–
        126
    Freudian, 18–20, 27–28

interpersonal affective
    tensions within early,
    20–25, 38–39
intersubjectivity, 253–256
knowledge and authority,
    244–249
omissions in, 7–8, 30, 228–
    229
paradigms, 263–265
post-Freudian, 28–29
progression of, 37–54
of public opinion, 238–242
rapprochements and
    conflicts, 293–302
social extensions of, 259–262
total composite, 237–238
unification of, 4, 8, 51–54
unity/pluralism within early,
    25–26
World War I, 26–27
Psychosomatic medicine, 95–99
Public opinion, psychoanalytic
    theory of, 238–242, 262

Racker, H., 243
Rado, S., 100
Rangell, A., 167, 272
Rangell, L., 5, 8, 46–47, 49,
    51, 53–54, 71, 76, 89, 91,
    94, 102, 104, 107, 117,
    119, 133, 136, 137–138,
    150, 151, 152, 155, 157,
    164, 170–172, 188–190,
    193–196, 202, 205, 225,
    229, 237, 239, 251, 252,
    258, 261–262, 269–270,
    291, 302, 306, 311
Rank, O., 19, 20–21, 23, 30, 31,
    38–39, 99, 109, 220, 229

Rapaport, D., 5, 77, 78, 92, 98, 105–107, 112, 124, 125, 142, 144, 189, 195, 201, 280, 281, 294
Rationality, theory development, 39–40
Recovered memory, 291
Reed, G. S., 59
Reich, A., 74
Reich, W., 21, 59, 74, 170
Reichmayr, J., 58, 74
Reider, N., 34
Reik, T., 17, 75
Relational theory, drives and, 7
Renik, O., 12, 244, 252, 254
Richards, A. D., 32, 77, 105, 218, 219, 304
Ritvo, S., 160, 161
Robbins, L., 85
Rodman, 236, 297
Rogers, C., 118
Rome Congress (IPA, 1969), 144–155
Romm, M., 92, 103, 104
Rosen, V., 63, 66, 84, 93
Rosenblatt, B., 182, 303
Rosenfeld, H., 130, 133
Rosten, L., 86
Rothstein, A., 252

Sampson, H., 194
Sandler, A. M., 182, 222, 225, 237, 245, 286, 297
Sandler, J., 77, 78, 181, 182, 189, 222, 225, 245, 267, 268–270, 286, 289, 292, 296, 297, 298, 303
San Francisco, California, 278–279

San Francisco Congress (IPA, 1995), 236
Saul, 100
Savitsky, N., 64, 70–71
Schafer, R., 142, 144, 196, 245, 248, 252, 279–285, 291, 299, 302, 304
Seduction theory, 291, 293
Seeley, J., 86
Segal, H., 130, 132, 133, 155, 279, 284
Self-disclosure. See Therapist self-disclosure
Self psychology, 146–155, 186, 206, 300
Shatzky, J., 73
Shaw, G. B., 194
Shengold, L., 77
Shevrin, H., 143
Simmel, E., 27, 64, 89, 91–92, 96, 100, 101, 103
Sociocultural realm, 112
South America, 152–153
Spence, D. P., 299
Spezzano, C., 245, 252, 254
Spitz, R., 77, 93, 161
Stanford University Center for Advanced Study in the Behavioral Sciences, 118–120
Stein, M., 155, 214
Steiner, R., 9, 59, 177
Stekel, 21, 109
Stoller, R., 240
Stolorow, R. D., 10, 133, 220
Stone, L., 77, 79, 93, 108, 109, 237, 282, 289, 296, 311
Strachey, J., 255, 260, 264

Sullivan, H. S., 5, 29, 30, 31, 109, 126

Tarachow, S., 32, 64, 92
Target, M., 292, 293
Tartakoff, H., 163
Theory. *See* Psychoanalytic theory
Therapist self-disclosure, recommendations for, 6–7
Thompson, C., 29–30, 32
Tidd, C., 91
Topeka, Kansas. *See* Menninger Clinic (Topeka, Kansas)
Total composite psychoanalytic theory, 237–238
Training. *See* Psychoanalytic education
Transference, role of, 6–7
Trauma, 292
Truth, narrative/historical truth, 257
Tyson, R., 266

Valenstein, A., 175
Van Dam, H., 72, 161
Van der Heide, C., 91, 93, 120
Van der Leeuw, 150, 151
Vanggaard, T., 251
Vienna Congress (IPA, 1971), 156–157, 159, 161, 162–165, 168, 171, 175–176, 183, 269
Vienna Psychoanalytic Society, 23

Waelder, R., 6, 77, 98, 99, 143, 194, 195, 200, 218, 219, 238, 244, 264, 277, 281, 305–306
Waelder-Hall, 100
Wallerstein, R., 5, 77, 78, 153, 182, 219, 221–224, 256, 263, 267, 292, 296–299, 303
Watergate scandal, 133, 134, 197–198, 200–201, 240
Wechsler, I., 62
Weigert, E., 32
Weigert, 100
Weiss, J., 194
Wexler, M., 141, 207
White, W. A., 29, 31, 109
Wills, F., 133
Winnicott, D. W., 31, 170, 210, 217, 236, 262
Wolf, E., 147, 149, 209
World War I, 26–27, 89
World War II, 57, 74, 83–86
Writing, 68–73, 89

Yorke, C., 297
Young-Bruehl, E., 154, 156–157, 159–162, 163–164, 166, 168, 169–170, 172, 173, 180, 182, 183, 184, 270

Zetzel, E., 77, 282
Ziskind, E., 63